This gem of a book is the result of what happens when you combine heartfelt spirituality with a lifelong love of medicine, patient care, and life itself.

WISDOM COMES will provide genuine wisdom and life lessons for all those that read it.

Dr. Mark Moyad
Jenkins/Pokempner Director of Complimentary and
Alternative Medicine,
University of Michigan, Ann Arbor, Michigan.

'WISDOM COMES' is a memoir of a life well lived, penned by Dr. Mahmood Hai narrating his journey from India to the US, to his very successful decades long practice in surgery. He writes thoughtfully and with candor of the many ups and downs along the way. It is full of learning and reflections that will inspire not only those in the practice of medicine but all who seek to live a full life and give back.

S. Qaisar Shareef
Author of "When Tribesmen Came Calling".
Former Country Manager,
Proctor & Gamble International.

Every medical student and healthcare practitioner should read this book!

And everyone will enjoy reading this great surgeon's journey from native India to the United States where he became famous for developing the GreenLight Laser that made possible near-bloodless prostate surgery. Dr. Hai writes, "As long as you work hard, are honest and professionally competent, your reputation will grow and you will be recognized." Indeed, Dr. Hai was recognized by his peers worldwide, yet he has remained humble and shares gripping stories of the compassionate and creative care he provided for his patients. Whether rich or poor, every patient received the best care possible. He says, "Success in these difficult cases requires love, hope, and faith." Dr. Hai's spirituality, faith, and integrity are on every page and worthy of emulation. Also, the book includes his personal reflections on the practice of medicine, including the business of medicine and medico-legal issues. Every page is filled with wisdom. Finally he shares how he and his beloved wife, Annette, have given back to their community. The book ends with this observation: "Life is a journey with problems to solve and lessons to learn but most of all experiences to enjoy." Read and be blessed.

Dr. John K. Graham, M.D., D.Min., MSc.,
President and CEO
Institute of Spirituality and Health,
Texas Medical Center, Houston, Texas.

In all my years in medicine, I have found but a mere handful of people that I would call true 'Humanitarians' and Dr. Mahmood Hai is one of these. I have had the honor of knowing him, and he has been an inspiration with his work and life which comes from his heart and soul, not just from the brain and his medical expertise. It's not just the words in his book – it's the feeling behind the words that impel them. This is rare in life and certainly rare in medicine and every page pays tribute to his care and compassion as a human being.

In this remarkable book, a memoir and inspirational guide combining grippingly written case histories, personal recollections, and a frank and insightful discussion of professional issues such as burn-out and medico-legal issues, Wisdom Comes is a must-read for all, especially those in medicine seeking, as Dr. Hai puts it in his introduction, "a guide to a healthy, honorable, successful, and prosperous life."

At the end of my first consultation with Dr. Hai, he welcomed me into his 'family'.

And so it has always been since, with myself, my wife and the patients I have referred to him. As you read him, you too will be welcomed, from his heart. Welcome to his 'family of humanity'.

Dr. John Diamond, M.D., FRANZCP, MRCPsych.
Renowned Physician, author, philosopher and poet.

This is one of the most useful memoirs I have ever read. In it, a brilliant doctor who remains a humble man takes us on a journey from his youth in northeastern India to a long distinguished career as an American physician.

Equipped with a true moral compass, the hands of a born surgeon, and a lively fascination with the quirky human race, Mahmood Hai delivers this remarkable report of a life devoted to adventurous service marked by the invention of certain surgical techniques that have permanently advanced his chosen field.

Lucky for us, the book's central chapters are layered with dozens of case studies and well drawn patients' portraits, providing the reader a window into the very personal business of curing people and saving lives. The clear-eyed writing is spiced with the wit of a sharp but compassionate observer who, whether taking the measure of cancer or of human folly, knows whereof he speaks.

This book is intended for professionals in the medical field and other walks of life.

It really should be read by everyone.

> Michael Wolfe
> Scholar, Author, Film & TV producer and Journalist.

WISDOM COMES

Life's Lessons
Learned

Mahmood A. Hai, MD

Printed in the United States of America

First Printing, 2019

ISBN: 978-1-54399-081-2 (Print)
ISBN: 978-1-54399-082-9 (eBook)

Bookbaby Publishing
7905 N. Crescent Blvd.
Pennsauken, NJ 08110

www.bookbaby.com

Dedicated to God Almighty
The source of all knowledge and wisdom

*In memory of my beloved parents and with gratitude to
my siblings who nurtured my educational foundation
and showed me by example how to live a virtuous life.*

*To my lovely wife Annette who has been an
important part of all my ventures, providing
love and strength to face the realities of life.*

*To our children, Yusuf, Ayesha, Charlie and
Matt and their spouses who have always given
me their unquestionable love and support.*

*To our beautiful grandchildren who keep
me active and young at heart.*

Acknowledgement

I am deeply and sincerely indebted to my dear friend, Michael Wolfe, who despite being extremely busy, found time to edit the book and guide me through the process of completing it.

S. Qaisar Shareef also reviewed the manuscript thoroughly and made several corrections for which I am very thankful.

I owe a deep sense of gratitude to my spiritual brother, Dr. John Graham, for reading the book several times, and offering his comments and suggestions. His beautiful editorial leaves me humbled.

To Dr. Mark Moyad for his review and suggestions. Over the years, his professional advice has been invaluable in helping us lead a healthy life style.

To Dr. Sherman Jackson, who initially encouraged me to undertake this project and has helped guide me with his suggestions.

Lastly my special thanks to Dr. John Diamond, a friend and a mentor, who has over the years lovingly guided me till the completion of this book.

Patrick Aylward and his team at BookBaby publishing have greatly helped in completing this mission.

A very sincere thanks to my wife, family and friends who have patiently supported me over the last few years.

CONTENTS

Introduction

This book is a summary of many life experiences that molded my career as a surgeon. No doubt there were many cultural, environmental, and other factors, beyond my control and not accounted for here, that have also had their influence. This book is addressed to professionals, in both health industry and other walks of life, as a guide to a healthy, honorable, successful, and prosperous life in a world with all kinds of meanness, calamities, and turbulence. It is never too late to learn and become wiser. As Sir William Osler said, "The hardest conviction to get in the mind of a beginner is that the education upon which he is engaged is not a college course, not a medical course, but a life course, for which the work of a few years under teachers is but a preparation."

Seeking knowledge is exciting and there is no doubt arts, science, medicine, and technology have dramatically improved the lives of millions of people. But wisdom is quite different from knowledge. Socrates (c. 470 – 399 BCE), one of the founders of western rational tradition, believed that wisdom was not about accumulating information and reaching hard-and-fast conclusions.

At the end of his life, Socrates believed that the only reason he could be considered wise was because he knew that he knew nothing at all.

The life of a surgeon is a lot like that of a high-performance athlete. The day-to-day challenges are both physical and mental. The job has to be done with sound judgment and the greatest possible efficiency, ethically, yet *in collaboration* with a team. Successful surgeons are mentally tough. They have the hardiness and fortitude to push through life's disruptions. *Good* surgeons have to go beyond the barriers of what is comfortable. There *has to be* resilience and a willingness to go beyond the point of exhaustion, to secure excellence outside the bounds of mediocrity.

Elite surgeons have the uncanny ability to find the positive in everything. It is not that they do not have down moments; they absolutely do. But when those down moments occur, they let them pass, and then improvise and bounce back. They put a positive spin on things, find a silver lining, and resume their quest for professional and personal excellence yet with realism about success and failure. And they realize that the outcomes of surgical care are wholly dependent on the following:

- The quality of the team they work with, in which each member is equally important, with defined responsibilities (and able to cover for each other if the need arises);
- The availability of facilities and equipment;
- Time and focus;
- Ability to improvise and overcome deficiencies;
- Maintaining their cool and staying unruffled by surprises; and
- Follow-up care.

During a procedure, the surgeon is truly like the conductor of an orchestra and has the leadership of his team. Knowing the role and responsibilities of each member of his team, he has to keep in mind the capabilities of each individual. The outcomes depend on the team effort.

It reminds me of Ernest Shackleton who was the leader of an Antarctic expedition of the South Pole. His ship was literally frozen in place, and he led his twenty-eight-person crew on a two-year journey of survival. Amazingly, the entire crew survived. They credited their survival to the teamwork, to the humanity and mutual reliance that Shackleton led with, and to the sense that they were all responsible not only for themselves but for each other.

In an Oncology Times article "Evolution of a Successful Physician," Dr. Joseph Simone describes three stages of development of a physician.

(1) Gaining knowledge and experience: It is the basis of all the rest.

(2) Intellectual insight: It combines experience and knowledge acquired from all sources, practice, books, journals, conferences, research, etc.

(3): Humility: Knowing the boundaries of one's ability and common sense to act accordingly leads to wisdom (opposite of know-it-all).

Medical residency and fellowship programs in the United States and Canada are great training programs, well structured, graduated, and comprehensive. They objectively evaluate each surgeon as he or she is nurtured and mentored toward the given standards of practice over three to ten years, depending on the specialty. During this training, residents are given increasingly demanding responsibilities under the supervision of their mentors and peers. At the end of the program, they are thoroughly evaluated for their ability and competence, and before going into practice, they have to pass a state certification exam and a national board exam. Finally, the credential committee of the hospital where they plan to practice evaluates them not only for their qualifications and certifications, but also for their human characteristics. When a surgeon finally gets operative privileges and starts performing surgical procedures, he or she is under the supervision of a senior surgeon, who vouches for his or her competence. Throughout their careers, surgeons are re-certified and re-credentialed to current standards of practice.

I feel greatly privileged to have been born in a well-educated family with a father who was a physician of repute and two siblings who also pursued medicine. A good education at an English-medium school run by American Jesuits laid a strong academic and moral foundation, which was further reinforced by a structured home where learning and *humanity* were given top priority.

After graduating from medical school and obtaining a post-graduate degree of Master of Surgery, I came to the United States in 1973 to pursue further training in surgery in Boston and later in urology in Detroit. I started practicing urology in a community hospital in 1978 and completed forty years in June 2018. In the year 2000, my pioneering research with lasers in urology led to FDA approval of the GreenLight laser for removing obstructed prostate tissue. It also gave me a great opportunity to travel around the world teaching this new technology. As of December 2016, one million of these surgeries had been performed around the world and I have visited and taught laser surgery in thirty-two countries.

My guiding premise for many years has been that life on this earth is never going to be perfect. We need to learn how to be happy and content. At any given time in our lives, there are hundreds of things going right and hundreds of things going wrong. We have to decide which ones we want to focus on, and that will determine our attitude toward life. Contentment has to come from within, and no amount of material wealth and possessions can make it better.

There is a well-known saying that life is not measured by the breaths you take, but by the moments that take your breath away. So, live your life fully. Cherish each and every second of your life. Love your near and dear ones unconditionally. Do all the good you can, and try not to harm anyone intentionally. Take care of your health and your body, so you do not become a burden on others. Do something each day that you love to do. Laugh when you can. Spread goodness and happiness. No one is responsible for your happiness or misery but you yourself. Take time out to thank the Creator who gave it all to you. Stay happy, stay blessed.

My life has been a very interesting and challenging journey. I have learnt a lot, and continue to do so every day. My close friends and colleagues, who feel I have a treasured story to tell, have repeatedly urged me to write about these interesting life experiences and their outcomes, as a guide for those who are in the field of health care and other professionals. I do not know how my story will influence you, but it reminds me of the words of Edna St. Vincent Millay:

"My candle burns at both ends;
It will not last the night;
But ah, my foes, and oh, my friends –
It gives a lovely light."

Mahmood Abdul Hai
November 22, 2019

PART ONE

Early Life

CHAPTER 1

Early Life in India

I was born on December 4, 1946, in Patna, capital of the state of Bihar in northeastern India, just a few months before India gained independence from the British.

Patna is one of the oldest cities of India, located on the south bank of the Ganges river. The ancient city was called Pataliputra, which was founded in 490 BCE as a small fort. It became the capital of major powers in ancient India, including the Maurya Empire, during which it became one of the largest cities of the world with an estimated population of four hundred thousand. From 273 to 232 BCE, it was the seat of the government under the famous Buddhist Emperor Ashoka. History tells us that it was among the first cities in the world to have a highly efficient form of local self-government.

Extensive excavations carried out by the Archeological Survey of India has revealed an ancient university called Nalanda that existed from about 401 to 1200 CE. It was the seat of learning of two major world religions: Jainism and Buddhism. A museum at Nalanda houses many of the treasures found in the excavations, and in 2016, the ruins were designated a UNESCO World Heritage site. In 1538 CE, King Sher Shah Suri took control from the Mughal Empire, made Pataliputra his capital, and changed the name to modern Patna. The city later became a part of the British Empire. After independence, Patna deteriorated, and sometimes I wish it had retained even a fraction of its past glory.

The subcontinent was already enduring the turmoil that would culminate a year later in independence from British colonial rule. The British Raj, as it was called, had transformed India from a largely rural economy to a rapidly developing one with modern technologies including railways, roads, canals, bridges, and telephone and telegraph links. These in turn promoted international trade, but most key positions and gains were taken by the British. Although India benefitted from modernization, many Indians still believe they were robbed by the British.

At the same time that they were pushing for independence, negotiations were taking place between the two leading political parties, the Indian National Congress and the Muslim League. The big question was whether to leave India as a single nation or be divided into several fractions: India for Hindus, Muslims, Sikhs, and Christians, and Pakistan as a homeland for the Muslims. After division — known as the Partition — was decided on, many millions of Hindu, Muslim, and Sikh refugees trekked across the newly drawn arbitrary borders created by the British hierarchy. Extreme communal violence broke out, leading to one of the largest population displacements in human history. Between one and two million people are estimated to have died during that time. Today I strongly believe that, from all perspectives, an undivided Indian subcontinent would have been the best for all.

I was the youngest child in a family with two elder brothers and one sister. As far as my memory goes, it was a very happy and fulfilling childhood. Life was easy for a child in an upper-class family. All four of us were born within six years, and we remain close even today. An English nanny, Miss Connelly, was totally in charge of all our daily activities.

Our parents were exceptional in their own ways. They were very kind and honest people. My mother's father was a well-known barrister, trained in England. The family had both wealth and status. My mother was very young when we were born, yet extremely responsible, and she lovingly took care of all our daily needs. Although we had servants and cooks, our mother made sure we had a delicious and balanced meal on the table. In her spare time, she kept herself busy sewing our clothes, knitting sweaters, and managing a large household of relatives and servants. She was extremely kindhearted, always giving to the needy and taking care of everyone's problems. What I loved most was that I could always get change for ice cream or chocolates from her dressing table drawer.

My father, by contrast, was a self-made man who had worked his way through college and medical school by his own earnings. As a medical student, he would make house calls on his bike to give penicillin injections to rich people who could afford the new wonder drug. After a few years as a practicing physician and a teacher at the medical school, he saved enough funds to go to England to gain membership in the Royal College of Physicians. He also obtained a degree from Wales as a specialist to treat tuberculosis, which was rampant in India.

On his return, he became well known as the "TB specialist". He worked relentlessly from 7:00 a.m. until midnight, taking care of thousands of patients, saving the lives of rich and poor. I would hear his patients say, "He heals more than he cures." To cure a patient, he felt, was a question of medical technology while to heal a patient was a spiritual matter. He was a man bound by his principles and high moral standards. He lived an austere life based on the values of the great leader Mahatma Gandhi, and he believed and practiced social justice. He wore hand-woven *khadi* clothing, became a vegetarian at an early age, and, despite the extremely hot weather in Patna, did not even have a fan in his room. He spoke very softly, but every word was a pearl of wisdom. Loved by his students, adored by his patients, he soon gained great respect in the community. He became the personal physician to two presidents of India. In 1962, he was awarded one of the nation's highest awards, the Padma Bhushan award, for his services to humanity.

My life at home was very structured and disciplined. We were indeed privileged to have a phenomenal parochial school run mainly by American Jesuits, the St. Xavier's High School. I had just turned six when I started first grade in 1952. The school had a very balanced academic and sports program. The Jesuits and all the teachers were exemplary, with high scholastic and moral values. I strongly believe that who I am today, and my successful life, are outcomes of the foundation they laid in my education and the polish I got at home, where day-to-day life was based totally on the principles of faith and morality.

St. Xavier's was a small school, with only thirty-four boys in our 1962 batch. With the excellent education we received, a large number of us became physicians. One became the Foreign Secretary of India, another a higher-up in the United Nations General Agreement on Tariffs and Trade, yet another a Harvard professor and the author of a textbook on immunology. Those who went into business and the professions were extremely successful, too. As a group we are still very close, and we communicate regularly through our cell phones. My experience has been that old friendships only grow stronger with time. I remain in touch with most of my classmates, and I'm proud to report that at our fifty-year reunion I was awarded the Distinguished Xaverian Award.

After finishing Senior Cambridge, I enrolled in a two-year premedical program, joining my two elder brothers at the Prince of Wales Medical College in Patna. All three of us were very studious and meritorious throughout our college years. Academics and clinical learning totally consumed our lives, leaving little time to socialize with family and friends. In those days, there were no televisions or video games to distract a young person.

I still recall vividly my first assignment as a medical student. The summers of 1966 and 1967 were extremely hot throughout India. There was no significant rain for two years, leading to widespread drought, especially in my home state of Bihar. In July 1967, I was a fourth-year medical student at the Prince of Wales Medical College in Patna, and the Rotary Club was looking for volunteers to go to the drought-stricken areas to vaccinate people against cholera and typhoid. Five of us signed up. Late one Friday, we took off in the jeep that Rotary provided. The heat was unbearable, and the rural roads were rough and unpaved. By the time we arrived, our hair and faces were so covered with dust that it was difficult even to recognize each other. We were stationed in a two-story government bungalow. The first floor was all offices, plus a kitchen and dining area. We were given a room on the second floor. After a good shower and a simple meal, we were done for that day of our arrival. The next morning, we went out into the villages, setting up tent camps where people would line up to be vaccinated. The poverty was visible in every aspect; with their emaciated bodies and faces, they looked like skin-covered skeletons. You could not see an ounce of fat anywhere, not even in the children. Their eyes were sunken, and you could see each and every rib on their chest walls, like pictures we've seen recently from war-ravaged districts in Syria and Yemen. Barely a remnant of clothing covered their bodies. Hungry children lacked the strength even to cry. When we gave the injection, we had to take care that the needle did not hit their bones.

After a long, hot, tiring, and depressing day, we returned to the bungalow and showered, and then sat on the second-floor balcony, sipping a cup of tea and pondering the devastation the famine had produced. It was about seven o'clock, the hot sun was still high above the horizon, and I saw a large group of villagers approaching the building. It was then that I remembered that this building also served as a food distribution center. The people sat down on the ground in rows, most of them without plates or bowls to receive the food. They swept the dust aside on the ground in front of them and the meal was served, a scoop of steamed rice and corn, maybe with a little salt. The unfortunate recipients shoved the tasteless food in their mouths as if it were manna from Heaven. They picked up and ate each and every morsel of food from the ground. They knew this was all they would get to eat until the next evening.

Unconsciously, tears rolled down my cheeks. These people were as low as it seemed possible for humans to be, subsisting on the basics for human survival. The moment at first shocked me and then moved me, confirming my decision to become a doctor and the conviction to alleviate human suffering. The Hippocratic Oath flashed in front of my eyes. This indeed was a turning point in my life: I was not just going to be a doctor but a missionary for the cause.

I returned from our mission in the countryside fully confirmed in the purpose of my life. With a strong foundation in the practice of the medical sciences and great clinical opportunities, I graduated in 1969 with honors in anatomy and surgery. Soon after, I began my teaching career as a Demonstrator in Anatomy and also registered for the post-graduate Masters in Surgery program at Patna University. Life was extremely busy, but immensely rewarding.

The following year there was a government takeover of the medical school, and academics was overtaken by politics. I was appointed the family planning officer for Jahanabad, a small town about thirty miles away. It became my first exposure to the day-to-day reality of practicing medicine in India. The train ride to Jahanabad took anywhere from two to four hours one way. There was hardly any work to be done at the clinic, so I spent my time studying and completing my thesis, which involved going to the veterinary school to do surgical experiments on dogs.

It was there that I had the distinctive privilege of operating on a lioness from the zoo. The professor of surgery called me one day to say that a lioness had been brought to the college with her rectum prolapsed, and he had no idea how to fix it. I knew how to treat the problem in humans and offered to do the surgery. The date and time were fixed, and I arrived rather scared. I had brought all the instruments sterilized from the surgery department. The lioness was tranquilized by an injection, but I refused to go into the cage with her, sensing that this might be the end of my career, or even my life. After much debate, I agreed to operate from outside the cage as long as they would position the animal for me to work between the bars. The procedure went well, but as I was putting in the last few stitches, the lioness began waking up. I quickly finished the job and went my merry way. The professor later informed me that the surgery had cured the problem, thank God.

Soon after that, I had an eye-opening experience. I received an official letter that the chief medical officer was scheduled to visit the clinic. I had no idea how to prepare for his visit.

The gentleman arrived in a jeep on a hot and sultry day. He must have weighed nearly four hundred pounds and was totally drenched in his own sweat. He could barely walk without losing his breath. He sat down, enquiring as to how many vasectomies I had performed as the designated family planning physician. I informed him that very few villagers were agreeing to undergo a surgical procedure for family planning. Instead of being upset, he was actually delighted. "That means there are a lot of unused supplies," he said. I nodded, but at first I didn't understand. He instructed me to have all the supplies loaded in his car and to juggle the books that all the supplies had been used in surgery. I vehemently refused. He pulled me into an adjacent room and whispered, "You fool! Don't you understand? This is my time to make money. Your time will come in a few years."

I refused to comply and do anything immoral or illegal. At this point he slammed the door in my face and left. Later I learned that he had written a long report about my incompetence and disobedience. I began to realize that it would be impossible for me to survive in so corrupt an environment. I became desperate to get out.

In 1971, I passed the Educational Council for Foreign Medical Graduates (ECFMG) test, the qualifying exam for foreign medical graduates, which was a requirement to pursue my training in the United States. Upon receiving the certification, I started applying to surgical residency programs. In 1972, I completed my master's and was accepted to a program at Boston University beginning on July 1, 1973. The university program gave me a year of credit for all my post-graduate work. My happiness knew no bounds.

I took the twenty-four-hour flight on Pan Am and arrived in Boston late on the night of June 28, 1973. My very dear friend from Patna, Dr.

Shamshu Rizvi, was at the airport to receive me and brought me to his apartment near Kenmore Square. The Indian government had allowed me to carry only $100 in foreign exchange, and after travel expenses, I had just $27 left in my wallet. The next day I caught up on sleep, adjusting to the new time zone, and then walked to the square and took a trial run on the bus to Boston City Hospital where I would be starting work the following day, Sunday, July 1. At the hospital, there was a short orientation and I was thrust into work. Everything was different from what I had learned and trained for in India, and I knew that this was a new beginning. I was told that I would be on call that night. Surgical residencies were very demanding in those days. To obtain the most clinical experience, we had to be on call every other night and every other weekend. I worked all day Sunday, was on call all night, and had a full working day Monday. The resident who was on call Monday night had missed his flight from Brazil, so I had to stay in the hospital for an additional night call.

After working all of Tuesday, it was my scheduled night to be on call again. Wednesday being the Fourth of July holiday ended up as a long operating day because of emergencies. At the end of the day, while I was looking forward to getting back to the apartment, I was informed by the chief resident that, because it was a holiday, I would be on call again that night. All of Thursday I pushed myself, using all my willpower to get the job done. Finally, I returned to my apartment in total exhaustion. It then dawned on me that I had worked straight through five days and four nights, with hardly any sleep. I wondered: is this what I had opted for?

I had left the great comfort of my home, family, friends, culture, language, and food to this crazy, hectic, totally consuming life of an American surgical resident.

CHAPTER 2

Life as a Resident:
From Boston to Detroit

I cherished my two-hundred-square-foot studio apartment overlooking the Charles River as a refuge from the crazy life at Boston City Hospital. It was summer, and I would come back late in the evening, open the windows, and look out. I could hear the Boston Pops orchestra playing melodious tunes in their outdoor auditorium. People were out walking and playing on the greens. Many were sailing and rowing boats on the river. Most days I was so exhausted, I would lie on the sofa and within minutes would be out, to wake up early the next morning to start another day. As a first-year resident, my contracted annual salary was $8,000. We received a paycheck every two weeks for about $275, after taxes were withheld. That was surprisingly adequate, as the hospital had free food and living quarters, and we lived in scrubs every day. As a matter of fact, after a few months I had $400 in my bank account. On a free weekend I bought my first TV set, a 20-inch color Sony, which was a source of great entertainment for years.

In the early seventies, we had a room reserved in the Emergency Room for all the drunks and drug addicts in town who would be brought in or walk in with falls, hits, fights, and all kinds of injuries. We had to evaluate them, clean them, stitch them, and give them whatever treatment they needed. A bus would come early in the morning from the Pinewood Center, pick them up, and take them to their facility. There they would get a shower and a good meal and be sent back out onto the streets. Some of them were regulars, while others wandered over from different parts of town.

As residents rotating through the ER, we were on call twelve hours a day four days a week, and we would get every other weekend off. Time passed quickly, as there was never a dull moment. One Saturday I was getting ready to end my shift, when a big African-American gentleman was wheeled in. He was totally intoxicated and was being held down by four EMTs. He was bleeding profusely, and the pressure dressing put on his head had soaked through with blood. I ran over to him, and we wheeled him into the designated treatment room. With a lot of help we were able to restrain him, tying down his extremities so he could not swing at or kick someone. I took down the dressing and there was a deep gash, about eight inches long, all the way across his forehead. His eyes were fiery red, and alcohol vapor was coming out with each breath. I gently cleaned the wound and numbed all around with local anesthesia so that he would not feel any pain. Facial wounds have a lot of blood supply and tend to bleed a lot. Because of the deep nature of this wound, it had to be stitched in layers.

I set up a surgical tray on the Mayo stand with everything I would need. Since the ER was crowded, I had no one helping me. I finished suturing the first deep layer, and the bleeding slowed down considerably. The next suture was loaded, and I had just started suturing the second layer when the patient opened his blood-shot eyes, looked at me, and blurted out, "You son of a bitch." I totally ignored it and kept doing what I was doing.

He took a few deep breaths, and what came next was one of the worst insults I have faced in life. With a mouthful of saliva mixed with the alcohol he had regurgitated, he forcefully spat a full blast all over my face. I could feel my face turning red and my head pounding with anger. Immediately my inner voice said, "Get away." I dropped everything, ran toward the sink, turned the cold water on, and washed my face over and over for ten minutes, until I calmed down. I had been slapped and hit and kicked by patients before, but the fury of this insult knew no bounds.

Then I went back, set up another sterile surgical tray, and asked the nurse to give the patient a small dose of sedation. He fell back into his slumber. The alcohol vapor was still strong, but I completed stitching the tear in his forehead, and then cleaned and dressed it. I had been there three hours past my time. Finally I drove home, warmed up some food, and sat looking out the window. I felt really proud of myself: I had conquered my anger and overcome the desire for revenge.

A great opportunity came up during the first year of my residency. A new requirement was established, that every community hospital had to have twenty-four-hour emergency room services. For the smaller community hospitals, the only solution was to have residents moonlight at their facility. Dr. Rizvi and I contacted a small community hospital called Nashoba Community Hospital in Ayer in north-central Massachusetts, about an hour's drive from Boston City Hospital. They interviewed us and gave us a contract that would pay us about $1,000 for a weekend of coverage. This was about ten times what we were paid in our residency program. It seemed we had hit a gold mine. We adjusted our schedules so that one of us would be available to moonlight every other weekend that we were off from residency calls. The sacrifice was that we would not see each other for months. At the hospital, the doctors and nurses treated us like royalty. We could catch up on sleep, eat gourmet food, and have a sort of social life. The workload was a joke compared to the residency program, and there was a lot of time for R & R. It was great financially too. In a short time, we built a decent saving in our bank accounts.

I distinctly remember my last day working at Nashoba. I was finishing my surgical residency in Boston and moving on to a urology residency in Detroit. I was really sad and depressed. Around 6:00 p.m., I received a call from the kitchen: the chef had fallen down and injured himself, and I was needed there urgently. I ran down to the kitchen, which was in the basement, and — to my utter surprise — the whole staff, including all the doctors and nurses, were there to bid me farewell. A sumptuous dinner was set up and in the middle of the table was a huge cake depicting me working in the ER. The chief of staff presented me with a $1,000 check and a beautiful Lladro sculpture of a Spanish doctor, which I still adore forty years later. I came to realize how much they loved and respected me.

Growing up, I had become fond of hunting. My parents gave me a Daisy air rifle when I turned twelve. There were a lot of trees in our orchard, which attracted different kinds of birds. With practice I had become a good shot. During high school and college, several of our friends would go on deer-hunting expeditions. At that time there were no permits or time limitations on hunting in India. I would borrow my dad's shotgun, and we would camp in the wild.

An incident during my residency in Boston brought an end to this sport for me. It was my second year as a surgical resident, and I was rotating through Beverly Hospital, north of Boston. The mid-November hunting season had just started. After finishing all my work at the hospital, I had just returned to the resident quarters, which was just a ten-minute walk. I was on call that day. The beeper went off, and it was the ER calling to come immediately. I ran down and met the nurse at the door. We went to the cubicle where the patient was on a stretcher. It was a beautiful blonde fourteen-year-old girl. I touched her. The body was cold; there was no pulse or heartbeat. She was clearly dead.

The EMTs who had brought her were standing right there. The story I got from them threw me into tears. The young girl had returned home from school and told her mother she was going biking in the woods in her backyard. It was just beginning to get dark. Some crazy hunter was out in the woods looking for deer. He was probably drunk. He had seen something moving and, without confirming what it was, had taken a shot at it. The rifle bullet had gone right through her head and probably killed her instantly. A neighbor who had seen the girl on her bike heard the gunshot and saw what had happened and immediately called 911, and the EMT got there right away and brought her to the hospital. They had no time to go to the house to inform the family or anyone. She was dead on arrival at the ER. The hunter had absconded, and no one knew who he was.

So it now became my duty to call the family. I gathered myself and called the home phone number. Her mother answered the phone. I said, "Mrs. Johnson, your daughter has been brought to the ER at Beverly Hospital, and she is in critical condition. You need to come to the hospital right away."

"It is not my daughter," she replied, and hung up. I called again and tried to tell her that we had identified the girl and that she was indeed her daughter.

"It can't be true," she insisted. "My daughter just came back from school and went bike riding while I was preparing dinner." I insisted that she come to the hospital right away. After much persuasion, she agreed to get her husband and come to the hospital. I had never faced a situation like this before, and there was no prep time. The parents arrived within fifteen minutes, and I had to be the bearer of this terrible news. They were absolutely devastated. That day I promised never to hunt, and since then I have never pulled the trigger of a firearm.

I have realized that one of the toughest things to do in the life of a physician is to pronounce someone dead, and then walk up to the family and give them the bad news. I have always hated it. The worst is sudden death, especially when a child is involved. I have always tried to go to the funerals of my patients, and sometimes I have wept on their shoulders. It always reminds me that you cannot always win in this game. We are all mortals, and when our time comes, we have to go.

In May 1975, I was chief resident in the Surgery Department at Boston University. It was my final rotation through the Emergency Room at Boston City Hospital. The place was hopping, with all kinds of sick and injured patients being brought in. The EMTs had called on the radio to say that they were bringing in a body that had fallen out of a dumpster when it was being emptied by the garbage trucks. They were not sure whether the man was dead or alive. It appeared that he had been looking for food several days earlier, had fallen in the dumpster, and had been unable to climb back out. There was no information as to how long he had been there. When he was wheeled in on the stretcher, he was in a coma. The body was cold, and I could barely feel a thready pulse, with hardly any breathing. He looked like a young man in his twenties, severely dehydrated and emaciated. We first covered him with blankets and with great difficulty were able to start an IV. Just as an oxygen mask was being put on, we realized that there were maggots crawling out of every orifice in his body. There were loud shrieks, and everyone left the room.

I had to compose myself, because I was the chief surgical resident in charge of the ER. I double-gowned and double-gloved with surgical hat and mask, and then collected a bunch of sterile instruments and supplies ready to go in. Every member of the staff refused to accompany me. I had no choice but to go in alone. I turned on all the room lights, pulled up a stool, and got to work. By now, the monitor showed that he had a recordable blood pressure and was breathing more regularly. The saving grace was that he was still totally out. I started with his nose, and then his ears, literally pulling out one maggot at a time. A wave of nausea passed over me, and I overcame it with sheer willpower. After that, I was so engrossed with what I was doing that nothing mattered. Once in a while I could see eyes peering through the tightly closed doors.

Two-and-a-half hours had passed when the shift changed, and one of the younger nurses took pity on me and came in, gowned and gloved to help. Another three hours went by, and we turned the patient on his side. His entire back was devoid of skin. The maggots had got into the bones and his anal opening. We cleaned him as much as we could, covering the raw surfaces with ointments and bandages. By this time, he started opening his eyes. He was alive again.

We brought some bread and milk and he just scarfed it down, asking for more food. He was totally disoriented, behaving like an animal, and had to be restrained. Soon after, we transferred him to the ICU, where he stayed for a few days. I followed him through his recovery, and after two weeks he was discharged and walked out of the hospital. Another miracle had happened.

I learned never to give up and to do whatever service is demanded of me in the call of duty. Right from the beginning of residency, I always believed that my first loyalty was to the patient. I will be their advocate against everything. They have put their total trust in me, and I have to live up to it. Even today, I try not to get angry about anything at work. The only thing that angers me is when patient care is compromised and the patient suffers.

The surgical training program was a combined one consolidating Harvard, Boston, and Tufts universities. If I remember correctly, we had more than a hundred residents covering a large number of hospitals in Massachusetts, from Beverly in the North to Cape Cod in the South, as well as a few hospitals in Providence and Pawtucket in Rhode Island. I was the chief resident in surgery, rotating through one of the smaller hospitals in Pawtucket. One day in October 1974, the last year of my residency, I had just finished dinner in the hospital cafeteria. Looking out the window of the doctors' lounge, I found myself in absolute awe of God's creation. Fall colors were in full bloom, and set against a crimson sky it was just spectacular. Just then I received a page on my beeper and called the operator back. She informed me that I was needed immediately in the ER. I hurried down the corridors to the ER, which was on the same floor. In those days there were no locks or codes for security.

The patient was a thin twenty-two-year-old white female, writhing in abdominal pain and vomiting at the same time. I gave her a few minutes to settle down, and then introduced myself to her and her parents, who were at the bedside. The nurse had just finished recording the vital signs. I got the history that she had been having abdominal pain around the belly button since the day before. Today the pain had gotten much worse and had migrated to the right lower quadrant of the abdomen. The family had just sat down for dinner when she started throwing up, and the pain became much more intense. At that point, they rushed her to the ER.

After completing my examination and reviewing the chart, I ordered an abdominal X-ray and some stat blood tests. But the diagnosis was very obvious. There were no CT scans available in those days and we depended a lot on the clinical symptoms and signs to make a diagnosis. It was a classic case of acute appendicitis, and the X-ray and blood test would further confirm it.

Since it was after routine hours, I called the nurse supervisor and requested her to call in the OR crew on call, which included the anesthesiologist, scrub nurse, circulating nurse, and recovery room nurse. I also called the attending surgeon on call. He was at a party and sounded annoyed that it would disrupt the fun he was having. I duly apologized and told him that I would call back when things were ready to go.

I went back to the ER and reviewed the test results. The white blood cell count was very high, indicating severe inflammation. The X-ray showed a lot of abdominal gas trapped in the bowels, indicating that the bowels were paralyzed because of the inflamed appendix. I walked back to the patient and her parents and discussed the findings of the test and the most likely diagnosis. I explained that it was an acute inflammation of the appendix and that we needed to surgically remove the appendix under anesthesia as soon as possible. The patient and her family were very understanding. We talked in detail about the involved procedure and possible complications. The patient and her father signed the consent for the surgery. At that very moment, I felt I was taking full responsibility for the patient's journey through surgery and recovery.

By now it was around 9:30 p.m. The nursing supervisor informed me that the crew was all ready to wheel in the patient from the ER to the operating room. I called the attending surgeon, and he sounded very different than when I had talked to him two hours before. His speech was somewhat slurred, and all I could understand was, "I'll be there."

I walked into the operating room. The patient was there, and the anesthesiologist was explaining his part in the procedure and what she was to expect in the recovery room. Her face was pale and anxious and her eyes were rolling around, her wide pupils inspecting everything around her. I walked up to her, held her hand, and sensed relief. Our eyes met, and she gave me a smile. It felt as if she were saying, "I trust you. Please take care of me. Get me out of my misery." Since then, I have always made it a rule to be in the OR as the patient is being put to sleep and to hold their hand firmly. It gives them a sense of comfort and confidence. Compassion has a great role to play in a surgeon's life, although unfortunately physicians receive little formal training in the art of listening. As healers, our professional calling card is to listen carefully and treat patients with the dignity and respect they deserve.

My dad, who was an extremely compassionate physician, always reminded me that no patient should leave your office without physical contact, if only a firm handshake or a tap on the shoulder. He practiced for over fifty years as a general practitioner in Patna. He was trained as a tuberculosis expert, as the disease was rampant in those times. As a medical student, I would assist him in his clinic. On any given day, he would see sixty to seventy patients. One third of them would pay his full fee, which was less than a dollar. Another third would give whatever they could afford, and a few would pay him in kind with fresh vegetables, fruit, or rice. And yet there were a few who had nothing. My father would take out his wallet and give them enough money to buy medicines they needed.

Returning to the patient on the OR table, I waited until she was fully asleep under anesthesia, and then went back to the surgeon's lounge to see if the attending surgeon had arrived. He was there. I recognized him, as I had worked with him a couple of times before. He was a big, burly man, close to six feet tall and overweight, with a big paunch. He was trying to change into the OR outfit and failing miserably. His face was red as a beet, and within seconds I knew he was drunk. I immediately confronted him, pointing out that he was not in a stable state to go into surgery. He shouted back: "I have to be there!" I pleaded gently, to no avail. Then, in a sterner voice, I asked him to sit down. The anesthesiologist walked in to let us know the patient was ready. The surgeon growled back at both of us, "I am okay!" Time was ticking away, with the patient under anesthesia. In a loud and firm voice, I said, "You are not okay, and I *will not* let you touch my patient." By now he was in my face, and I could smell the alcohol even more strongly. He shouted back, "How dare you question my authority!" At this point I had no choice but to call the hospital security officer, who promptly arrived and sat him down. After much persuasion from the three of us, he agreed to stay in the surgeons' lounge and let me perform the appendectomy. I had asked the security guard to stay with him in case he changed his mind and barged into the operating room, which would have been a disaster in the middle of surgery.

During my surgical training in India I had done many appendectomies, and I had completed the master of surgery program at Patna University. As chief resident, I had guided other residents in performing many surgeries. I was very confident that I could do this surgery with the help of the surgical nurse who had already scrubbed in. Thank God the patient was thin and the appendix had not ruptured. There were no complications. The procedure went very well, and I was done in thirty-five minutes. I immediately walked back to the lounge and informed the attending surgeon of the successful surgery. I also advised him to sleep in the lounge or have the security guard drive him home. His arrogant personality would not accept either piece of advice. He put his jacket on and rushed out of the room, saying, "I will take care of you tomorrow."

I said to myself that I had done the right thing given the circumstances and went back to the recovery room. The patient was waking up, and I gave her the good news that it was all over successfully. I then stepped out to the waiting room and gave the family the same glad tidings. They were happy beyond bounds and expressed their relief and gratitude.

After writing the post-operative orders and dictating the operative report, I returned to the residents' on-call room. The whole incident had been physically and emotionally very challenging. I lay down in bed and began analyzing the incident step by step. Despite what had happened, I had subordinated a senior surgeon. If he reported me to the hospital board and the chief of the residency program, it could be the end of my surgical career. What should be my next step? Should I have called the chief of surgery before I reacted? I went to the desk, picked up a pen and paper, and wrote exactly everything as it had happened, including the exact exchange of words. Thank God I had two other witnesses. I remembered how it was always stressed in the residency program: "Documentation, documentation, documentation! If it is not documented, it was not done." I fell asleep, anxiously thinking of the days to come.

The next morning I awoke early, as we made our rounds with the residents and interns at 6:00 a.m. before going into the OR at 7:00. The appendectomy patient was doing fine. Her white blood count was down, and she was hungry. I did not mention to anyone the confrontation I had had the night before. At seven I was in the OR, at the scrub sink, when the chief of surgery showed up. I could not wait to unload everything on him. I pulled him aside and related the whole incident in brief. His response was, "Mahmood, you did the right thing, but I wish you had called me." He advised me to document everything and was happy to know that I had already done so.

The next few weeks I was on pins and needles. Sure enough, the senior surgeon filed a written complaint against me. I filed my written report and was called to appear at the next hospital board meeting in two weeks. My fate was in their hands. I lost four pounds and could not get my mind off what was coming.

The board meeting was held in a large conference room. There were fifteen members. I was called in after they had finished a sumptuous dinner and my case came up on the agenda. I was given a seat at the end of the table and grilled by nearly every member. I had broken a "protocol" and set a bad example. When I left the room after an hour, I was in tears and felt the wolves had torn me apart.

The next morning, the chief of surgery paged me to his office. I was trembling and waiting to be fired. He was a kind man and gently asked me to sit down. He told me that after I had left the meeting, there was a heated discussion for another hour. The chief had been fully supportive of me and my actions. Luckily, he was aware of two other episodes confirming that the senior surgeon had walked into the OR under the influence of alcohol. The board had finally taken a firm and bold decision. I was severely reprimanded for my behavior, and the surgeon lost his privileges to practice surgery in the hospital. I took a big sigh of relief and thanked God that truth had prevailed. For several months thereafter, until I returned to Boston, I lived in fear that someone was out to kill me.

Earlier in the year, I had decided to switch specialties from cardiothoracic surgery to urology. A series of events had led to this. While at Quincy Hospital, I was rotating through and had a chance to discuss my future with two of the cardiothoracic surgeons on staff. Open heart surgery and coronary bypass were still in their infancy. After this major surgery, the surgeon had to stay in the hospital until the patient became stable, and there were times when the surgeon had to take the patient back to surgery urgently to remove clots in the coronary artery. Both of the cardiothoracic surgeons indicated that it was very demanding, and both of them were going through divorces. I met another surgeon at Boston City Hospital who told the same saga. I loved cardiothoracic and vascular surgery and had the privilege of working with giants in the field, such as Dr. John Mannick and Dr. Robert Berger. Dr. Berger had a position for me in the Boston University program, but after much deliberation, I decided to change my specialty to urology. Of course, this meant finding an approved residency program. I made many phone calls, and everyone had finalized their list of new residents at least two years in advance. But two of them would let me interview for the following year: Wayne State University in Detroit and Rush Medical School in Chicago.

The interview in Detroit turned out very interesting. The chief of urology was Dr. James Pierce, who was well known for his strict mannerisms. The chief resident told me bluntly, "He has medical students for breakfast, interns for lunch, and residents for dinner." With that in mind, I walked into Dr. Pierce's office with all my documents. He was a big man, over six feet, who loved sailing, especially in the annual Mackinaw race. A beautiful picture of his yacht hung behind his chair. He reviewed my credentials and papers for a few minutes, and then abruptly looked up. "Can you do research during the residency?" he said in a harsh voice. "Yes, sir," I promptly responded. He continued: "We are setting up a study to evaluate the effect of pre-treatment of cadaveric kidney transplants." I reached into my bag and pulled out a paper I had just finished writing. "Dr. Pierce, here is a study I did on that subject." He looked at me with total distrust and snatched the paper out of my hand. As he read through it, I could see the change in his demeanor. After a few minutes, he smiled and said, "We will let you know in a week if we have a position for you starting this July." I walked out of his office, thanked the secretary, and knew in my heart that I had lucked out. A week later, I received the full contract for the urology residency program at Wayne State University.

Starting the urology residency was another new beginning. Since everything had happened so fast, I had no place to stay when I arrived in Detroit. There was a small room in the research building across from Hutzel Hospital, and Dr. Pierce told me to stay there until I had found a place to rent. The building was very noisy, because the basement housed all the dogs we used for our research. The barking and howling went on all night. After dark, downtown Detroit was very dangerous. As recently as 1967, the city had suffered a major riot, and here I was in the middle of it. With the help of the office secretary, I found a one-bedroom apartment on Jefferson Avenue, right across from the Belle Isle bridge. It was a rather shady area, and you had to watch out for every shadow around you.

My first rotation was at the Detroit Receiving Hospital, which was in the worst area of downtown, a playground for drug dealers and criminals. The emergency room was one of the best places in the country to learn how to treat all kinds of trauma: gunshot wounds, stabbings, motor vehicle accidents. There were two very well-known specialists in the field, Dr. Anna Ledgerwood and Dr. Charles Lucas. They were really pioneers in this field, and I had great opportunities to learn from them.

My interest in doing human research continued in Detroit when I started my urology residency. Whenever we encountered a patient with major kidney injury, the rule was to surgically explore the degree of damage and try to repair as much as possible. Many times, the moment we opened the Gerota's fascia, a tight covering around the kidney, the tamponade (compression) effect was lost, there was excessive bleeding, and in most instances, we would have to remove the kidney entirely. I had reviewed all the literature and presented my thoughts at the Urology Journal Club. I suggested that we try conservative management and see if we could save the kidney by keeping close observation and not operating on these patients. All the staff physicians and residents agreed. It was astonishing that, within just three years, we had 102 cases to review and were able to save over 90 percent of the kidneys by not operating. I presented my findings at the annual urology meeting, and later published a paper in the *Journal of Urology*. Over the next few years, other centers agreeing with our approach started getting equally good results. The conservative approach became the standard of care in years to come and is still part of the national guidelines.

I remember those days very well. When on call, we would sneak out to Greektown just two short blocks away. Zorba's had a great deal; for $1.99 you could have a full meal and drinks: lamb souvlaki wrapped in pita bread, rice, overcooked green beans, and a glass of Coke. Anything was better than the awful meal at the hospital cafeteria. Sometimes, while we were eating, we would hear gunshots followed by sirens and knew that it was time to run back to the ER.

One time, I had just finished a long shift and walked to the parking structure across the street. My car was on the second level. Just as I reached in my pocket to open the car, I suddenly felt someone behind me holding a hard object to my head, and heard a voice shout: "Give me your wallet!" I started pulling out my wallet, turned around, and immediately realized that the guy holding the gun, a young black male and a known drug dealer, was someone I had just taken care of and discharged that morning. "Johnnie, don't you remember me?" I shouted. "I am Dr. Hai." Johnnie looked at me in despair, lowered his handgun, and started running away, saying, "Sorry, Doc, I'm really sorry." I took a deep breath and gathered myself. God had saved my life once more.

One of the great advantages of the Wayne State urology residency program was the fact that I got to spend nearly nine months at the Children's Hospital with Dr. Alan Perlmutter.

Dr. Perlmutter was a world-renowned pediatric urologist. Trained at Harvard, he was a meticulous surgeon. He had great respect for human tissue during surgery. Even general surgery and plastic surgery residents and fellows would come to learn from him because of his superb technique. He had a phenomenal memory and was one of the examiners for the Urology Board. He had published many papers and several books. He was truly my greatest mentor. On the other hand, he was a very tough teacher and expected everyone to live up to his standards. It was not unusual for him to expel a resident from the operating room in tears. Surprisingly, I happened to be in his good books and learned a lot from him. I reasoned that I had nine months to learn from this great surgeon. I didn't have to live with him for the rest of my life. I promised myself not to be emotionally shaken up by his personality. So I learned a great deal from him, and the techniques he taught are still a valuable part of every surgery I perform. Even after completing my residency, Dr. Perlmutter and I remained in touch. At his retirement party, he invited me and my wife to visit him at his Cape Cod home. Unfortunately, we never met again after that, and a few years later he passed away with bladder cancer.

In 1978, I was the chief resident in urology at the Allen Park Veterans Hospital in the suburbs of Detroit. There were two patients who were like landmarks. Let us call them Leroy and Bob. Leroy was a sixty-two-year-old Afro-American gentleman who was a severe diabetic and had lost both his lower legs. During his last surgery, both his buttocks had had to be removed, rendering him unable to sit. He also had a urinary tube to empty his bladder, and a bag to contain his bowel movements. All day he lay on his stomach strapped to a short four-wheel stretcher. He would wheel himself all around the hospital, happily cracking jokes and constantly knitting. As a matter of fact, he made a beautiful afghan when my son was born. Bob was a sixty-five-year-old white gentleman, totally paralyzed from the waist down. He weighed over four hundred pounds and was confined to a motorized wheelchair — another happy camper.

One Saturday morning, making my rounds, I found that both he and Leroy were missing. I immediately ran to the nurses' station and enquired. To my utter surprise, I was told that they had both gone out on a pass for the weekend. I kept wondering how they would survive outside the hospital and what they could possibly do. Monday morning, they were both in their usual form, chatting in the corridor. I hurried down to talk to them, to find out that they had spent the weekend in a room at the Hyatt Regency. "We had a ball, doc," Leroy said. "We went to the bar, got drunk, watched movies all night. It was so much fun."

Bob chimed in: "And we're going to do it again, doc."

Here I had always felt bad for them and their physical disabilities. That day I learned that happiness is a state of mind.

Acie Brown was a veteran who was brought to the ER at the V A Hospital in Allen Park. He had been bleeding in his urine off and on for six months. This time his bleeding had continued for over a week, and he was passing large clots. He felt dizzy and had passed out when the EMT had to bring him in. He lived alone in an apartment and had not previously sought any medical help. He was emaciated, dehydrated, and short of breath. I admitted him to our urology service. His red cell count and hemoglobin was down by 50 percent. After a transfusion of several pints of blood, he looked better and his breathing improved. We started our workup. CT scans were available only at certain university centers, and we had to arrange for him to go downtown to have one done.

The reports came back three days later. It was very bad news. Acie had a very large left kidney mass involving nearly three-fourths of the kidney. The tumor had grown beyond the protective layer, the Gerota's fascia. The worse news was that there was a huge blood clot extending from the kidney vein to the big vein, the vena cava, which drains directly into the heart and which could even be invading one of the chambers of the heart. The disease had gone too far, beyond surgical cure. There was possibly a 5 percent chance that we could extract the large clot from the heart and the vena cava in one piece, and then remove the whole kidney.

The very likely scenario was that, while trying to remove the clot, a large piece would get loose and totally block the heart chamber, leading to instant death. If we did nothing, the tumor would continue to grow and do the same within a few weeks. Death was inevitable.

I sat down with Acie alone, as he had no family or community support. With the help of sketches and anatomical drawings, I was able to give him the real picture. He sat down, quietly absorbing all I had said. He then looked up and said, "Doc, do you know why they call me Acie?" I shook my head. "Well, Doc, they call me Acie because I am a gambler. You know, the ace in a pack of cards. I have always gambled with my life, and I will take my chances with the surgery." I reiterated: "But Acie, you realize that the chance of you dying on the operating table is 95 percent." But he had made his decision. I discussed the case with the attending urologist, who agreed that we had to abide by the patient's decision.

The day of the surgery was set. We knew there would be excessive blood loss, and I arranged for twelve units of packed red cells to be available in the operating room. I had also discussed the case with the cardiothoracic team, in case they had to open the heart chamber to extract the clot. Needless to say, I was extremely nervous that morning and made a special prayer for Acie. Once he was totally anesthetized, I opened him up from stem to stern, so we would have full access to his chest and abdomen. All the retractors were put in place, and we started exposing the big vein, the vena cava. The clot was totally filling it up. We made a longitudinal opening in it. There was no flow of blood. We carefully started to free up the clot, and a small stream of blood began flowing. My heart was pumping away, and I could feel beads of sweat running down my back. The whole clot started coming out, as we gently pulled at it. It was like cleaning a very delicate piece of crystal. And then it happened. The long piece of clot was in our instrument, and the other end broke off and floated into the heart chamber and disappeared. The heart suddenly stopped pumping. The cardiothoracic team, all scrubbed and ready, moved in. They immediately opened the heart chamber. There was blood all over. The bleeding was totally uncontrollable, and we knew we had lost the game. Despite all efforts by both teams, we could not get the heart going, and after ten minutes of trying to get the heart started, we had to stop. Acie had gambled his life again, but this time he had lost.

I was totally devastated. Acie was gone. There was no family or friend to talk to. This was the first death of a patient on the operating table in my career. For weeks I kept questioning myself: could I have done anything differently?

Thank God, I have never had another patient die on the operating room in my forty years of practice.

CHAPTER 3

Love Conquers All

My definition of love is to give or sacrifice without expecting anything in return. Grief and unhappiness come when you don't get the return of favor that you were expecting. I have always believed that, as a human, your duty is to do the best you can in any given circumstance. You have complete control over what you do. On the other hand, you have no control over what the other person or group does in response. This goes against the basic principles of our material world, where most of what we do is a barter. But if you look at true love — for example, a mother's love for a newborn — she does everything possible to keep the baby happy and fed, and what she gets in return is crying, lack of sleep, and a dirty diaper. Yet the happiness she gets in holding the baby is divine. Similarly, in life, when you do an act purely from the goodness of your heart, expecting nothing in return, the sweetness of the reward is amazing. I am in no way suggesting that this is what I always do, for I am as human as anyone. But I definitely strive toward it.

Roget's Thesaurus uses nearly fifty different words to describe love, from "delight" to "idolatry." When we talk of "love at first sight," we are really talking about infatuation. Love grows over months and years. In the practice of medicine, you have to be devoted to the level of passion. Once you commit to becoming a physician, that becomes the primary role of your life. Practically everything else is secondary. There were many occasions when

I had to miss important family events, or leave in the middle of dinner, to go to the ER, to the dismay of my family.

You have to learn to love what you do and whom you serve. I have always said that when a patient comes to me, he or she becomes a part of my extended family. When dealing with them or planning their treatment, I have always thought, *What would I do if this were my uncle or aunt, grandmother or nephew, brother or sister?* And the answer would be very clear. All other factors had to be removed from the equation. This is what develops mutual respect and love between the patient and you.

When I was younger, in my twenties and thirties, I read poetry, especially the translations of poems by the great philosopher Rumi. And it all sounded abstract.

"Gamble everything for love, if you are a human being."

"Your task is not to seek love, but merely to seek and find all the barriers within yourself that you have against it."

"Yesterday I was clever, so I wanted to change the world. Today I am wise, so I am changing myself."

Over the years, as I grew wiser, it all made sense. As human beings we have the capacity to love or hate, and I found that love is so much easier and more fulfilling. I started to look at the goodness in people, and to overlook and ignore their weaknesses. I realized that everyone has good habits and bad habits. We all make good decisions and bad decisions. I began to step in the shoes of the person who wronged me or hurt me, and to look at things from their perspective. It started making some sense. I came to the conclusion that there are very few people who are truly bad or evil. Most of the time it is just bad choices or circumstances that lead to bad behavior. I started accepting the fact that indeed all of human creation has an innate goodness, and we are all the same in the eyes of the Creator.

An old quote comes to mind:

"The heart is a very good fertilizer; anything we plant: love, hate, fear, hope, revenge, jealousy: surely grows and bears fruit. We have to decide what we want to harvest."

In the last year of my urology residency, I began looking for a job or partnership. The chief of my urology department had offered me a faculty position, which would make me an associate professor and the staff in-charge of the VA hospital. But I hated the way academia worked. There was so much politics, backscratching, and backbiting. I just wanted to be out of it. When I refused his offer, the chief became extremely angry. He categorically told me that I had no chance of surviving in the private sector: I was a foreigner, English was my second language, and I did not understand the culture of the patients I would be caring for. I apologized and asked him to give me a chance. If I failed in private practice, I told him, I would definitely come back and accept his offer. I understood that he said what he said not in vengeance or to hurt me, but in an effort to retain me for the Urology Department. A few years later, when we ran into each other at a urology conference, he was delighted to learn that I was doing very well.

One of the very busy community urologists, Dr. A, approached me as I was nearing the end of my residency. He had been in private practice for many years and had been very successful in every way. He told me that his health was bad, mainly with cardiac issues, and that he wanted me to buy his practice. I was rather naive about the business of medicine. He took me to an attorney, who prepared all the documents specifying that I would purchase his urology practice at a fixed price. He would continue practicing at a slow pace, get me privileges at the local hospital, introduce me to the patients and referring physicians over the next six months, and then quit. I had to go to the bank to get a loan to pay my attorney bills.

On the first day of July 1978, I started working in his office and at the Annapolis Hospital. Life out of residency became even more fun. I loved it. The work was very busy and demanding, but the gratitude of the patients and the income were great. Dr. A was my best friend and advocate, telling all the patients and physicians how great I was. The office staff and the nurses were all delighted to have a young physician join the practice, bringing in new techniques and procedures. My brother was at that time a cardiologist on the faculty at Northwestern University in Chicago, and I referred Dr. A, now my senior partner, to him. He was given a complete medical evaluation at Northwestern and placed on a treatment plan. He started feeling much better. Our practice was flourishing, with lots of new patients, who themselves became a great source of referrals.

I remember the day very clearly. It was Thursday November 30, 1978. Dr. A and I were walking out of the office after a long day of work. He stopped, looked at me point blank, and said: "Mahmood, you don't need to come back to work from tomorrow. My health has settled down and I feel great. I will take care of my practice. You need to find another hospital and office and start your practice." It felt as though someone had pulled the rug from out under my feet.

In shock, I looked at him and mumbled, "What do you mean? What about the legal documents we signed?"

"They don't mean anything to me. Throw them in the garbage," he replied, and continued walking toward his car. I stood there for several minutes, in total disbelief. Then I gathered myself and drove home to tell the family that from tomorrow I had no job.

All night I was awake pacing the floor, trying to understand what it all meant and what my next step should be. Yet with all the black clouds, there was one silver lining. I was on call in the ER that night, and quite unexpectedly ended up with nine new patients admitted to my service. A new day had begun.

The next morning, I made a work list and made several phone calls. My accountant and medical supplier assured me that they would find an office and set it up for me within a week, and indeed they did. On Friday, December 8, I started seeing patients in my office. A majority of the physicians at the hospital were very sympathetic and helped me by sending patients and referrals. A few of the patients from the old practice found out and started seeing me in the new office. From that day onward, I have never had a dearth of work.

I called my attorney and gave him the news. He exploded: "I can't believe it! Let's sue the bastard for a few million dollars. You just have to sign a piece of paper, and I'll take care of the rest. When we win, we'll split the money fifty-fifty." I thought about it, but the decision in my mind was a clear no. I hadn't gone through school and fifteen years of training to get into a legal battle. If I worked hard, I told myself, I should be okay.

The next few years were quite a struggle. While I was applying myself to growing my practice, my ex-partner was doing everything to uproot me. He created false allegations against me and sent them to the ethics committee and the executive committee, requesting them to take away my privileges to practice. All his buddies were on the committees. My only assets were the truth and the fact that I had not done anything wrong. Verbally he was telling everyone how bad I was. I fought back with documentation from patients and other physicians who knew the allegations were a result of jealousy. Because truth usually shines through, the verdict was in my favor. After looking at all the evidence, the ethics committee concluded that I had done nothing wrong and, based on that, the executive committee also cleared me. Word got around, and it further boosted my referral base. I learned that being good is not good enough. When evil strikes, you have to fight back.

Unfortunately, my ex-partner faced many tragedies. Years later, he suffered a severe heart attack and had a coronary bypass surgery at a downtown hospital. I paid him a visit and took flowers. He was surprised. Two years after that, he went through a bitter divorce. He was thrown out of his house, and his wife and children left him. One day in the surgery lounge, he told me the whole story. I had tears in my eyes. He was homeless and the court had given most of his assets to his wife, who had supported him through his urology training. I felt pity for him. Words from my St. Xavier's

High School days kept coming back to me: Matthew 5:43-48, in which Jesus says, "But I say unto you, Love your enemies, bless those that curse you, do good to those that hate you, and pray for those who speak evil about you, and persecute you . . . that you may be children of your Father in heaven."

That evening when I got home, I rearranged a room in my house and asked Dr. A to come and live with me. He agreed and was delighted by my generosity. But on the day he was scheduled to move in, he received a call from his brother to go live with him in Germany until matters settled down. Dr. A secretly flew to Germany and spent the next few months there.

A few months later, in a department of surgery meeting, Dr. A got up and publicly apologized for his behavior toward me and asked for my forgiveness. I was overwhelmed and assured him of my love and friendship forever. Dr. A closed his practice and left town. We remained good friends for many years to come.

All faiths insist that compassion is the test of true spirituality and that it brings us into a relation with God. As Karen Armstrong states in her book 'Twelve Steps to a Compassionate Life,' the Golden Rule in all religions is "Always treat others as you wish to be treated yourself - and you cannot confine your benevolence to your own group; you must have concern for everybody — even your enemies."

CHAPTER 4

Bev's Story

When I went to medical school and did my residency, no one talked about how to run a medical practice. In the previous chapter, I explained how I got started in the practice of urology immediately after finishing my residency. Exactly five months after I began practice, I was thrown out in the field to start my own solo practice. With the help of my accountant, Larry Brown, and medical supplier, Robert Green, I was able to set up an office at the corner of Venoy and Palmer Roads in Wayne, Michigan. Fran, who was Dr. A's office manager, was very sympathetic to me after how terribly Dr. A had treated me. She sent her younger sister, Beverly, to help me with answering the office phones. Bev was forty-nine years old and worked in the meat department of the local grocery store, Farmer Jack. She had no idea how to run an office. Her husband, George, was a truck driver delivering products to Farmer Jack stores in northern Michigan. George had been a bachelor in his mid-forties when he fell in love with Bev at work. Bev had recently been divorced and had to support her three boys. She and George now had a small house only five minutes from the new office.

Very soon I realized that Bev was not only honest to the penny but also punctual, and that she had no demands on her time at home. Three days after we started, I sat down with her and had a very candid discussion. I told her, "Bev, I am thirty-one and you are forty-nine, and neither of us has any idea how to run a medical practice. So, let us learn it together." She readily agreed, with one condition: "You can fire me any time you feel I am not doing my job right." We started off on a handshake and the rest is history. There were no contracts, no papers, no signatures.

In those days, there were no computers. Patients started calling, and Bev would give them an appointment and pencil them in on our black diary. When the patient arrived, she would put them in the examining room with a manila folder and a blank sheet of paper. I would write down the patient's history, examine them, note the findings, and draw out a plan that the patient agreed to. In the right lower corner of the page, I would scribble down the fees: $10 for a new patient, $5 for a follow-up, and $0 if the patient requested not to be charged. The patient and I would then walk up to the desk where Bev sat. She would give them their paperwork for lab tests and X-rays, and note on a different piece of paper if any procedures had to be scheduled. Any prescriptions needed were handwritten by me. Bev collected the fees, and the patient was on his way home. Life was simple.

We designated Wednesday afternoons as billing day. Our main guide was the Urology Coding book, a skim volume with a few hundred codes commonly used in urology. I would select the right code, and Bev would fill in the standard billing form on the typewriter. Letters were sent in the mail, and within a few weeks we started receiving checks from Medicare and other insurance companies. It seemed like magic.

I had opened a checking account at the local bank, and they had sent me a deposit book and a book of checks to write. Once in a while, Bev had to call the insurance company if the payments did not come in time. She had also developed a network of other office managers to share her successes and grief.

Initially, when things were slow, and to keep myself busy and polish my skills, I would assist the OB/GYN surgeons when they did major surgeries. Sometimes I would be helping them when they were called to do an emergency caesarean section or to deliver a baby, and I had to complete the operation. This turned out to be a great blessing in disguise, as I learned to do many gynecological procedures very well. I have learned over time that any talent, experience, or education you acquire never goes to waste. Because of this additional training, all through my forty-one years of practice, I was able to help my urology patients who also needed some gynecological surgery.

Working at Annapolis Hospital was exciting and lots of fun. All the years of training as a surgeon and urologist were now being put to good use. I developed a respectful relationship with other physicians, nursing staff, and even the janitors. I tried to take the time to address their questions and concerns about the patient's care, realizing that everyone was part of the team and their clinical performance would be better if they understood the rationale and reasoning behind my decision. As a part of my educational efforts I started giving a monthly talk to the nursing staff on different aspects of urology.

I first met Annette Clement in July of 1979 when she started her nursing career as a graduate nurse in the ICU at Annapolis. One of the patients under her care was unable to pass urine and the admitting cardiologist had asked me to see the patient in consultation. After examining the patient, I determined that he needed a Foley catheter to relieve his urinary retention while recovering from his heart attack. I asked Annette to bring the catheter and necessary supplies. After explaining the procedure to the patient, we got everything ready. "Annette, why don't you put the catheter in", I said. "I know how to do it but I have never done it before," Annette replied. "Well then let this be the first time," I said. Although nervous, Annette successfully catheterized the patient, the cloudy dark urine started to drain into the bag, and you could see a proud smile on her face. "Thank you, Dr. Hai," she beamed. "You did a great job. Welcome to urology," I said. The patient was totally relieved of his misery. A year later, Annette transferred to the operating room because of her interest in surgery. Little did I know that it was in God's plan that, eighteen years later, this graduate nurse would become my wife.

Over the next few years, the practice grew rapidly, thanks to referrals and word of mouth from patients and their relatives. The days would start early with surgery and end late in the office. With her enthusiasm, Bev kept pace with me and kept learning new skills every day. Our bond grew, and I could feel a mother-son relationship developing. I was about the same age as Bev's own children. They were all living away from home and doing well, and I became her new baby. Nearly every day when she went for lunch, she would bring me a salad or something light to eat, knowing that I would be rushing to the office after finishing the surgeries with no time to eat.

Since the late 1960s, I had been closely following the debate over how computers might enhance the practice of medicine. During the 1980s, computers improved dramatically, leading to the creation of Health Level Seven (HL7), which set a standard for the electronic exchange of clinical, financial, and administrative information among health-care-oriented computer systems. With my philosophy of staying up-to-date with cutting-edge technology, I took a few courses on computers. During a national urology meeting in Chicago, I saw three vendors selling computer systems for medical billing. It aroused my interest, and I asked if I could visit an office where the system was in use. I was told that nobody in Michigan was using it, but that we could see it in action in an office in Chicago.

After returning to Michigan, I discussed it with Bev, and she was agreeable to looking at it functioning in an office. IBM seemed to have the best system, and Bev and I flew to Chicago to attend a full day of demonstrations in a medical office there. The whole experience was amazing. After getting Bev's consent, I ordered the system from IBM. It cost more than $20,000, but the company gave us a big break if we would allow them to use our office for demonstrations. All the paperwork was completed and signed.

It was not until late October 1985 that the huge IBM boxes arrived at the office. They were stored in one of the examining rooms. A weekend was scheduled at the end of November for instructors from IBM to set up the system and teach us how to use it. On Wednesday of that week, when I sat down at my desk, there was a long letter from Bev giving her resignation. The letter stated, "You need to hire somebody young and smart to run the computers. I will not be able to do a satisfactory job."

I nearly fell out of my chair. All throughout the decision-making process, Bev had been very enthusiastic and agreeable. What had caused her to change her mind?

I called Bev into my office, and she broke down in tears. Between sobs she said, "I feel so bad to put you through all this. You've been so good to me and have put up so much money for it, but I just can't do it." I went around to her side of my desk and gave her a big hug. Now she was crying with hiccups. I put my hand on her back and said, "Bev! Calm down. Let's talk about everything sensibly. These computers are your servants. They'll do what you want them to do. You're still the boss. Don't let them intimidate you."

She looked up at me and said, "You're not angry and upset with me?"

"Not at all," I said. "Leave the computers in the room. I will cancel this weekend's training, and you just think about it. Let's talk about it after a few weeks, and if you really don't want it, we will send those damn boxes back to IBM for a refund." A smile suddenly came across her face, because she loved the rare occasions when I used a swear word.

In mid-December, I got a call from my eldest brother in India, saying that our father was not doing well. I booked a flight and left the next week. I returned to the office on Monday, January 6, 1986. To my utter surprise, Bev had set up the whole computer system, taken the two-day training, and practiced for two weeks. She was ready to go. When I asked her what had changed her mind, she said, "You told me I was still the boss and the computer was my servant." We were one of the first medical practices to use computerized billing. Bev was not only efficient on the IBM computer, but also trained many people from other offices as they acquired the system.

One day in the spring of 1988, when I came to the office, Bev was sitting in her chair. She just didn't look right. Her complexion was pale, and there were dark shadows under her eyes. "Are you okay?" I asked her.

"Yes," she said, but dragging out the word.

"You are not. I can see it. What's going on?"

"I've been having heavy bleeding in my stool all week."

I scolded her: "Why didn't you tell me? I am taking you straight to the ER. Call George and let him know."

When we got to the ER, we found that her hemoglobin had dropped to nine grams. I called my gastroenterologist friend, Dr. Rao, and asked him to come down and see Bev in the ER. It was Friday afternoon, and we decided to give her two units of packed cell blood transfusion overnight and get her ready for a colonoscopy and biopsy the next morning. Throughout the procedure, I stayed with her, holding her hands and praying for her. Dr. Rao found a cancerous lesion in the descending colon, the size of a small strawberry. The bleeding was coming from that site. He took several biopsies, and then stopped the bleeding with cautery. I immediately called my surgeon colleague Dr. Don Largo. "Don, what do you have scheduled for Monday?" I inquired.

"I have a full day of surgery," he replied.

"Well, you need to add one more bowel resection," I told him. "It's my secretary, Bev. She has a malignant mass in her colon. Dr. Rao has biopsied it, and we will have a confirmation Monday morning. And Don, let me know when you are available to talk to Bev and her husband George."

Sunday morning, Dr. Largo and I met with Bev and George in Bev's room at the hospital. I had made all the arrangements that were needed prior to the surgery.

Bev called me around 2:00 p.m. "I'm okay with everything," she said, "but do you mind talking to my three sons and answering all their questions?" I took their phone numbers and talked to them at length. Two of them worked with the airlines; one was a pilot with United, and the other worked for Delta. They both decided to fly in Sunday night. On Monday morning, the pathology report confirmed the mass to be malignant. I met with the whole family in Bev's room and answered all their questions and concerns.

Monday afternoon, the surgery went very well. I had scrubbed in with Dr. Largo, and thank God the cancer was confined to the bowel and we could remove it all. I had cancelled my office that afternoon and stayed with Bev in the recovery room until she woke up. She looked at me and squeezed my hands tightly. Tears were rolling down her cheeks, and I couldn't hold in mine either. "It's all done and you did great," I said. "Let me get George, Bob, and Jack back to see you."

Bev was discharged and went home five days later. She was recovering well, and Dr. Largo had advised at least three weeks off work. Every day after work, I would pick up some food for Bev and George and stop by to see her. Two weeks later, when I got to the office, I was surprised to see Bev sitting at her desk opening the mail. "And what are you doing here?" I said.

"I was awfully bored at home, so decided to come back to work," she replied.

"I am sorry, I need to see a doctor's note before you can start working," I replied firmly.

"Don't be ridiculous!" she retorted.

"No, I am serious, and I want you to go home and rest," I replied. Knowing that she would not get her way on this issue, she wrapped up and went home. A week later, she started working full time and got back into her busy routine.

In the first week of July 1989, Bev came and talked to me. George had retired from Farmer Jack two years back and had a decent pension. Every day when she got home, George would complain that he was bored to death all day and angry with her for still working. Soon she would be turning sixty. She had never got back her full energy since the surgery over a year earlier, and she was finally giving up and wanted to retire. She had trained another secretary, Sue, and a medical assistant to help run the practice. I told her I was fine with her decision.

The following weekend, I took Bev and George out to dinner. After thanking her for all she had done for me, I asked them their retirement plan. They wanted to move to Miami where one of her sons, Dale, and his wife Theresa lived. After driving a big truck through icy roads and snowstorms, George wanted nothing to do with the terrible Michigan winters. I talked to Dale and Theresa, and they had found a nice two-bedroom condo complex on the water in the $100,000 range, but the whole amount was required in cash. I talked to my financial consultant to see how much money we had put in Bev's pension plan, and it was $17,074.27. I requested him to have a cashier's check for that amount sent to Bev. She was thrilled to receive the check and called me with lots of thanks. She and George sold their house and, after paying the real estate commission and closing costs, they netted about $53,000. They still needed another $30,000 to close the deal.

Before they left for Florida, we threw a big barbecue party in our back-yard and invited all of Bev's relatives and friends, the people that she had worked with, my family and close friends, and of course Dr. Rao and Dr. Largo. It was a beautiful evening, and we all had lots of fun. I had picked up a large musical clock from Things Remembered, which was personalized with Bev's name. She loved it, and I last saw the clock in her Orlando home when I visited her there in early 2019. Bev and George moved down to Miami and started living with her son Dale while all the condo negotiations were going on. A few weeks later, I flew down to see them and the condo. It was in a great location, on the bay where all the cruise ships would turn to dock. It was a great pastime for the condo owners to sit and watch the ships go by. After some time, the residents knew exactly what ship would be in port at what time. There was a nice public park next to the property, too.

After seeing their intense desire to move into the condo, I knew I had to do something to make it happen. I told Bev that I would arrange for the balance of $30,000 right away and they should plan on closing next week.

I had my broker sell some of my stocks to raise the amount and send the check to Florida. Bev and George moved into the condo right away, and their happiness knew no bounds.

The most interesting thing happened at the end of November that year. It was a weekend, and I was looking at the financial picture of the practice for the whole year. When I looked at the pension plans, it struck me that I had been putting a lot into Bev's pension plan because of her age, so why was it only $ 17,000 at her retirement? On Monday morning, I called the financial consultant and explained my concern to him. Two days later, while I was in the midst of seeing patients, he called me back. "I found the problem," he said. "We had a plan that we closed a few years back and Bev has $30,020.41 in that plan. But now that she is happily gone, I will just roll it into your account." Furious, I shouted back, "It is her hard-earned money, and we need to send it to her ASAP!"

I called Bev immediately and asked her forgiveness for delaying in paying her due pension. I told her that she would be getting another check for that amount. I could hear her shouting out to George, "Honey! We won the lottery and we don't owe anything to anybody!" Bev told me to keep the check and pay off the money I had lent her. It was amazing how God had quickly paid back an act of kindness.

In the midst of all this, I was going through a major crisis in my personal life. I had got married in late November of 1975 during my second visit to India. My in-laws had lived in Ypsilanti, Michigan, for many years. A year later, my father-in-law passed away suddenly with a major heart attack and, as I had promised him, I assumed full responsibility of my in-laws. On fifth November of 1977, our son Yusuf was born, and nearly a year later, our daughter Ayesha was born on October twenty-six,1978. To make it more convenient for everyone, I purchased a large house in Dearborn Heights, Michigan, and moved my mother-in-law and sister-in-law to live with us. Life had suddenly become very busy and complicated. Many day-to-day arguments and disagreements had started between me and my wife, and over the years, we both felt we were growing apart. We went through years of marriage counseling to no avail.

I went to see my brother in Chicago. He saw me and said, "What's going on with you? You look terrible." Being a cardiologist at Northwestern University, he took me to his office and did a complete evaluation. The EKG showed some changes, and he immediately scheduled a cardiac catheterization. One of my major coronary arteries was significantly obstructed. I underwent cardiac catheterization and dilatation of the blocked artery. It was like magic — I immediately started feeling better.

The following day, my brother sat down and had a serious talk with me. He knew all that was going on in my life. "Mahmood, you just cannot go on like this," he said very seriously. "The stress is going to kill you. You have to take some decisions in life and make changes, whatever it takes, even if you have to go through a divorce." It was July 1996, and when I returned to Michigan, I filed for divorce.

The only good thing was that our children had grown: Yusuf was twenty and at the University of Michigan in Ann Arbor, and Ayesha was nineteen, had just graduated from Country Day High School, and was getting ready to start at the University of Michigan, too. When they were toddlers, I had invested into the Michigan Education Trust (MET) program that guaranteed them four years of college in the state of Michigan. It turned out to be an absolute blessing in those trying times.

It was at this time in my life that an angel came to help and guide me. His name was Sahal Kabbani. Sahal had obtained his engineering degree from MIT in Boston, had married a local girl, and had gone back to his homeland, Saudi Arabia. There he started a plastic pipe manufacturing company, which proved successful and made him wealthy. I first met Mr. and Mrs. Kabbani in the late 1980s, when Sahal had come to see me as a patient. He was a tall, handsome man in his late sixties who looked very accomplished in every way. He was extremely kind, humble, and exemplary in his behavior. I had fallen in love with his overall personality, and he had become like my favorite uncle. Sahal and his wife in turn became very fond of me. He got involved in my Michigan Educational Council project and put me on the board of some of the philanthropic work that he was doing in the United States.

Every summer, Sahal and his wife would spend a few weeks in Michigan and we would have a great time together, going to eat and talking for hours on different subjects. He had gradually become my life mentor. In the early 1990s, he had met Annette in the office and was greatly impressed by her talent and personality. He even got her home telephone number and would call her and talk to her for hours, sometimes giving her fatherly advice. Mrs. Kabbani also liked Annette and would go shopping with her. In late August 1996, when he came for his summer retreat, I told Sahal about my heart issues and divorce. He was very sad, and hugged me and whispered in my ear, "You have to be strong and have faith. God has a better plan for you."

In the first week of August, Sahal and I flew to Washington, D.C., for the two-day meeting of an organization where we both served on the board of trustees. We were staying in a nice hotel in the suburbs. After a long day of meetings and dinner, Sahal called me in my room. "We need to go out for a walk," he said. "How about meeting in the lobby in an hour?" I agreed. With an hour to kill, I stretched out on the couch. *My life is in such turmoil. What do I do to settle everything down?* My thoughts were heavy on my mind.

It was a beautiful evening. Sahal and I walked out of the hotel and across the street to a nice park with green grass and flowers in bloom. We followed the path toward the central fountain. Light music was playing in the background. We sat down on a bench on the quiet side of the park.

"Mahmood, I know you are going through some very difficult times," Sahal said to me. "The last few years have been miserable for you." It seemed he was reading my mind. "But God puts us through these trials to test our faith. He has a plan, and I will tell you what I think you should do." I looked up into his face and focused on his eyes, which looked big through his thick glasses. "Me and my wife have known Annette for several years. She had gone through a divorce few years back and is raising her twin boys, Matt and Charlie. Life has been extremely difficult for her too. Both your elder brothers are well acquainted with her. She had helped your family plan the hospital in your home town in Patna, India. You need to marry Annette." There was a pause. I was totally taken aback. "The two of you deserve each other, and she will bring you happiness and peace of mind and together you can raise all the children in a happy family." He waited for my response.

"But we just know each other professionally," I objected.

"And that's where my wisdom comes in play," he insisted. "I know the two of you very closely. She is a single mother raising two young kids, and you need a stable, supporting, and loving companion." The old man had given his verdict.

"Well, thank you for your advice, but there is a lot for me to think and deal with," I told him. That was the end of our conversation on the subject, as we walked back to the hotel.

When I got back the next day, I asked Annette to stay back after work. I sat down and told her the whole episode with Sahal. After listening to everything, she said, "Yes, he called me this morning and told me the same thing. I do respect him very much, but this is not an easy decision for either of us."

We left the office with a promise to think about it seriously over the next few weeks.

I talked to my brother in Chicago. His advice was, "If you know her well and feel it will work for you, don't waste too much time." My elder brother In India was also very supportive of the idea. They had both known Annette from the time she had helped us in planning the hospital in India — it was named "Hai Medical Research Institute" and was built as a legacy to our parents. Over the next few months, I talked individually to some of my very dear friends in the community. Not knowing Annette personally, they said, "You definitely need stability in your life and work. The community and all of us need you, and if you think she is the right person, you have our unquestionable support." After discussing all aspects of this union, Annette and I finally took the decision to get married in July 1997. We had a simple ceremony at the Fairlane Club in Dearborn, with just our close friends and family. Sahal could not be with us because of Mrs. Kabbani's sudden illness, but his happiness knew no bounds. It has now been twenty-three years, and we have never regretted our decision. Annette became not only a wife, but a true companion in every venture we have gotten into. Sahal Kabbani's wisdom and foresight were unerring.

Over the years, I kept in touch with Bev and George. In the late 1990s, they sold their condo and moved to Orlando, to a small duplex near Sea World. Her youngest son Jack and his family lived very close. They had two boys who brought a new cheer into Bev's life. Whenever I called Bev or she called me, we would talk about the good old days and then all about the boys. I had made it a routine to visit her whenever we were in the Orlando area, and she developed a great fondness for Annette knowing that I was taken care of so well.

As years went by, George grew weaker and eventually became totally dependent on Bev. One day as I walked in the office, the office manager came up and said, "Your mother called from Orlando, and she wants you to call her right back." When I called, Bev told me that George had passed away in his sleep. They were bringing the body to Michigan for the funeral. We attended the funeral and the burial in Westland. Bev had lost her long-term companion and friend.

Over the years, Bev would send me emails, remembering the good old days, wishing me and my family love and happiness. On Wednesday, December 3, 2014, she sent me this:

"HAPPY BIRTHDAY TOMORROW

I want to wish you a very wonderful day on your 68th birthday. You are a very special person and I am glad we have known each other all these years.

Hello to all and love to you and Annette.

A few words from Steve Maraboli as advice to you.

The wise will admire you

The wishful will envy you

The weak will hate you

This is the reality for those

Who dare to be epic.

Love Bev"

Throughout her life, Bev always depended on me for her medical care. In early 2017, she called me with the bad news that she had swollen glands in her neck and was having marked difficulty in swallowing. I told her to have her primary care doctor refer her to a hematologist/oncologist, and that as soon as the specialist had completed his testing, I would discuss everything with him. Unfortunately, the diagnosis came back as lymphoma. After much deliberation, we all agreed that she should have chemotherapy. She had a phenomenal response to the first dose. Although she was weak, the neck swelling disappeared and she could swallow and function much better. I called her regularly to see how she was doing and advised her to take some supplements to give her more energy. Overall, she felt much better. I visited her around Christmas, and she looked better but remained mostly confined to home.

The lymphoma struck again in June 2018, and this time with a vengeance. The oncologist suggested a clinical trial chemotherapy that was extremely toxic. There was not much of a choice at this time: either have a miserable death from the disease or die from the chemotherapy with a small chance of complete remission. Always a fighter, Bev chose chemotherapy. She was given the first dose and became deathly sick, ending up in the intensive care unit. She was in the hospital for months, and finally ended up in a nursing facility. It took her three months to regain enough strength to be discharged home. At this time, both Jack and his son Cody, Bev's much-loved grandson, decided to move in with her to help with her day-to-day needs.

On January 21, 2019, Annette and I drove to Orlando to see her. Before we got to her house, we stopped at Red Lobster and picked up lunch for everyone. I knew Bev loved seafood. Normally we would mail her Christmas present, but this time we brought it with us. She loved the outfit Annette and I had chosen for her. She was close to ninety now and still in great spirits, though weak. As we were leaving, she hugged me firmly and just kept crying and whispered, "Please take care of yourself. I love you." Tears were running down my cheeks too. An inner voice told me that I would never see her again.

Thirty-eight days later, early in the morning of March 1, 2019, I received a call from Jack to say that Bev had passed away in her sleep. Her body was brought to Westland, Michigan, where she was buried next to George. Bev always loved building birdhouses in her spare time and would give them out as gift to everyone. In her memory, we sent a beautiful birdhouse with flowers to the family. The message said, "You were like a mother to me: loving and protecting. May God grant you the peace you deserve. Annette and I will miss you forever."

I miss her immensely and tears are flowing as I finish writing this chapter.

CHAPTER 5

A Proud Citizen

M_y Pan Am flight from India arrived in New York on the afternoon of June 28, 1973. I had all the hospital paperwork with me to apply for Permanent Resident status on arrival. The papers were processed right at the JFK Airport, and I was given temporary documents so I could start work as a surgical resident when I arrived in Boston. A few months later, I received my Green Card in the mail, and I carried it with me at all times.

A month after my arrival, I was told by my fellow residents that I needed to buy a car, because my next surgical rotation would be outside Boston and I would need to be driving on my own and could not depend on the subway and buses. I started looking at ads in the newspaper. In those days, you could buy a decent new American-made car for under $3,000. I was attracted to a more compact German car, and I ended up at the Audi/Porsche dealership. As I stepped into the showroom, a middle-aged gentleman welcomed me and introduced himself. I shook his hands and said I was a resident at Boston University. "Please, doctor, we have a great selection of cars, and with your employment we should have no problem getting your loan approved," he assured me. I was really impressed by the respect and professionalism he showed to me. In general, Indian residents and physicians had a very good reputation. They were known to be hard-working, well-educated, and mostly fluent in English. An hour later, after a test drive, I signed up for a new bright green Audi Fox. In my mind, I had decided not to pay more than $4,000, and, to my surprise, the final number was

$3,990. The loan payment was stretched over three years, which made the monthly payment very doable. I had always driven a stick shift, and it was very easy to learn the automatic shift. I loved that car and drove it for five years, finally selling it in 1978 for $5,000.

In late 1975, I decided to make a visit back to India to spend two weeks with my family. Immediately on landing at Delhi, the endemic corruption in my homeland hit me in the face. The customs officer openly asked for a bribe to let me through. When I refused, he decided to keep some of the gifts I was bringing home. It was a rude reminder. *You are back in India, Mahmood!* I said to myself. A few more incidents happened on my flight to Patna, and the reasons I had left India came back to me in a flash.

It was great to see family and friends at home. The thing I remember enjoying most was my mother's cooking. Every day she cooked my favorite dishes, and I ate without end. After a few days, when I was well rested, my father sat down to talk to me. He was a very wise man, and he spoke sparsely in a very soft voice. After listening carefully to my achievements and success stories, he gave me a piece of advice that decided my entire future. "Mahmood, my son!" he began. "God has been very good to you. He gave you a great opportunity and you have worked hard to do very well. If you do decide to come back to India, there are only disappointments and frustrations waiting for you. If you continue on the path you are on, and put forth your best efforts, you will not only have contentment in life, but also can make a positive difference in the lives of many humans. I will be happy whatever you decide and wherever you dwell, but I would like you to be excellent in what you do."

He continued: "You are going to live in a great country, the United States of America. There will be times when you will feel on top of the world — 'I am a great physician, have a big house, beautiful cars, great respect, and so on.' Look up, and there will be many who have much more than you, and it will humble you. Then there will be times when you will feel down and depressed — 'I wish I had this mansion, a private jet, unlimited wealth, and on.' Look down, and you will see many who are struggling to get the basic necessities of life, and it will uplift your spirits. At whatever station of life you are, thank God for what He has given you and be content."

I returned to America, and for the next eight years, I totally forgot about my immigration status. Then one day, a friend asked if I had become a citizen. I had decided to do so long ago, but had never completed the application. I had already started living the American dream, and becoming a citizen would further confirm my long-term commitment. So I went downtown Detroit to the Immigration and Naturalization office and picked up an application. It read:

"Become a U.S. Citizen: To be an American Citizen means becoming a part of one of the most culturally diverse and most exciting countries in the world! A place where you have endless opportunities and the freedom to create a better life for you and your family. Do not wait anymore to start living the American dream as a Citizen!"

I filed the application for citizenship along with all the supporting documents. It was now 1983, and I had finally gotten around to it. After reviewing all the papers and submitting to a personal interview, I received a letter from the Immigration and Naturalization Service stating that all the requirements had been fulfilled, and that I was eligible to become a citizen. All that remained was for me to take the oath of allegiance at a swearing-in ceremony. The date for that was set for October 1, 1984. I told my office staff to keep that morning free, so I could go finish the process and be back in the office by ten o'clock.

I headed downtown early to avoid the morning rush. But when I arrived at the US Immigration center on Mount Elliot Road in Detroit, I was told that the swearing-in ceremony would take place at 9:00 a.m. at Cobo Hall, and that President Reagan would be there. I knew Cobo Hall well, from attending the Detroit International Auto show every year. When I got there, it was still only eight o'clock. I was the very first person to enter when the doors opened, and I took a seat in the front row, dead center. Before I knew it, the hall was packed and bustling with activity. The stage was full of dignitaries and popular figures from the news and television media.

And at exactly 9:00 a.m., the president walked onto the stage. The national anthem was sung, and US District Judge John Feikens administered the citizenship oath. After we sat down and the speeches began, I was intently studying the president. He looked fresh and energetic, and very handsome in his dark blue suit and red tie. Lost in this gaze, my eyes met his, and he winked at me with a smile. It was like magic. Even after thirty-five years, that memory remains vivid to me: a newly sworn-in citizen and the president of the United States sharing an accidental private moment.

Soon after, the president got up and gave one of the most remarkable speeches I've ever heard. It has remained forever engraved in my memory. It had such an effect on me that I want to share it with you in full:

> "My fellow Americans; and I'm very proud to be the first to address you with those words, my fellow Americans welcome to your country. Of all the things that a president does, nothing is as rewarding as events such as this. This is a ceremony of renewal. With you, today the American dream is reborn.
>
> As you were saying the Pledge of Allegiance, it was clear to me, even from up here, that you weren't just reciting words that you'd memorized. You spoke with belief, and it was good to see, because the pledge not only contains the best definition of our country, it contains our greatest hope: to always remain 'one nation under God, indivisible, with liberty and justice for all.'
>
> Today you've joined a people who are among the freest on the face of the Earth. We're a nation greatly blessed. We were founded by men and women who wanted it said of our country: here the people rule. They created a philosophy of freedom that is expressed in the document by which our

country was established, the preamble of which was read to you, the constitution.

Now, I know that most Americans are immigrants from other countries, and most of those countries have constitutions. I haven't read all the constitutions of all the nations of the world, but of all that I have read, I've noticed a difference that is so subtle it almost escapes you, and yet it is so tremendous it describes the difference. Those other constitutions give the people, or grant the people, in most instances, many of the same rights that our constitution says are yours. But those constitutions say that government grants you those rights. Our constitution says we, the people, have those rights by grace of God by our birth, and we, the people, will grant to the government the following rights.

Our government, now your government, has no power or rights that we, the people, have not freely given to it. Now, this may seem a small distinction, but as I said, it is everything.

You've joined a country that has been called 'the least exclusive club in the world with the highest dues'. America was founded by men and women who understood that freedom doesn't come free. It has a cost. But I don't suppose anyone would know the cost of freedom, the price of freedom better than you who have taken this oath today.

Some of you came from places that, sadly, have not known freedom and liberty. Some of you have come from places that don't offer opportunity. Some of you are probably here because you are, by nature, adventurous. And some of you have no doubt come here for a new start, to wipe the slate clean and begin your life anew.

These strike me as all good reasons. In fact, they're the very same reasons that our forefathers came here. And they did pretty well; so well, in fact, that two centuries after they invented this country it is still what they intended it to be: a place where the oppressed, the lost, the adventurous, can come for sanctuary and comfort and chance.

It's long been my belief that America is a chosen place, a rich and fertile continent placed by some Divine Providence here between the two great oceans, and only those who really wanted to get here would get here. Only those who most yearned for freedom would make the terrible trek that it took to get here. America has drawn the stoutest hearts from every corner of the world, from every nation of the world. And that was lucky for America, because if it was going to endure and grow and protect its freedoms for two hundred years, it was going to need stout hearts.

Fifty million immigrants came to this country in the last two hundred years. Some of the most recent have crawled over walls and under barbed wire and through mine fields, and some of them risked their lives in makeshift boats.

And I know that all of them felt as the immigrants of the early part of this century felt. So many of them steamed into New York, and as they would see the approaching skyline and the Statute of Liberty, they'd crowd to the side of the boat and say, 'America! America!' And in that word they heard the sound of a New World. In that word they heard everything.

And all of them have added to the sum total of what your new country is. They gave us their traditions. They gave us their words. They enlivened the national life with new ideas and new blood. And I urge you, you probably don't need to be urged, but I'll urge you anyway, just for fun urge you to remember, as they did, the land of your birth. Bring to us its culture and its heritage. We don't reject them. We need them. They enrich us.

You know, man can take unto himself a wife. A wife can take unto herself a husband. That doesn't mean that they abandon their mothers and fathers and forget them. So, you know, every now and then academics talk about assimilation and how our various ethnic groups have, with time, dropped their ethnicity and become more 'American'. Well, I don't know about that. It seems to me that America is constantly reinventing what America means. We adopt this country's phrases and that country's art, and I think it's really closer to the truth to say that America has assimilated as much as her immigrants have. It's made for a delightful diversity, and it's made us a stronger and a more vital nation.

But our diversity is not only ethnic. You'll find, if you haven't already, that this country is full of different and, sometimes, conflicting ideas and philosophies. Walk by a newspaper stand, and you'll see scores of magazines and newspapers arguing this point and that. Listen to television and radio, and you'll hear more than enough opinions with which to agree and disagree. In fact, if you don't over the next several years find one time, at least, when you feel like taking off your shoe and throwing it at a television screen, then you will have missed out on one of the great American moments. [Laughter]

Arguing is something of a tradition here. We like to disagree. But it's usually pretty good-natured arguing, and it doesn't tear us apart. I think you'll find that for all our disagreeing, Americans remain united around certain shared ideas and shared dreams which takes me back to where I began. All of us want one nation under God . . . with liberty and justice for all. Most of the disagreeing just has to do with the best ways to secure liberty and justice and the best ways to protect them.

And so, today you join a happy country that is happier for your presence. You're adding your voices to the chorus, and in doing that you've become part of a great unending song.

And I want, as president, to thank you for something before I leave. There have been times in our recent history when some of our citizens have doubted if America is still all she was meant to be. They've wondered if our nation still has meaning. And then we see you today, and it's an affirmation. You, standing here, reveal we all must still stand for something."

He ended by saying, "I know that the eldest among you is ninety-two, and the youngest among you is two. And we thank you all for the compliment of your new citizenship. Thank you all, and God bless you."

Cobo Hall has a capacity of about twenty thousand. As soon as President Reagan finished speaking, all twenty thousand of us stood and applauded. He smiled back as he turned and walked off the stage and out of the room, while the applause continued for several long, loud minutes.

And for me, that day was one of renewal of loyalty and commitment to activism. I promised myself that I would do my utmost to fulfill the oath I had just recited, by contributing to making our nation a better place for everyone.

By the time I got to the office, it was close to noon, and I started seeing patients immediately to make up for lost time. By four o'clock, calls were coming in from patients, acquaintances, and well-wishers, congratulating me. I was perplexed: how did anyone know? It turned out the president's appearance had made the local television news, and people had seen me sitting in the front row. The next day there were photographs of the ceremony in the newspaper. And there I was again, in the front row.

My Certificate of Naturalization came in the mail a few weeks later. I was now a bona fide citizen of the United States of America *with full commitment to give my services with pride, love, and compassion.*

CHAPTER 6

Formation and Development of the Michigan Educational Council

"Whoever follows a path in pursuit of knowledge, God makes his way easy to Heaven."

—*Hadith*

On the morning of Saturday, June 30, 1984, we were in Ann Arbor celebrating our annual holiday, Eid-ul-fitr, at the end of the holy fasting month of Ramadan. Everyone was dressed in festive clothing to attend the sermon in the hall at the Michigan Union at the University of Michigan. The young man giving the sermon totally mesmerized me. His name was Dawud Attauhidi, a PhD student at the university. After the ceremony, I introduced myself and exchanged phone numbers with him. It was the beginning of a long and purposeful shared journey.

Dawud was born into a Christian family in Philadelphia. While at Lehigh University, he started an inner quest, searching for the meaning of life. He studied many religions and philosophies and, in 1972, at the young age of twenty-one, he converted to Islam and changed his name from David to Dawud. Once committed, he wanted to learn everything about Islam. He studied Arabic at the University of Philadelphia, and proceeded to the most renowned Islamic university in the world, Al-Azhar University in Cairo. There he studied all the classic books, took many courses, and graduated in 1980 with an immense knowledge of Islam. He could read, speak, and write Arabic like a scholar. On his return to the United States, he completed his master's degree in Islamic studies at the University of Michigan in 1983, and in 1985, he completed his doctoral candidacy examination in the same field. He was absolutely brilliant.

I learned a lot from Dawud over the next twenty-five years. We spent a lot of time together, discussing and planning the future of children's education. I had always believed that the best gift you can give a child is education. It is a treasure that will give him or her a better life overall with a good understanding of the very purpose of our existence. I felt I had a good understanding of education, but talking to Dawud, I realized how little I knew. My own education had begun.

I am reminded, in a small way, of a transformative episode in the life of the famous Persian poet Rumi. Jalal-ad-Din Muhammed Rumi was born in September 1207 in Balkh, Persia. His family later moved to Konya in Turkey, and he became an accomplished Islamic scholar, theologian, and jurist. On November 15, 1244, while Rumi sat next to a large stack of books, engrossed in his reading, he saw a man in dirty clothes weaving baskets and selling them on the streets. The man's name was Shams-al-Din Tabrizi, and he was a traveling merchant. Passing by, Shams asked Rumi, "What are you reading?" Regarding him as an uneducated stranger, Rumi scoffingly replied, "Something you cannot understand." At that moment, Rumi's stack of books caught fire, and he hastily asked Shams, "What did you do?" Very politely, Shams Tabrizi replied, "Something you cannot understand." Rumi quickly rescued the books and, to his utter surprise, they were undamaged.

The encounter was transformational for Rumi. For the next few years, he spent all his time with his new teacher, Shams. The exact nature of their conversation is not known, but the intensity of his relationship with Shams catapulted Rumi into a vision of the universe as experienced through the eyes of divine love. He plunged into the wellspring of creativity, and poetry and music began to pour out of him. Shams had kindled in him a love of the divine that was henceforth to be Rumi's guiding light and the inspiration for all his achievements.

In a very short period, I was totally convinced that Dawud was a great educationist who had a holistic understanding of religion and education. In addition, I had lost faith in the public school system. Very soon, we rounded up a group of committed parents who were concerned about their kids' education, and in 1985, a small parochial school was started in an existing building on Plymouth Road in Ann Arbor. It was a temporary solution, and plans for an independent school in a central location became the top priority.

In 1987, a group of six individuals committed themselves to the establishment and development of the school. The organization was registered with the state of Michigan as a 501(c)(3) nonprofit and named the Michigan Educational Council. The composition of the group was very interesting. Of course, Dawud was the educator and driving force. There were also a psychiatrist, an engineer, a professor, a director of laboratories, and me, a urologist. In our first meeting, I said something that still resonates in my mind. "Let us put our hearts, minds, and resources together," I said, "and if one good human being walks out of this institution, I will feel that all our efforts were rewarded." Everyone agreed, and the work started with great enthusiasm.

Our first challenge came a few months later. A very dear friend, Sultan Mohiuddin, had purchased nearly twenty acres at the corner of Palmer and Lotz Roads in Canton with plans to build single family homes. This was the exact location we had been looking for. I called him right away, "Sultan Bhai, can you sell us a part of the land to build our school and community center?" With extreme generosity he replied, "Mahmood Bhai, you can have whatever you want and I will not take a cent more than what I paid." We quickly decided on eight acres at the very corner with access from both streets.

We *now* had to come up with $82,000 urgently. Everyone in the group pitched in, depending on their capacity, and we purchased the land. Next, we started looking at architectural firms that specialized in building schools. After interviewing several of them, we agreed on TMP, which had built more than five hundred schools around the country and had also built the airport in Riyadh, Saudi Arabia. After several meetings, with Dawud leading us in needs and designs, a few sketches were presented. The next battle was with the Canton township and the neighbors at a public hearing. We all strongly believed that truthfulness and transparency were the best way to approach these matters. The township's main concern was traffic control, as the building itself would be governed by the state's rules and regulations.

The plots of land around the school property were still fairly rural. A great idea came up. We invited all the neighbors one afternoon to have tea with us at the Canton public library, where we gave an open presentation about who we were and what we were planning to do. I told them that one thing was for sure: their property values would go up, and it was much better to have a school at that corner than a factory or a commercial building. We received total support, except for one old lady who came up to me.

"Doctor!" she said. "How are you going to make money on this deal?" I very politely assured her that this was a nonprofit venture, and that our intent was not to make money. She did not seem fully convinced, but she agreed to support us at the public hearing. Things ran fairly smoothly after that, and we feverishly worked on the architectural design. We had to meet pretty much daily, and sometimes late into the night. Decisions had to be made on the spot to keep the project going. There were times when we would get into heated arguments, but we had all agreed on one thing: when we walked out of any meeting, every decision had to be unanimous.

Until then, we had been able to cover all the costs. But now the big question came up: how were we going to fund the whole project? The estimate for completing the building and equipping the school was close to $2 million, and that was an uphill task. We started approaching everyone who we thought agreed with our plans and was ready to give a helping hand. The strategy was to talk to individuals who would donate and appeal to the community at large. Every dollar was valuable at this time. For many of those we visited, all we received was coffee and cookies. A few gave outright support and wrote a check, while others pledged their support over a period of time.

We held several fundraising dinners. We invited guests to come and listen to our story, look at the plans, and donate what they could. We and our families would cook the food at home, bring it to the hall, and set up the tables and drinks. Then we would get dressed in our suits, ready to beg and borrow. After everyone left, we would get back in our street clothes and clean all the dishes and mop the floors, to leave the hall as we had found it. They were long and tiring days, but soon we got used to it.

Once we had $500,000 in the bank account, our group decided to start construction, with the hope that seeing brick and mortar would stimulate more people to donate. The groundbreaking ceremony was a great success, as we had invited some dignitaries, city officials, and community leaders. We arranged a big fundraising event at a Dearborn school where the famous singer Cat Stevens, now Yusuf Islam, was the guest speaker. That night was highly successful, and we raised $223,000. Our hope and joy knew no bounds.

A few months after the foundation was completed, the first wall of the central hall was erected. Just looking at a structure above ground was so exciting, and we were all there taking pictures of the new beginning. One Saturday morning, I arrived at the construction site just after sunrise. There had been heavy rains and thunderstorms overnight, with strong gusts of wind. One whole wall of the main hall had collapsed to the ground and lay totally shattered. It was heartbreaking to see love's labor lost. As I stood there depressed and crying, the construction crew showed up. They had been working weekends to keep up with the building timeline. Seeing me in the state I was in, the construction manager walked up to me and, in a very consoling tone, said, "Don't worry, Doc! These things happen. But the good news is we can reuse most of the material to build it again." I drove home with less despair.

The project went on successfully, and we passed through all the state and township inspections. Some more funds came in, but we were still far behind in collection of the pledges that had been made. In the early fall of 1991, the building was finally completed. We were waiting for the final inspections from both the township and the State of Michigan. Our funds were totally depleted and, we knew the "30-day net bill payment rule," that all bills must be paid within thirty days of the completion of the work. We were short by $1 million. Every day our anxiety level went up. Fifteen days passed, and now we started getting nasty calls from the suppliers and different trades that had completed their jobs. And then, with only five days remaining to make the final payments, two of us in the group got threatening calls: "We know where your kids go to school, and we will kidnap them as ransom." I had never imagined it would get so bad that *our children and family would be on the line.* That night I just could not sleep. I prayed all night: "God! Please help us. I don't know what to do next."

We were living in Dearborn and did all our personal and business banking with the National Bank of Detroit. One branch was right around the corner from us, and I knew the branch manager from previous dealings. After dressing in my best suit, I drove up to the branch, and took a seat right in front of the manager's office. He saw me and came out right away. "Can I help you, Dr. Hai? You look really upset."

"Yes, I am," I told him. "I need a million dollars to pay off all the bills on the school construction."

"And how soon do you need it?" he asked calmly.

"Today!" I said, and went on to explain to him how many of the pledges had not come through, and that I was getting threatening calls.

Without blinking he said, "Alright. You come back to the bank at four o'clock this afternoon, and I will have a check for you."

I looked at him in disbelief. "You're kidding, aren't you?"

"No, I am giving you my word. Just give me a few hours to work every-thing out."

I rushed to my office and called all the members of the group to inform them what had happened. After seeing patients, on my way back I stopped at home and picked up all the documents of assets in my possession. With another member of our group, I arrived at the bank exactly at four o'clock. In the back of my mind, I was thinking of all the excuses the bank manager could use to tell me the funds were not available. But he greeted us with a smile, invited us into his room, and called his secretary, Miss Gandhi. "Can you kindly give the check we have prepared for Dr. Hai?" She passed me an ordinary envelope, and I clumsily opened it and pulled out a cashier's draft in my name for $1 million. I could not believe my eyes. God had fulfilled His promise to support the project. I took the manager's right hand and clasped it tightly between mine. "Thank you, thank you! You are an angel! Here are all my assets. Keep them as collateral." I passed over my bag to him. Refusing to take it, he looked at me and said, "Dr. Hai, don't worry about anything right now. Go pay off all the bills, and we will meet and talk next week."

I called the attorney who was handling all the contractors, and he was overwhelmed by the news. "Now that we have cash," he said, "I can deal with all of them to settle for a lesser amount." Within a few days, he had met with the contractors, and everything was paid off for $800,000. I promptly paid $200,000 of the $1 million loan back to the bank.

The following week when I met the manager, he was again very kind. "Dr. Hai, just meet with your group and determine how much you can comfortably pay on a monthly basis, and I will write up the papers accord-ingly," he said. The next week we agreed on an amount, and the documents were written for a $10,000 per month payment that would take approx-imately eight years to pay off the full sum. He did not want any of my possessions as collateral, and when I questioned him, he just said, "Dr. Hai,

I know you and trust you, and I also know the sincerity and commitment of your group."

The bank manager had only one request: "They are opening a new NBD branch in Saline, and I would love to be transferred there. It is only two miles from my home." All our prayers were answered when, two years later, God fulfilled his wish, also. *His miraculous generosity strengthened our friendship.* We even attended Miss Gandhi's wedding at the Hilton in Chicago. With everyone's hard work at fundraising, the whole loan was paid off in three years, and the Michigan Educational Council was free of any debts or liabilities. We were all a big happy family for many years.

The Crescent Academy International school was registered as a 501(c)(3) nonprofit organization to serve the community as a private college preparatory institution. I had had my schooling, from elementary to high school, at a parochial Catholic school run by American Jesuits in India, with the motto "For God and Country." Our own children had started their education in the Montessori system and later went to Divine Child School in Dearborn. That was the image of a school that I had in my mind. Dawud and the newly formed board of trustees wanted to make sure we met the educational and spiritual needs of children growing up in America. The motto selected was, "Lord, increase us in our knowledge." The mission statement clearly stated the basic principles: To educate and raise young people imbued with a complete personality, devotion to the Almighty God, care and service to others, understanding their role in contemporary society. To educate students who are empowered and live as effective, conscientious, and upright citizens in the national and international community, contributing to the betterment of humanity.

Dawud was very emphatic that we provide education of the total person, with integrity, honesty, industry, cooperation, enthusiasm, responsibility, appreciation, and faith as the basic principles guiding our endeavor. He truly believed that, starting at an early age, we could mold the children's personality with good core education, moral behavior, and actions, and with the teachers acting as excellent role models.

The school opened its doors with eighty students in 1991. There were so many things to plan and execute: selection of teachers and books, bussing arrangements, school budget, fee collection schedule. Dawud would spend hours and hours planning everything to its minutest details. The school was his life and existence. Sometimes the depth of his thinking amazed me, but then I would remind myself that it was Dawud. If any of the board members ever criticized him for spending too much time on a project, I would raise my voice in defense. He was indeed my hero, the master of human education.

Within a few years, the school was among the top 20 percent of schools in Michigan. Students were coming from all over: Grosse Ile, Dearborn, Ann Arbor. By 1997, the student population had grown to 165. We had deliberately kept the fees at a reasonable level, to ensure that families from all income groups could participate, and we even had scholarships for those who could not afford it. Initially, we had to collect nearly 50 percent of the budget through donations and fundraising. The local community had joined hands and contributed to the project, and in return they were given the privilege of using the building when it was not in use by the school. Issues did come up, but they were handled amicably.

Within a few years, the school building had reached its full capacity and there was more potential for growth. Temporary portable classrooms were added to accommodate the growth, but very soon the necessity for a second building was loomed over us. There was pressure from the administration, the parents, and the community. After much deliberation, the board agreed to build the second phase. We prepared ourselves mentally for a grueling campaign, and the plans began in 2004.

The new building would be a modern school, with up-to-date amenities all of us could be proud of. We had learned a lot from our previous venture. Dawud was back at the drawing board. The good news was that, over the years, we had grown into a strong school family, primarily as a result of the great education plan Dawud had developed. A large group of young professionals had joined us. Among them was a successful engineer who had a large construction company, doing work for the big three automakers in Detroit. He and Dawud, as a team, took it upon themselves to take the lead and make the new school happen. There was a bond of love and respect between them. Of course, we were all there, the old guard and the new blood, to provide whatever support they needed.

The new building was approximately 60,000 square feet and would cost close to $8 million. By the time it was completed, it came close to $9 million. Dawud was in his glory, working even harder, focusing on everything: the quality of the tiles, the paint color of the various classrooms. He made all his decisions on the basis of first their educational value. Construction started in 2005, and was completed in 2007. Many selfless new champions came out of the group, without whom the project would have never reached completion. Another young and dedicated engineer, Mahmoud Omais, took it upon himself to make sure the project was completed and done exactly to Dawud's specifications. Despite all the cost-cutting measures and extensive fundraising, we ended up with a $5 million mortgage. The big difference was that now the institution itself was standing on its own two feet. The valuation of the whole property was close to $10 million, and altogether the buildings added up to nearly 88,000 square feet. The school finally became financially stable, with the help of some finance professionals and CIG Capital Advisors, a boutique finance company in the community. The new school increased its capacity to five hundred students.

Over the years, Dawud continued to promote his educational program. In 2005, he had the phrase "Integrated Learning Model" (ILM) registered as a trademark. He introduced the curriculum in five other schools in the United States and a few schools internationally. To promote further growth of his educational program, he travelled to the Middle East and the Far East. He strongly believed that education is a dynamic process and that we need to advance it constantly with the newest tools available to us, while always keeping in mind the principal mission.

In late 2007, Dawud suddenly developed a chronic cough and saw blood in his sputum. Further investigations at the University of Michigan were done, and in June 2008, he was finally diagnosed with extensive high-grade lung cancer. Although he had never smoked, this terrible monster totally devastated his health. All the treatments and chemotherapy made him weak, although he retained his mental faculties. I spent many hours at his home, discussing the future of the school and his education plans. As part of his wisdom, he had already trained a protégée, a young lady named Pembe Yasarlar who had graduated with a master's degree in education from the University of Michigan. Pembe had not only trained under Dawud to run the school, but was truly and deeply committed to Dawud's philosophy.

The following years were very difficult for all of us. It was so painful to see this mastermind melt away, losing all his faculties one by one. On May 23, 2010, at the young age of fifty-eight, Dawud passed away into his eternal life, leaving a legacy for us to carry on. As the scripture says: "We have all come from God, and unto Him we shall all return." I was reminded of a beautiful couplet in Urdu:

"Bulbul hi ko bahar ke jane ka gham nahin
Her berg hath malta hay gulzar ke liye"

My translation: "It is not just the birds that are singing sad melodies, but every tree and plant in the garden has lost hope that spring will ever come."

Dawud's funeral itself was a testament to his achievements and contributions, not only to our community but to the whole world of education. Throngs of people came from around the country to show their love and pay their respects to a selfless man who gave every bit of himself for the cause of education. I have always believed that Dawud, with his degrees and brilliance, could have been in the limelight of any world-class institution, but instead he sacrificed his whole life to his belief that the field of education needed a major turn in its course. Not only was his life devoted to children's education, but he taught many lessons to the teachers and parents and all of us. I personally learned from him the quality and value of humility and servitude. He proved to me that by sticking to your high ethical and moral values, you can achieve excellence in whatever you do, and that one man's selfless devotion could create a legacy for many years to come. Dawud was buried at the Knollwood Cemetery in Canton, and I still often go and stand in front of his grave, praying for him and deriving inspiration from his soul. I will never personally know a man of his stature, with so much grace and grandeur.

After Dawud was gone from our midst, it took us some time to gather our wits together. There was no true replacement for him. We had also lost another very devoted member of our group, Khurshid Hussain, in August 2004. Then, on July 10, 2013, a sudden death took from us our beloved Mahmoud Omais, the devoted engineer who had worked very hard to oversee the school project to completion. Three new and exceptional members were added to our group, and a very well-functioning board of directors was developed. Pembe Yasarlar, the protégée Dawud had trained over the years, was appointed the new Director of Crescent Academy International.

In 2016, a refinancing of the school loan had to be done. We approached several banks and had a very good response, considering that schools are not money-making businesses. PNC Bank, which had given favorable rates, wanted to have their team, including the vice president and finance officer, visit the school. We had set the time for 3:00 p.m., but by the time everyone got together, it was 3:30, time for the children to be dismissed from their classrooms. As we were walking through the main corridor, children were beginning to come out. Seeing us coming down, they stopped and said, "Good afternoon, sir. Please go ahead." They patiently waited for us to move forward, and then came out one by one in a very orderly fashion.

The vice president of the bank called me the next day and thanked me for the visit. He very candidly remarked, "Dr. Hai, I have visited many schools, and if you happen to be in the school corridor at dismissal time and you're not careful, you will be knocked down and run over in the stampede. What are you teaching your children that leads to such good behavior?" I told him that we incorporate good moral values into their personality. Needless to say, we got a great deal from the bank.

It was the middle of winter in 2016, and my son and his wife had to be out of town for a long weekend. Annette and I stayed with their kids overnight Thursday, and Friday morning the children got dressed and had Grammy's yummy breakfast. I had the responsibility of dropping them off to school on my way to work. The snow was coming down heavily, with strong gusts of cold wind. I carefully drove up to the drop-off point near the back entrance of the school. A young lady bundled up in winter clothes came up to the car to receive the children. I recognized her. It was Pembe, the director of Crescent Academy International. "How come you are out here?" I asked. "The teachers do it by rotation, and it was my day today," she replied with a smile. Humility and service are what make an institution great, and it flows down from the top management. Pembe is like the pied piper with the kids, and the love and respect her staff and teachers feel for her are obvious.

The school's twenty-fifth anniversary celebration in March 2017 brought great joy to all the founders, long-term supporters, alumni, staff, teachers, and students. We have all been members of a large extended family. Students from Crescent have gone on to attend Harvard, Yale, the University of Michigan, and many other excellent universities, carrying their ethics and moral values with them. As of 2019, there are 480 students and 55 teachers, and nearly all the faculty have advanced degrees. The average class size is twenty, and you can easily see the love and respect between the teacher and the taught. The reality of Dawud's vision lives on, and it gives me immense pleasure and pride to have been a part of his educational adventure. I have come to realize that institutions become great not because of buildings or money, but thanks to individuals who selflessly sacrifice everything for the success of the organization they work for.

Nothing comes easy in life. It is only by contributing time, money, and hard work and sacrificing our egos that we can build organizations and institutions which in one way or another contribute to the betterment of our community, society, and the nation. But if we are passionate about what we want to achieve, it does become easier.

"The world is but a canvas to our imagination."

Thoreau

CHAPTER 7

Development of GreenLight Laser

My interest in research started very early, as a first-year medical student at the Prince of Wales Medical College in India. I was in the anatomy dissection hall one day, working on the blood supply to the kidney. "Sir, the arterial supply to the kidney in this cadaver is very different from what is described in Cunningham's book on anatomy" I noted to my anatomy instructor. "Well, there are a lot of variations we see but I can't tell you how often it happens," he replied. The next day, I asked him if I could dissect out the blood supply of twenty kidneys and get an answer. He was happy to see my enthusiasm and authorized me to do so. I was excited, but soon realized that it meant working an additional hour every day after school for twenty days. Since I had committed to it, I took on the challenge.

After a month, I had the data I needed. It took another week to analyze it all and reach a conclusion. The classic description of the renal artery and its divisions, as described by the famous anatomist, Graves, was present in only two-thirds of the kidneys, while one-third showed variations. My anatomy instructor was delighted, and in due course, my first research paper was published in the scientific magazine of the medical college. My love for human anatomy became a passion, and I passed with honors in anatomy. My first job after graduating from medical school was as a teacher of anatomy. That became a stepping stone into surgery, which is essentially an application of anatomy. I passed the final medical school exams in surgery with honors.

The next big research project I took on was the work for my doctoral thesis. This involved going to the veterinary college, trying out different surgical techniques on dogs, and reviewing the long-term outcomes. The dogs survived very well and provided us great insight to improve surgical outcomes in humans. I was awarded the Master of Surgery degree from Patna University in 1972.

While working as a surgical resident in Boston, I encountered another major surgical problem. Many patients came to the emergency room at Boston City Hospital with severe injuries to the pelvis and lower extremities, bleeding to death. I was doing my surgical rotation with Dr. Berger in the cardiothoracic surgery department. He designated me and a surgical fellow to work at the Boston University dog lab on a project where, after anesthetizing the dog, we would create a major artery injury in the groin. We would immediately make an incision in the abdomen and totally clamp the main artery, the aorta, with a temporary device. This would give us time to repair the groin blood vessel, releasing the clamp and thereby saving the dog from bleeding to death. The experimental outcomes were great, but unfortunately, I left Boston before I was able to use the technique in injured patients.

One of the most common ailments that urologists see in men is benign enlargement of the prostate, commonly known as benign prostatic hyperplasia or BPH. It occurs in practically every male to some degree and is considered the most common medical problem in men over fifty. By age sixty, over 50 percent have symptoms from it, and this increases to 90 percent by the age of eighty-five. Common symptoms are weak or slow stream, frequent urination, and nocturia, getting up at night several times to urinate. With the prostate enlarging, there is a gradual increase in obstruction to the flow of urine. If not treated, it can progress to complete urinary retention and other serious complications such as urinary tract infection, bleeding, bladder stones, and even kidney failure. Treatments include fluid management, medications, and surgical interventions, depending on the seriousness of the condition.

In the early 1970s, when I was in residency training in urology in Detroit, the most common surgical treatment was transurethral resection of the prostate (TURP), in layman terms referred to as "roto-rooter," for small- and medium-sized glands. When the prostate was markedly enlarged, the only way to relieve the obstruction was to make an incision in the lower abdomen and physically remove the prostate. Both procedures were fairly traumatic and painful and had both short-term and long-term complications.

In 1976, Caine and associates reported the first results of medical treatment, but it was not until the late 1980s that randomized, double-blind, multi-center, placebo-controlled studies showed the safety and efficacy of two groups of medications. By 1990, medical treatment for BPH became an accepted standard of care. Although it did not provide a cure for the problem, it gave much symptomatic relief, especially in mild to moderate cases. For more severe cases, TURP remained the gold standard of surgical treatment.

In 1988, I had been in practice for more than ten years and had mastered the TURP surgery. The outcomes were very good, but the procedure had to be done as an inpatient procedure, under general anesthesia and with significant blood loss. After surgery, the patient had to live with a catheter for a few days, which was quite painful. Once in a while, there were major complications, and a few times after discharge, the patient ended up in the ER with excessive bleeding. The recovery period was long and kept the patient away from work. I started thinking about other techniques for treating BPH problems. My wife Annette, who was then a surgical nurse working with me, also began wondering about alternatives. Lasers had just been introduced to the medical field. We first tried experimenting with different lasers on pieces of steak, and then joined a course on lasers at the veterinary school in Lansing, where we studied the effect of different lasers on a bull's prostate. In 1991, Laserscope, a company from California, came out with a clinically approved laser machine. We started using it in our clinical practice and got good results for small to medium prostates. By 1995, we had done over five hundred successful laser procedures for the treatment of BPH. That November, we were invited by the 13th World Congress of Endourology, in Jerusalem, to talk about our work with lasers in urology. My presentation, "Laser Ablation of the Prostate using only KTP Energy," was the first paper on this subject and received wide acceptance by the urologic community.

I asked Laserscope several times to develop a KTP laser machine with a higher power. Finally, in 1998, Eric Reuter, the new CEO, sent a young man named Henry to my office. The company had decided to build a prototype 80-watt KTP laser machine for me to do the necessary FDA studies and to get an approval for clinical use. To this day, I wonder why they chose me over all the big universities and renowned professors in the field. Despite running a very busy practice, Annette, Henry, and I got down to work on the task ahead.

After two years of hard work, we received approval from the Food and Drug Administration (FDA), and a few months later from the Centers for Medicare and Medicaid Services (CMS). We were all overwhelmed by this success. The annual meeting of the American Urological Association was scheduled for May 2000 in Anaheim, California. With Henry in the lead, Laserscope started planning a grand debut for our laser machine and the new procedure. More than three thousand invitations went out worldwide to urologists who were planning to attend the meeting. About four hundred sent RSVPs saying they would be there.

The day we had all been awaiting finally arrived. We had booked a big ballroom at the Hilton to accommodate up to five hundred people. The presentation would be followed by a phenomenal dinner. Laserscope's CEO, board members, and engineers were with us, everyone one of them excited to usher in this great new device. A total of seven urologists showed up. Henry was literally in tears. I gave my presentation as planned, and three of the seven were impressed enough to sign up to purchase the machine. After everyone left, I hugged and congratulated Henry for all his efforts and convinced him that it was better than four hundred attendees with no machines sold.

I had made it clear to the company that, on principle, I wanted no conflict of interest and would not be involved financially in any way. I would do all the presentations, teaching, training, and writing about the new technology and its outcomes. They would pay me for the work and travel expenses. I had also insisted that the new laser technology for BPH needed to be made available to everyone, not just the rich and the elite. In 2001, we held a press conference at Annapolis Hospital in Wayne, Michigan, to let the public know that this new technology was now available.

At first, we encountered serious resistance from academic urologists as they had had very little to do with the development of this technology. The one exception was the Mayo Clinic, where Dr. Reza Malik and his team had worked on it in 1996. He and I did several publications and presentations together. There were lots of naysayers who needed to be convinced. The task of promoting the new technology was daunting. We traveled all around the United States and abroad to introduce it to urologists by sharing our successful data. Like all new technologies, the initial phase encountered a lot of friction. But a few good things happened, too. I was giving a course in London, and Professor Gordon Muir and some well-known British urologists came and were very impressed by the laser. They came across the pond to our center in Michigan, learned the technique, and started doing a large number of cases in the United Kingdom. A young urologist from New York, Dr. Alex Te, came, saw me performing, and got on the bandwagon. The domino effect started as they began teaching other urologists, and the GreenLight laser started gaining popularity.

Another breakthrough happened in 2003. There was a long-distance call to the office, which nobody could understand, and the phone call was passed on to me. "I am the Surgeon General of China, Dr. Wu. Can I talk to Dr. Hai?" said the voice in a very strong Chinese accent.

"Yes, this is Dr. Hai. How can I help you, sir?" I replied.

"I have read about all the work you have done with lasers, and I want you to personally come to China and do my prostate surgery and teach my Chinese urologists how to do the surgery." It sounded more like a command than a request. Later I found out that he was a high-ranking officer in the Chinese army.

"It will be my absolute pleasure, sir, to fulfill your request," I said.

I thanked him for his call, hung up, and sat quiet for a few minutes, in disbelief. Then a sudden excitement came on. We had just been offered a great opportunity to spread the laser work in a country of more than a billion people. I called Henry and Eric Reuter, the CEO of Laserscope. Overwhelmed by the news, they said, "Don't worry, Dr. Hai, we will make it happen."

Three months later, our whole troop landed at the airport in Beijing. We were treated like royalty and taken to the Grand Hyatt hotel. The surgery was planned for the following morning. It was decided that I would do the surgery, and Annette would assist and also teach the Chinese nursing staff.

A good night's rest got us over the jet lag, and after a sumptuous breakfast, we were taken to the main army hospital, where we met Dr. Wu and all the top-brass physicians. We could sense the high level of security all around us. Although our trip was planned as two days of work and two days of sightseeing, Dr. Wu had a different schedule in mind. His order was that we do surgery and training for the whole week, with one day of free time. Not familiar with the culture, I was not prepared to contradict him and readily agreed. "I want all of us to get back home safely," I told Annette.

Thank God all the surgeries went well, and we were able to train four hundred Chinese urologists in this short time. Every night we were entertained at different high-end restaurants. The more sophisticated the restaurant, the crazier was the food. We had fish bladder soup, boiled webs of duck's feet, sheep eyeballs floating in brown gravy. Annette and I instantly became vegetarians. One night we escaped and had a great salad at the Hyatt, and another night we went to McDonald's and had fish tacos. Fast food had never tasted better. There was great appreciation for our work, and we all returned happy and satisfied.

The next few years were extremely busy. We were flying all over — England, Canada, Germany, Austria, Turkey, Italy, India — teaching the technology and finding good mentors who would educate the next generation. We visited Australia, Indonesia, Malaysia, Hong Kong, and returned to China. We gave lectures and did surgery in the United Arab Emirates, Saudi Arabia, and Bahrain. GreenLight laser became extremely popular worldwide. Interest came from South America, and off we went to Argentina, Colombia, Brazil, Panama, Bolivia. Scientific papers started being presented from all these international groups. Everyone wanted to hear and learn from us. We were treated like celebrities everywhere, and I had to keep my ego under control. I refused to melt in this limelight, but I had to work to maintain my humility. It wasn't always easy.

Another extensive teaching trip was planned for different cities in China. This time a major conference was arranged in Beijing. The chief of urology at the big army hospital, Professor Chen, was in charge of the planning. The huge auditorium was packed with physicians, dignitaries, and media. I gave a lecture with a slide presentation, and everything was translated into Chinese. Professor Chen and I went to the operating room and did two laser surgeries that the attendees viewed onscreen from the auditorium, and then we returned to answer questions from the audience. I was handed a list of 120 people who had signed up to have the GreenLight laser surgery performed by me. It was an awkward situation. I said to the audience, "Ladies and gentleman, thank you for showing such great confidence in me. We have already trained a large number of Chinese urologists. They will do an excellent job and will also be able to explain everything to you in Chinese."

I was really impressed by Professor Chen's hospitality. He was a tall, well-built gentleman, and I felt honored, if a little crushed, when he gave me a bear hug. He took us all to a very good Chinese restaurant, where the food was excellent. By now he had figured out our taste. To top it all off, he said, "Now, Professor Hai, to prove how happy we are that you are my teacher, we will complete our Chinese tradition with a one-hour foot massage for all." Truly, as I lay there having my foot massage, all my fatigue drained away. Since then, every time Annette and I have gone to China, Taiwan, or Hong Kong, we end the day with a relaxing foot massage.

In total, we taught in over thirty-five countries and some places more than once, with different languages, cultures, and religions. What we learned very clearly was that people are the same, wherever you go on this earth. They are kind, respectful, and thankful, and if you treat them nicely, they will reciprocate. Traveling indeed brings great education and wisdom. To write about our experiences around the world would take another book.

One time, we were teaching in the rural town of Tarija in Bolivia, a region with fewer than 170,000 residents. The urologist could not understand English, so he had arranged to have a lady, the professor of English at the local college, as our interpreter. Despite the language barrier, we did quite well. The day I was leaving, the urologist asked an interesting question through the interpreter: "Dr. Hai, why did you take the trouble to come all the way here to teach me?" I replied, "For two reasons. One, that you wanted to learn. And two, that I love to teach." I also told him that when I developed the GreenLight laser technology, I had promised myself that I would make this treatment available to everyone. Another urologist in a small town in Indonesia asked a similar question, and I gave him pretty much the same answer. During a visit to Shanghai, a Chinese urologist asked in broken English, "Your government hate mine, why you come here?" I very politely answered, "I don't represent the US government. As Americans, we love all the people of the world. I am an ambassador of the American people, and we want to share all that is good for humanity."

During this time, I was also working with the engineers and the research team to further improve the laser. The second generation of the machine, called the HPS laser system with 120 watts, was released in 2006. We soon realized that there were some major issues with it. The machine was breaking down more frequently and the laser fiber was unable to handle the higher power. We formed a board of advisors and regularly met with the engineers for further advancement into the next upgrade of the machine and fiber. By now, a large number of urologists from all around the world were involved.

Over the years, I remained deeply involved in the progress, and in September of 2010, I was privileged to receive the first machine of the third generation, the XPS machine with 180 watts. We also introduced a new water-cooled fiber that gave the fiber great longevity and efficacy. We now had the ability to take care of prostate glands of all sizes and all conditions of prostate obstruction. It was indeed another major milestone in the history of urologic laser treatment, and I fondly called it "a beast of a different order." The GreenLight laser had become the new gold standard for treating prostate obstruction.

While all this was going on, financial troubles loomed. Laserscope was an aesthetic laser company started in 1984 in San Jose, California. It had been floundering for nearly a decade. In 1999, its stock price was down to under a dollar. The board decided to hire a new CEO, a young engineer named Eric Reuter. Eric started looking at medical uses for the laser technology, and that's when they found me and we started working together. Eric had gambled when he gave me the 80-watt KTP prototype laser machine. After using it on a few patients, I was amazed by its efficiency and lack of bleeding. I asked Eric to create some funds to do the FDA study. He was very reluctant, and said, "I would rather spend the money in improving our aesthetic lasers, where I know we have a market share." I pleaded on the phone, "Eric, just come and see me doing a few cases, then you can decide." A few weeks later, Eric came on a scheduled day, with a few engineers from Laserscope, to observe the effects of the laser on a live prostate. As I started doing the surgery, they could not believe how effective the laser was, and Eric shouted, "Oh my God! It really works!" I knew I had convinced him to do the FDA study. Once we got FDA approval and the machines started selling, Laserscope's revenue, which had dipped to $35 million in 2001, rose to $43 million in 2002 and $57.4 million in 2003, with a net profit of $2.5 million.

With national and international sales starting to boom, Laserscope got onto the radar of other medical equipment suppliers. In June 2006, the company was sold to Minnesota-based American Medical Systems (AMS) for $715 million, with a share value of $31 per share. It was payday for Eric, Henry, and all the engineers and investors. As I mentioned, I had no financial interests in Laserscope, but I had known AMS for many years and had used their products for men's health and urinary incontinence. Personally, I was very happy that the GreenLight laser would now enjoy much greater support and growth. AMS had a great reputation among urologists worldwide, and they had a large sales force. Under the AMS banner, the GreenLight laser flourished and, in August 2010, the third-generation laser machine, the XPS with the new MoXy fiber, was released. There was a whole new level of enthusiasm for the use of GreenLight laser for BPH. I was totally overwhelmed by requests from all over the world to demonstrate and teach how best the new laser could be used. It was during these years that I met and came to work with some great human beings like Matt Valencic and Jeff Smith who had their heart and soul in this new technology. Not only did they know the business world at its best, but were also men of great integrity. I am proud to say that I learned a lot from them.

Unfortunately, AMS had some major financial problems resulting from class action medical lawsuits involving another product. They had to be bailed out. In April 2011, a pharmaceutical company, Endo Pharma, purchased AMS for $2.9 billion, which included paying off $312 million in debt. This was not a good move for the laser because, although Endo Pharma was a successful national drug company, they had no idea about laser technology or the international market. It took them a while even to understand the technology. I remember spending a whole afternoon with some of their high-level corporate executives, explaining what lasers are and how they're used in urology.

Endo Pharma soon decided that urology lasers were not their cup of tea. In March 2015, Boston Scientific Incorporated purchased the AMS urology portfolio, which consisted of men's health and prostate health, for $1.6 billion. Thank God, the laser was back in the hands of a very large international company that was totally wedded to urology and urologists. They had products in the fields for stone disease, BPH, men's health, and urinary incontinence, and their corporate level and sales force were very familiar with laser products. The GreenLight laser technology has indeed prospered under their banner and continues to do so. In recent years I have made several trips to China and Taiwan, teaching the technology and training the trainers there.

In 2014, a large multicenter study, called the Goliath study, was done in eight countries in Europe. It definitively proved the superiority of the GreenLight laser over the traditional TURP procedure. In 2015, I had the privilege of being the principal investigator for a large retrospective study with close to a thousand patients, conducted in collaboration with four centers in the United States and McGill University in Canada. These two studies confirmed that the GreenLight laser treatment, with the new XPS laser system and the new and improved MoXy fiber, was indeed the new gold standard for treating BPH obstruction.

In December 2016, I was informed by Boston Scientific that we had done more than a million GreenLight surgeries worldwide. It gives me immense pleasure that, starting from a very humble beginning, this technology has had a major impact in giving relief to suffering humanity, and that I have been part of it. I had the privilege of treating many celebrities and world leaders on one hand, and multitudes of common people on the other.

Greed always finds its way whenever there is fame and recognition. Many of the medical reps informed me that some physicians in academic centers were charging large amounts for doing the GreenLight and other procedures, because of their claim to rank and results. They implied that I should also increase my charges and take advantage of my pioneering and expertise and the fact that I had done the largest number of GreenLight procedures in the world. I constantly resisted this temptation and repeatedly told them, "My charges are the same for the rich and the poor, and I accept the payments made by all insurances, including Medicare, Blue Cross, Medicaid, and Obamacare." In the mid-2000s, word got out in the Amish and Mennonite communities that the laser procedure was much better than the old TURP, and that they could get back to work much quicker. At first a few of them came from Ohio and Pennsylvania. I was truly impressed by their faith, honesty, and simplicity of life. They worked very hard for a meager income. I talked to Annette, who was managing the office, and the rest of the staff and decided to give them a 50 percent discount on their whole medical bill. This news spread to all their communities and, by word of mouth, we had hundreds of them coming to our center for the GreenLight treatment.

In 2008, a well-known multi-millionaire businessman from Saudi Arabia was referred to me for laser treatment of his prostate. He came to Michigan with his whole entourage. An entire floor of the Ritz Carlton in Dearborn was booked for them. He was brought to my office by the Ritz limousine, accompanied by his personal urologist from back home. I examined him and explained the whole laser procedure and recovery plan. After a two-hour discussion, the laser surgery was scheduled for the following morning. Thank God the surgery went very well and he returned to his luxurious hotel for recovery.

The next morning, he was scheduled to come back for the removal of his urinary catheter. His personal urologist called, saying that the patient was tired and did not want to come to the office and asked that I arrange instead for a nurse to go to the hotel and remove the catheter. He also requested that all medical bills be sent to the hotel for payment. I asked Annette to go to the hotel, remove the patient's catheter, and give him the medical bill. An hour later, Annette called the office in a frenzy: "I need to talk to Dr. Hai right away." I got on the phone and blurted out a string of questions: "What happened? Did the catheter come out okay? Is he bleeding?"

Annette answered in a whisper. "No, everything went well. The catheter came out easy, and there is no bleeding."

"Then what is the problem?" I wondered.

"When I handed him the bill, he looked at it and went into a rage."

"What did he say?"

"He threw the bill at me, saying it was an insult to him to be given such a small bill, and he would have paid much more if he had his surgery done in his own country."

I asked Annette to hand the phone to the rich patient. "This small amount is an insult to me, Dr. Hai," he shouted.

Calmly, I replied: "Well, sir, we have one standard charge for everyone, rich or poor. But if you are feeling insulted, I will give you the names of a few local charities that will gladly accept your donation and put it to good use." He calmed down, and then sat at the table and wrote two checks, one for our small medical bill, and one for $50,000 to one of the charities I had suggested. Thank God the conflict had a good resolution: we got paid, the charity got a good boost, and our rich patient felt satisfied. The following day, he and his convoy flew back to Saudi Arabia.

Many new technologies are currently on the horizon for treating obstruction resulting from BPH. Other lasers have been used, but none have gained the popularity of the GreenLight laser. Stapling devices, steam, and water jet therapies have recently been approved by the FDA, and I have continued to take a keen interest and to participate in their development. Time alone will tell which of them will successfully replace the GreenLight laser in the coming years.

What I learned over all these years is to develop a passion for what you do. There will be many ups and downs, as I faced with GreenLight, but the key is to always remain focused. Success comes to those who work hard and remain honest in their endeavor. As scientists and researchers, our loyalty should always be to the patients who we serve, and not to any technology or companies supporting it. We need to maintain an arm's length to any conflict of interest in these issues and yet be honest and compassionate.

PART TWO:

Challenging Cases

CHAPTER 8

Introduction to Challenging Cases

One of my patients had given me a plaque with beautiful calligraphy that hung in my office for many years. It was from Khalil Gibran (1883–1931), the famous Lebanese mystic, poet, dramatist, and artist who lived his last twenty years in the United States of America.

"When you work you are a flute through whose heart the whispering of the hours turns to music. To love life through labor is to be intimate with life's innermost secret. All work is empty save when there is love, for love is work made visible."

Life is full of challenges, and each one makes us stronger, wiser, and more resilient. The few years of medical school give us a strong foundation in understanding the human body, how it functions, and what diseases can do to it. The way I have always looked at it is that God has created every human being to be unique, the very opposite of cars coming off the assembly line. Therefore, we have to tailor our treatment differently for each individual because their anatomies are different and their responses to treatment, be it medication or surgery, are different. We have to look at many factors, including their general health, environment, attitude, family dynamics, and ability to heal. Over the years I have learned to overlook chronological age, because the person could represent an old car well taken care of or a new car badly abused.

Even when I order tests to be done, there has to be a good reason for it, and I try to think one step ahead: how will it change my treatment plan?

Once the test results are back, I look at the treatment options. Conventional wisdom is great, but we have to think outside the box in order to be innovative and progressive. After I have thought through all the options, I sit down with the patient to educate him or her adequately, to help make the right decision. The practice of medicine should not be dictatorial, but rather a collaborative decision with the patient and his or her family, because at the end of the day, it is his or her body. When it becomes a joint decision, and the patient acknowledges the possible outcomes, the results are improved and the chances of medico-legal issues are lessened.

In this section, I share some of the challenges that I had to face in my career and how I dealt with them. For the sake of some form of order, I have grouped them into three categories — kidney, bladder, and prostate — with the first two stories remaining uncategorized.

Serious infections still happen

As a schoolchild, every weekday morning I went with my siblings for tutoring at the house of Mr. and Mrs. Halge. Mrs. Halge was our third-grade teacher, and Mr. Halge worked in the administration office at the St. Xavier's High school. My dad had made this arrangement to further reinforce our education. The Halges had two sons and a daughter: Keith, Raymond, and Valerie. Keith was close to my age, about nine, and Raymond was my eldest brother's age, thirteen or fourteen. Valerie was still in the cradle.

One morning while we were there, Keith was complaining of fever and stiffness in his body. Mr. Halge took him to the family doctor, who diagnosed him with a mild flu and sent him home with some aspirin tablets. The next morning his body stiffness had gotten much worse, to the point that he could not even get dressed for school. I had a feeling something serious was going on. Mr. Halge took the day off and brought him to the main hospital. The doctor immediately transferred him by ambulance to the infectious disease hospital, and by late afternoon we got the word that Keith had a full-fledged case of tetanus and was in critical condition. We all made special prayers for him, but the next morning he passed away.

The funeral was held at the school chapel. The grief and pain in everyone's heart was immeasurable. I never saw the Halge family ever smile or laugh again. For months, we all worried that something would happen to us too. I have always wondered whether, if the family doctor had suspected tetanus on the first day, Keith's life might have been saved.

The lesson I learned stayed forever: never take things for granted.

New life for an old lady

In 1984, visiting Pakistan for the wedding of one my cousins in Karachi, I arrived a few days early. An older gentleman I had operated on in Detroit the year before was from Faisalabad in Pakistan. He was a very rich landlord, and he had requested that I visit him during this trip, even if for a day. He had sent his son to fetch me, and we flew from Karachi to Faisalabad. I received a big welcome at the airport and was driven in a brand-new Mercedes to my patient's palatial home. He showed me around town and took me to the big charity hospital that he had built, and then back to his palace for a twenty-course dinner.

As we sat drinking tea, he asked for my advice. His mother was in her seventies and was dying of stomach cancer. "Can you just see her? And make a special prayer for her," he pleaded. All the local doctors had given up, concluding that she had a few days to live. I saw the old lady in her bed, where she had been confined for several weeks. She was thin, frail, and extremely pale, but in no pain. Her pulse was very weak, and she could barely say a few words. I then started going through all her medical records. The gastrointestinal specialist had seen blood in her stool, had felt a lump in her upper abdomen, had looked in with a gastroscope, and had labeled her as suffering from "advanced gastric cancer". But no biopsy or pathology report had been done stating a diagnosis of cancer. Her hemoglobin was down to four because of the stomach bleeding, and there was good reason for her to be in the condition she was. I examined her and, through her thin abdominal wall and emaciated body, could not feel any lumps or masses. I discussed the case with the GI specialist on the phone. "How can you diagnose cancer without a pathology report?" I asked firmly. "Sir, we know her well, and that is our diagnosis," he replied. I was totally unconvinced.

I thought for a few minutes and came up with a plan. In my opinion, the old lady had gastric bleeding from an ulcer and was now dying of anemia. I sat down with the family and explained my thinking. They had an unwavering trust in me. "Then what should we do, doctor *saheb*?" asked my host. "I would like to give her four units of packed blood cells over the next eight hours and see how she responds," I replied. A phone call to the blood bank at the hospital was all that was needed, and everything was there at my disposal. I started the intravenous line with normal saline, and then slowly hooked up the bottles of the packed red cells. It was a long night, and I stayed up with her until the morning call to prayer. When I returned from prayer to check on her, she looked like a totally different person. Her face was fresh and pink, and her eyes were wide open. She looked at me and smilingly said, "Son, can you help me sit up?" And as I propped her up with pillows, the whole room was silent and in awe. It seemed as if she had risen from the dead.

And then loud recitations of prayers started. Every member of the family was coming up and hugging me with tears of joy. Indeed, a miracle had happened.

My return flight was at noon. I quickly dressed, and had a sumptuous breakfast. I was told that seven lambs had been sacrificed that morning as an act of charity, and that hundreds of poor and homeless people would be fed that night in gratitude to God Almighty. As I left the palace, throngs of people had collected on the streets. The word had gotten out, and they were all there to bid me farewell. I felt like a renowned warrior returning after a great victory. Indeed, the fight was against illness and frailty, and a new life had begun.

I was exhausted and slept through the flight back to Karachi. The wedding went well, with all the traditional pomp and glory. The rich gentleman wrote letters of gratitude to me, and we stayed in touch for many years. His mother passed away seven years later of an unknown cause. I had sincerely learnt that the diagnosis of cancer should not be made without a biopsy. Thinking outside the box and prayers had given a new life to the old lady.

CHAPTER 9

Kidney Cases

The dying Jehovah's witness

It was still in the earlier years of my practice that a twenty-three-year-old white man was brought to the ER. He was married with two children and was a member of the Jehovah's Witnesses. He had a large left kidney stone that had been removed by open surgery, which was the norm in those times before endoscopic surgery became popular. The procedure had been done at one of the major hospitals in downtown Detroit. The patient was discharged to his home in Garden City. Three days after coming home, he started seeing fresh blood in his urine. Initially the family was not concerned, but one morning when he looked pale and felt lightheaded, they brought him to the ER in my hospital. When the ER doctor checked his blood work, the hemoglobin was down to six — dangerously low. I was called to see him and take over his care.

He was thin, which made him even paler. The kidney X-ray showed good function in both kidneys, with no obstruction. There was swelling and evidence of surgery on the left side. My first thought was to talk to the family, admit him, give him a blood transfusion to build up his blood level, and try conservative measures. But they vehemently opposed any blood transfusion, because of their religious beliefs. I put him on complete bed rest and consulted a hematologist, and he also recommended a blood transfusion. The next morning the hemoglobin had dropped to four. I talked to the anesthesiologist about a surgical intervention, but he was not ready to take the risk of putting him to sleep without replenishing his blood. I pleaded with the family to talk to their church elders to make an exception for this dying young man. My appeals were totally rejected.

The next morning, he lay listless in the bed and was as pale as the white sheet. The hemoglobin was now down to 2.31. He was no longer a surgical candidate without transfusion. I could see myself being called in a few hours to certify him dead. I made a few calls to the university hospital to see if they would take him in transfer, but even transporting him might have been fatal. My senior colleagues had all thrown up their hands in despair. I went down to the hospital prayer room to meditate and try to think of anything else we could do. Time was running out fast. The picture of the young widow with two children flashed by.

As I sat there, suddenly an idea came to my mind: was there any way we could block the bleeding site? I ran down to the radiology department and talked to the radiologist. "Is there any way you can put an arterial catheter in the renal artery and advance it to the location where the bleeding is taking place?" I asked.

"We can try," he said. "But the risk is very high. And then how are we going to block the bleeding site?"

The question was very valid. My brain was working a thousand miles an hour. "If we can harvest a piece of his muscle, macerate it, and use it as a plug, it might work," I suggested. The very thought of doing all this on a dying man was very scary, but did we have a choice?

I ran back to the patient's room, met with his family, presented the idea, and waited for an answer. They had to consult the elders, yet time was running out. An hour later, I got the okay and they signed the consent form. I had specified very clearly that this was experimental, and that neither I nor the radiologist had ever done this before. With the help of the orderlies and nurses, we carefully transferred him onto a stretcher. It was like moving a dead body. I personally brought him down to the radiology room where the radiologists performed cardiac catheterizations for heart problems.

We gently transferred him to the procedure table. I cleaned and sterilized a small area in the middle of the thigh. When I put the needle in to numb the area, the young man did not even move or wince.

I made a small incision in the skin, and the muscle was right there. I cut out a small piece of the muscle. There was hardly any bleeding. I stitched the incision and put a dressing on it. I took the muscle tissue in a sterile dish, macerated it until it was emulsified, and loaded it up in a 5cc syringe. The easy part was done.

Under fluoroscopy X-ray guidance, the radiologist placed the arterial catheter through the right femoral artery in the groin and advanced it all the way into the kidney artery. He gave a flush of the contrast material and there it was, clear as day: the leaking artery. I switched over to the syringe with the emulsified muscle and injected 2cc of it.

To our utter surprise, the leak stopped. We could not believe our eyes. The radiologist removed the arterial catheter and pressure-dressed the wound. The bleeding had been stopped, and the patient had survived the procedure.

The very next morning his hemoglobin was up to 4.2, and within a week, it was over 9. The patient was discharged home. Another miracle had taken place. The happiness of the family and elders knew no bounds. They said, "We knew God would not let him die as long as we kept our faith in Him."

Jane's inoperable kidney cancer

Jane was a thin white female in her late forties, a healthy housewife totally dedicated to her husband and family. She had been admitted by her family doctor for a complete workup for blood in her urine. Other than minor colds and headaches, she had never been sick. Her husband was a plumpish middle-aged man who loved to eat, and Jane loved to cook. He had worked

at the General Motors plant for many years. Although they had totally opposite temperaments, they got along just fine. Their son had finished college
and had landed a good job with an accounting firm, and their daughter
was still in high school. Talking to her and examining her, I was already
impressed by her gentle nature and courteousness. I ordered some blood
tests and a complete CT scan of her abdomen and pelvis, and they were
done the following day. It was my routine, a habit I had carried on from
my residency days, to go down to the radiology department personally and
review the films with the radiologist. When a radiologist reads the films, he
is merely looking at shadows and does not know the details of the clinical
history that forms the other half of the story. Besides, two heads are always
better than one.

I walked in and asked Dr. Campbell to pull up all the films. We were
both amazed by what we saw. There was a solid mass, ten centimeters in
diameter, arising from the upper pole of the right kidney and growing right
into the liver, which was positioned above it. What was unusual was that
Jane had never complained of any pain or discomfort from it. We looked
at the tumor from all angles, and there was no question that it would be
impossible to remove it surgically. I called her family physician and gave
him the horrible news. "What a shame," he said. "We can't do much for
her." He and I both knew that in those days there were no good radiation
treatments or chemotherapy for kidney cancer.

We agreed to meet with the family together after office. I called the
nurse-in-charge to have Jane's husband and family meet us in the patient's
room at 6:00 p.m. Meanwhile, I had to run to my office and take care of the
crowd of patients waiting there. But all afternoon my mind was focused
on Jane: her terrible diagnosis and the poor prognosis. At 5:30 p.m., I sat
down to compose myself: What options did we have? What was I going to
tell this gentle soul and her happy family?

At six o'clock, the family physician and I met at the nurses' station.
We looked at each other; there was nothing much to say. I had the pencil

and paper I always carried to make sketches, as visuals are always easier to understand. The whole family was there. You could see the anxiety and fear on their faces. They sensed we had terrible news to tell them.

"Thank you all for coming on such short notice," I began in a low tone. "We have some bad news. The CT scan shows that Jane has a large right-sided kidney tumor, which seems to have invaded her liver too."

There was pin-drop silence in the room. The color of their faces instantly changed, as if someone had taken the most precious thing away from them. I pulled out my pencil and paper and started making a sketch of the kidney and liver. The first question came from her son: "Can you surgically remove it?"

"Unfortunately, it will not be possible because of the involvement of the liver," I replied. "I have thought about everything, and here is my advice." They all looked at me. Maybe I had a solution! "Since Jane is still young and healthy, I want to give her the best chance I can. I will explore her abdomen and see and feel what is actually happening. There is a very remote chance that the kidney mass may be just pushing into the liver, and not actually broken into it. On the other hand, if it has indeed grown into the liver, then I will take some biopsies from the mass and send them to the pathologist, who can give us more information about the nature of the tumor. Either way, it is a dangerous surgery and there are major risks." By this time tears were rolling down everyone's cheeks. The daughter had started sobbing loudly. Even Jane had an endless stream of tears coming down.

It has always been my practice that I never give seriously bad news on the telephone. I believe it has to be done face to face. The other most important thing is to give the patient and the family hope and the best possible option. No one knows the future. We all live on hope. There have been reported cases where a physician gave a cancer diagnosis on the phone and the patient committed suicide, feeling there was no chance of survival.

Jane broke the silence. "Dr. Hai, we trust you," she said. "When can you schedule the surgery?" It seemed she had made the decision, and that her family members were okay with it. I explained to her that I would call the scheduler in the OR and try to get the earliest possible time, and then let everyone know. Before leaving I looked at Jane and her family and said, "It is going to be a very serious operation and, as human beings, our team will do our best. But I would like you all to pray to God and ask for the best outcome." At this point, Jane opened her arms toward me and I leaned forward. She gave me a firm embrace and said, "We will leave it in God's hands."

The surgery was set for Friday morning, and I requested one of the senior surgeons to assist me. As usual, I had asked the blood bank for four units of packed red blood cells to be available for transfusion during the surgery, and I had booked a bed in the surgical ICU.

Once everything was ready, Jane was put under complete anesthesia.

Normally when we did kidney surgery, the patient would be positioned on the side and the incision made in the flank area, but in this case, we had no idea how extensive the surgery could end up. I opted for a supine position, in case I had to extend the incision. Once she was prepped and draped, I made a quick prayer, and then started with a long incision in the midline from the sternum to the belly button. Thank God she was thin and had very little fat to work through, and very soon I was in the abdominal cavity. The retractors were put in place, giving me good exposure. I started exploring the various organs. Then came the moment of truth. As I pushed the liver upward, with some restriction, I could pass my hand over the big kidney tumor. The tumor was still confined to the kidney; it was just physically pushing the liver, but there was no extension of it. I let out a big sigh of relief. Jane's prayers had been answered.

Now the task at hand was to remove this monster without causing any damage to the neighboring organs. Because of its large size, it had rotated the whole kidney and was now sitting directly on the two major vessels of the human anatomy: the aorta and the inferior vena cava.

I purposely did not want to manipulate the tumor too much before clamping the blood vessels, to avoid any chance of pushing a big clot or tumor pieces into the circulation. That could cause a complete block of the heart's circulation and would be the end of the game. I carefully and gently pulled the mass away from the midline, and there was the major blood vessel: the big fat vein that drains blood from the kidney. I could not see the artery behind it. My heart was pounding, and I could feel the sweat running down my spine. If this vein ruptured, the bleeding would be profuse, leading to instant death.

At this point, I have always relied on my tactile perceptions and on the three-dimensional anatomical picture that has been engraved in my mind since the days I taught anatomy at the medical school. Many a time I can close my eyes completely, and my fingers will transmit a full image of what I feel but cannot see. Although it is based on knowledge, I strongly believe it is a God-given talent. My wife Annette, who has done hundreds of surgeries with me, always told me, "Mahmood, close your eyes and tell me what you are feeling." In this case, I could feel a big kidney artery right behind the vein. With my eyes closed, I carefully started separating the artery from its surrounding tissues. It took a few minutes before I could feel the artery free and clear. I asked the nurse for a long vascular clamp and, purely by feel, advanced the clamp and clamped the artery. I then passed a suture around the big fat vein and tied it in three places. The blood flow to the kidney was now totally blocked. I breathed a sigh of relief. Then I tied off the tube going down from the kidney to the bladder. With careful dissection, the kidney freed out and the whole mass and kidney were removed from the abdomen. The tumor was larger than a softball. It had been totally removed, and there was no evidence of spread of the disease. In my book, Jane had won the game. She was cured.

It took me another forty minutes to put all the organs back in place and close the abdomen in layers. Because of the meticulous surgery, the blood loss was less than 100cc, and we did not need to give any blood transfusion. I ran out to talk to the family in the waiting room. The news of the successful surgery was met with many hugs and kisses. Jane would recover to live her life again, and thank God that He gave us two kidneys and we can lose one and still live a fairly normal life. I was very happy that I had taken a chance and not merely relied on the CT scan and the X-ray report.

After Jane recovered completely, she came back to the office one day and asked me, "Dr. Hai, since God has given me this extension of life, and the kids are all on their own, I would like to do some volunteer work. Is it okay?" I advised her to join the hospital auxiliary group, and she provided a great service to them for years. Now in her seventies, Jane still comes for her yearly checkup. She has six grandchildren and one great-grandchild. Tears fill her eyes when I remind her of the miracle that happened thirty years ago.

A crack in the renal artery

Ruth was referred to me by her internist for severe pain in the right flank area. An intravenous pyelogram had shown a very large stone in her right kidney, which was totally filling up the collecting system of the kidney.

Because these stones grow into each channel of the kidney, they are called "stag-horn" kidney stones. Before the advent of percutaneous fragmentation for the removal of stones and robotic surgery, they had to be taken out through open kidney surgery.

Since the kidney was quickly losing its function, the stone had to be removed as soon as possible. I explained the procedure in detail, and the patient and her family seemed to have a good understanding. Because Ruth was in her early eighties, any surgical procedure would be a high risk. In addition, she had extensive deposition of calcium in the walls of all her arteries. With all these factors, I impressed on them that the entire kidney might have to be removed. Her left kidney was functioning well and would carry the load satisfactorily.

The usual planning had been done, with blood available during the surgery and a bed assigned in the surgical ICU. I had also requested one of the surgeons, Dr. Largo, to be my assistant during the surgery. The procedure was going on well. I had exposed the whole kidney and the blood vessels, to gain control of the bleeding in case it became excessive. The kidney artery was extremely hardened and brittle because of the thick calcification. I had warned the surgeon assisting me to be extremely careful in that area.

As I was getting ready to open the kidney and remove the whole stone, Dr. Largo changed his posture, resulting in a slight tug on the artery. The big artery, which carries nearly one-fourth of the blood from the heart to the kidney, cracked open like an eggshell. A column of blood under high pressure shot up and hit the ceiling of the operating room. There was blood all over my face, and the whole surgical field was a pool of blood. The patient's blood pressure dropped precipitously. There was pin-drop silence in the operating room. My reflexes had worked instantly, and I exerted full pressure on the broken end of the artery. I had learned over the years that there is no bleeding you cannot stop by pressure. I gave a big sigh of relief and told everyone to relax. The situation was temporarily under control. Over the next ten minutes, we transfused four units and replaced the lost blood. The blood pressure came up. My left hand was still deep in the wound, putting pressure on the broken end of the artery against the spine. There was no active bleeding.

I asked the nurse for a big artery clamp and passed it toward my left hand. Closing my eyes, I could get a 3D picture in my mind and carefully placed the instrument on the broken end of the artery. Slowly, I retracted my left hand out of the wound. The bleeding was now totally under control. Using some big sutures, I completely sealed the end of the artery.

Following this, the procedure went smoothly. We removed the whole kidney with the large stag-horn stone inside. The incision was then closed in layers. All the patient's vital signs were back within normal limits. She was carefully transferred to the recovery room, and from there to the surgical ICU bed waiting for her. In that moment, I felt as if I had lost ten years of my life but, thank God, the patient made it through successfully. Ruth and her family were extremely delighted.

Later that afternoon, the assisting and circulating nurses came to me with a question: "How could you keep your cool through all that happened this morning?" I explained to them that when an episode like that occurs, you have to make a prayer, calm down, and quickly plan the next step. By getting upset and angry, you lose the power of rational thinking. You also create panic among the whole team, which breaks up the crucial line of communication. Life is an everyday learning experience: we get into a terrible situation, gather our wits, and come up to the occasion. These episodes are what makes a surgeon great.

Kidneys full of stones

Mr. A was the brother-in-law of one of the physicians in the Oakwood residency program. He was in his mid-forties and had been diagnosed with kidney failure. There were large stones in both kidneys, which had totally blocked and destroyed the organs. He was constantly falling prey to urinary tract infections, and no antibiotic was working. He had been advised to start dialysis and get in the long waiting line for a kidney transplant. I reviewed all his medical records and, even in the plain X-ray of the abdomen, you could see the whole contour of the kidney was built up with large stones. The blood tests revealed that the kidneys were functioning at a very low ebb. It was difficult to determine how much functioning kidney tissue was left and how much of it would recover after the stones were removed. Many questions were running through my mind. Was it even worth risking major surgery, to remove the stones? Would the kidneys ever recover? The patient himself was reluctant to go on dialysis, as it would consume a good part of his remaining life: eight hours a day, three days a week, hooked up to a filtering machine to clean out his blood.

After much thought, I met with the family and discussed the options. I could perform a major surgery, which would take four to five hours, and clean one kidney free of stones. There were no guarantees that the organ's function would improve. On the other hand, if we ran into extensive bleeding, we might have to remove the kidney entirely. With all the risks involved, Mr. A opted for the surgery, and the family was fully supportive.

Planning for the surgery, I was banking on two facts. First, from a study of the blood supply of the kidney that I had done as a medical student, I knew that there was a zone on the outer side of the kidney called Brodel's line. Brodel had discovered that if you cut into the kidney in that area, there was minimal bleeding, and my anatomical dissections had confirmed it. As a matter of fact, that had been the first paper I published in my career as a physician. Second, if we could freeze the kidney (hypothermia) before working on it, that would preserve the kidney from further damage, as the whole metabolism would slow down.

The surgery was scheduled for a Monday morning. Besides the usual preparations, I had frozen a few one-liter bags of sterile normal saline for cooling down the kidney. After fully exposing the kidney, using a sterile plastic sheath, I built a swimming pool for the kidney and filled it with slush made from the frozen saline. I clamped the main artery to the kidney, and the kidney blanched and turned cold. We had very limited time to work now. Making the incision along Brodel's line, I opened the kidney like a book. All the big stones were right there, staring at me. One by one I removed the stones, big and small, and felt around until they were all gone. Then I closed the kidney like a book and used some big sutures to hold it together tightly. At this point, I unclamped the main artery, blood started flowing, and the kidney turned pink again. There was bleeding from some small vessels, which I stopped with the handheld cautery device. The procedure went amazingly well. I removed all the slush, put the kidney back in its bed, and closed the incision in layers. The deed was done, but now he had to recover from the surgery. Then only would we know if we had had success in reviving the kidney's function.

The recovery was slow, but after a month, the blood tests showed remarkable improvement in his kidney function. Three months later, enthused by our success, we did the same procedure on the other kidney. The return of kidney function was even beyond my imagination. Mr. A felt a 100 percent better. One day, the family showed up at my office with a big box of gifts. I thanked them and told them it was not necessary, that I had just done my job.

Mr. A did well for many years on his own. A time came when he needed dialysis. Finally, he underwent a kidney transplant. I followed him through for many years. He was getting weaker from other ailments, but he would always hug me with utmost sincerity. In late July 2018, I received a call from his brother-in-law that Mr. A had passed away from cardiac arrest. I had the privilege of attending his funeral, and all the memories came flooding back. I had lost a dear friend and a well-wisher.

Surviving three cancers is no fun

Bob had just retired at the age of sixty-two, after putting thirty-five years with the United States Postal Service. His wife Betty had worked as a receptionist with one of the orthopedic surgeons at the hospital. When Bob saw blood in his urine, Betty asked her boss which urologist to see, and he recommended me. The routine workup for the presence of blood in the urine showed a suspicious mass involving the central part of the left kidney. A CT scan revealed a seven-centimeter-radius mass with typical features of kidney cancer. The tumor appeared to be totally confined within its own shell, with no evidence of spreading. A biopsy confirmed kidney cancer. Since Bob was otherwise healthy, I performed a left nephrectomy, a complete surgical removal of the kidney. His right kidney was totally normal and would take on the job of the lost kidney. The post-operative course was unremarkable, and within a few months, Bob felt great. Betty retired from her job too and the couple started traveling, which had been their plan after retirement.

Nine years later, Bob came in for his yearly checkup. His PSA level, the blood test for prostate cancer, had jumped up from 1.8 to 5.3. I did a prostate biopsy that showed a high-grade cancer just beginning to extend beyond the confines of the prostate shell, which we refer to as the capsule. Again, there was no evidence of metastasis. We received a medical clearance from the cardiologist stating that he was totally fit to undergo a complete removal of the prostate. During surgery, a few of the local lymph nodes had been harvested, showing extension of the disease. This meant we would need some additional treatment like external beam radiation to take care of the disease completely. I waited for three months post-operatively, and Bob had recovered well.

He was urinating with good control, and there was little change in his sexual function. Because of the extension of the cancer to the nearby lymph nodes, we referred him to a radiotherapist who agreed that the radiation would take care of any cancer left behind. Bob and Betty were always very compliant and grateful for the care they received.

When I saw Bob in the office again three months later, he looked good. He had tolerated the radiation well, but one new problem had developed. He had no control of his urine and was wearing diapers to keep himself dry.

We taught him pelvic muscle exercises and decided to treat the condition with conservative measures. Another three months passed. The lack of control was getting worse, and they were both getting frustrated with urine soaking through his clothes and all the linen and bedding. They had literally withdrawn from any social activity or traveling. Their son, who knew the situation, was the only one they allowed to visit. I did a complete evaluation with pressure studies and, on looking closely through the cystoscope, it was very evident that the urinary sphincter, the control mechanism, had been severely damaged from the radiation. Something had to be done soon, as Bob was getting very depressed and withdrawn. A week later, I sat down with the couple and went over the pros and cons of all the treatment options we had. After a long discussion, we all agreed that the placement of an artificial urinary sphincter (AUS) would give the best long-term outcomes, and Bob would be totally dry.

The artificial urinary sphincter AMS800, as we refer to it in our lingo, was developed in the late 1970s by Dr. F. Brantley Scott, a professor of urology at Baylor University in Houston. The device had been produced in association with a well-known surgical manufacturing company called American Medical Systems (AMS).

My memories of Dr. Scott are very vivid because of his personality. It was the early 1980s, and I had been in the urology practice for about four years. AMS invited a select group of urologists to attend the course on a new device developed for treating urinary incontinence. They had just started marketing it, and I would be one of the first few to learn the technology on the AUS and the inflatable penile prosthesis (IPP AMS 700). I met Dr. Scott just before the course at the breakfast table. He was a tall, well-built, handsome man in his early fifties, a true Texan, with highly decorated boots and a hat. Born in Texas, he had received his MD degree from Yale. He was a great inventor and an avid pilot. With this new invention, he had done well financially, and he had decided to retire and pursue his passion: building light airplanes. I remember that at the 86th annual urology meeting in early June 1991 in Toronto, AMS hosted a special lunch to bid him farewell. Less than three months later, Dr. Scott was flying a Quest-Air single engine plane that he had assembled from a kit, for a final test flight before taking it to the Oshkosh Air Show in Wisconsin. He was approaching to land, 150 feet above the ground, when the engine stalled and his plane crashed. His death came very soon after retirement, but I can just imagine the ecstatic satisfaction of successfully flying your own hand-built plane. We had lost a great urologist, inventor, and teacher.

The AUS AMS 800 is a completely concealed, implantable, fluid-filled hydraulic device made of solid silicone elastomer. Once surgically put in place, it mimics the normal sphincter function by opening and closing the urinary passage at the control of the patient. Bob was anxious to get his urine control back. Despite his previous surgeries and radiation, the AUS implanting procedure went well, and a month later the device was activated. Instantly it made him continent, and Bob couldn't have been happier. There was a learning curve with using the device, but within a few weeks, it became second nature to Bob.

A few years went by in bliss. Betty passed away, finally succumbing to lung disease, a result of her long years of smoking. I attended the funeral, and Bob was devastated. They had been married for nearly sixty-five years, and since their retirement, they had been together twenty-four hours a day, seven days a week. At ninety, Bob felt cheated. Luckily, the couple next door took up the responsibility of caring for him. They would bring him to the office regularly for follow-up. On one of his visits, we noticed a large amount of blood microscopically. I sent the urine sample for the cytology department to look for cancer cells. Lo and behold, it came back positive. Bob again had cancer in his urinary system. He had already lost his left kidney and prostate to malignancy. The blood had to be coming from his right kidney, kidney tubes, or bladder.

The next step was to do a CT scan of the kidney and take a look in the bladder. The scan came back negative, but when I looked in the bladder, there it was sitting at the neck of the bladder: a big mass, the size of a cherry. Bob was placed under sedation, and I biopsied it, and then totally vaporized it with the GreenLight laser. There was hardly any bleeding, because the laser seals the blood vessels before the tissue gets vaporized. I sometimes wonder if the radiation Bob had received could have initiated the tumor, but we will never know.

In November 2016, just after turning ninety-five, Bob started vomiting fresh blood. The neighbors immediately rushed him to the ER at the hospital. He was stabilized, and the bleeding stopped. The ER doctor told the nurse to place a Foley catheter in his bladder, to measure his urinary output. Bob was fully in his senses and told the nurse that he had an artificial urinary sphincter (AUS) in place, and that before passing a catheter it must be deactivated. He strongly advised her to call either me or the urologist on call. The nurse was rather careless and took no heed of what Bob was saying. She forcibly pushed the catheter through the inflated urethral cuff of the AUS. The catheter was left in place for three days while Bob recuperated from his bleed. When the catheter was removed, Bob was again totally incontinent of urine and back on heavy diapers. He was discharged home, very angry and depressed.

Two weeks later, he came to the office and told me the whole story. I was extremely upset. Despite Bob's reminder, they had caused totally unnecessary damage. They should have called me. By now, the whole system was infected. His entire perineal area and genitals were beef red and inflamed. The whole device would need to be removed, Bob would be incontinent on diapers for months to allow the area to heal, and only then could we try to put a new AUS in place. I called the nursing supervisor and made a formal complaint, insisting that they investigate and let me know how it had happened and who had done it. As a temporary measure, I gave Bob a device that fits like a condom over the penis and is attached to a tube that drains into a bag. At least this way the raw skin would not be constantly irritated by the acid urine, and the entire area would have a chance to heal.

Over the following six months, we periodically monitored Bob's progress. We performed a very careful cystoscopy. The tear in the urine passage had healed well, and the bladder was free of any tumor. In July 2017, I placed a whole new AUS system. I activated it a month later, and by God's grace, Bob was totally dry again. But what trials and tribulations he had been forced to endure in old age.

Bob is still alive as I write this, in 2019, and as cheerful as ever. In November 2019, he will turn ninety-seven years old. No one knows how much longer he will live, but I hope and pray that he makes it to hundred without any more major medical issues. He was unique, in that he had gone through three totally different kinds of cancer involving the urinary system and had been treated for urinary incontinence twice. Bob has taught me that there are no limits to human patience and resilience.

CHAPTER 10

Bladder Cases

The Ellen Carson story

I had been in my practice just a year when I saw Ellen in the office at 33000 Palmer Road in Westland, Michigan. She was a well-built woman in her mid-sixties, but she looked exhausted. Within a few minutes, she had given me her whole story. Three months back, she had seen a lot of blood in her urine and was totally shocked, because her health had been very good. She saw her primary care physician, who immediately referred her to a local urologist. After looking in her bladder and doing a CT scan of the abdomen and pelvis, the urologist had determined that she had extensive and aggressive bladder cancer that had invaded the uterus, lymph nodes, and other adjacent areas. He in turn referred her to the University of Michigan, where testing confirmed that she was not a surgical candidate and that they could give her chemotherapy only in an effort to slow down the tumor.

Ellen wanted nothing to do with chemotherapy, as she had heard enough bad things about it. At this point, she looked straight into my eyes and said, "Young man, I want you to get inside me and clean everything out. Just get rid of all the cancer. I know you can do it!" I thought for a few minutes, and then told her to come back with all her reports and her family.

Three days later she was back, with a thick folder of her medical reports and her daughter and son-in-law. I reviewed everything. Indeed, the tumor had grown out of the bladder into her uterus and the surrounding lymph nodes. Luckily the bowels and the rectum were not involved. I told her I would need to perform an anterior exenteration, which meant removing everything in the pelvic cavity other than her rectum. I would also need to work with a gynecologist for some parts of the procedure. The surgery could take up to twelve hours, and she could die on the table. Without a blink, she asked, "Where do I sign?"

It took a week to coordinate everything. I had talked to Dr. Marvin, an excellent gynecologist, who had agreed to help me in the surgery. We had reserved ten units of blood to replace blood loss during the procedure and also booked a bed in the surgical ICU. The day of the procedure came, and needless to say I was extremely nervous. Ellen was wheeled in to the operating room. I held her hand and talked to her. She was not the least bit worried and just said to me, "Pray to God, and He will help you." I did, as I needed all the prayers and help I could get for her surgery.

The surgery took nine challenging hours. The first five hours were spent meticulously removing the bladder, the uterus, and all the tissues and lymph nodes involved in the cancer. At this point Dr. Marvin had to leave, and I spent the next four hours reconstructing a urinary conduit, using a loop of the small bowel, attaching the tubes from the kidney, and closing up the abdomen in layers. Overall, the surgery went very well. We lost only four units of blood, which was promptly replaced, and the kidneys were producing large quantities of urine, which was now being drained into a bag in the front of the abdomen. Her vital signs remained stable throughout the procedure.

I was totally exhausted and sat down to have the traditional food in the surgeons' lounge: graham crackers with peanut butter and coffee. It was 5:00 p.m. The phone rang and it was my secretary, Bev. She was delighted to know that Ellen's surgery had gone well. Then she said, "And remember, you promised that you'll do the runway fashion show for the secretaries' charity dinner tonight." I almost fell off my chair. "Yes, of course, Bev," I replied. That evening I did change into a fancy suit and walked on the runway; I don't know how well my hips were swinging, but Bev told me the next day that they had a good collection at the charity ball.

The next morning when I saw Ellen in the ICU, she looked amazingly good. The nurses told me that she had refused to take any pain medications. Her recovery was remarkable. Two weeks later she came to the office for a follow-up, and she looked like a new person. She gave me a big hug and told me, "From now on I will be your local mother, since your real mother is in India." She had brought two big jars of homemade jam, and the supplies continued every month for fifteen years. Ellen had turned over a new leaf. She started doing a lot of volunteer work at a local church, cooked for hundreds at the Salvation Army, and gave every bit of herself in service. When I urged her to slow down, she said, "God has given me a new lease on life, and I want to thank Him every moment of my life."

After fifteen years, she died of a heart attack. I went to her funeral and cried. Even today, when I think of her, my eyes tear up. My adopted mother had passed away into the everlasting gardens of Heaven.

I learned a lot from Ellen. When you are determined and pray for God's help, He can change your fate in life, and the best way to pay back is to give service to humanity. It amazes me how He can create love in the hearts of strangers, even in a young Indian doctor and an old American lady. Even now Ellen's daughter, Pat, brings homemade jam to my office, and Ellen's memory lives on.

What auto accidents can do

Joey was a tall, handsome man in his early forties when I first saw him. Two years previously, he had been involved in a very serious car accident. Besides having fractured ribs and lung injuries, he had a severe crush injury of the pelvis. The EMTs had brought him to the emergency room at the University of Michigan, and after his vital signs were stabilized, he was taken to the operating room with a team of trauma and cardiothoracic surgeons. The urologist on call and the chief resident were also requested to scrub in the surgery. The fractured pelvic bone had extensively damaged the bladder, and the urethra had been totally severed. They were unable to pass a catheter into the bladder and had to divert the urine by placing a catheter directly into the bladder, a procedure referred to as a suprapubic cystostomy. Luckily, his kidneys were unharmed.

A week later, when Joey was out of the intensive care unit, they took X-rays to further evaluate the damage to his urethra, the tube that connects the bladder to the outside. The bladder was healing well, but there was a big separation of the urethra immediately below the prostate. A surgical procedure was performed in which the urologist made an incision in the perineal area, drained all the collected blood, and with great difficulty reconnected the two cut ends of the urethra. They were now able to pass a catheter from the opening of the urethra to the inside of the bladder. After a month in the hospital, Joey was finally discharged wearing two catheters: one draining the bladder directly, the other passing through his urethra. He was warned that his bladder control mechanics would most likely never function again. Not only was life at home with the two catheters painful, but the stench of urine was unbearable.

When Joey came back to the university clinic the following month, as his urethral catheter was being removed, his urine started leaking instantly. He was sent home with some heavy-duty absorbent diapers. At home he had to change them at least six times a day. Gradually over the next few weeks the dribbling of the urine stopped, and all the urine was draining from the direct catheter in the bladder. When he went back after three months, Joey was told by the urologist that unfortunately the repair had not worked and the scar tissue had closed up the passage again. Several surgical attempts were made, but with no success. Joey was told that he would have to live the rest of his life with the suprapubic catheter and a urinary bag to drain his bladder.

During my history taking, Joey told me that he had developed such severe depression that he was planning to commit suicide. Because of the urine smell he would stay away from everyone, including his wife and children. A friend of his had told him about me and my expertise with lasers. He came to see me as his last hope.

After assessing the whole situation, I sat down with Joey and his wife and explained the complexity of the problem. First, I would have to open the channel between the bladder and the urethra through all the thick scar tissue. I could use the laser for that. Then I would place a titanium stent to prevent the scar tissue from blocking it again. Even after the channel was open, he would still be leaking urine continuously. To fix the incontinence problem, I then proposed to put in place an artificial urinary sphincter. This whole process would have to be staged over at least six months, if all went well. Joey listened very carefully, and then looked at his wife and said, "Honey, I have no choice. I cannot go on living the way I am." His wife had tears running down her cheeks. She reached out and hugged him, saying, "Baby, I will be with you through everything." And she truly was.

Success in these difficult cases requires love, hope, and faith.

The surgeries went as planned but were long and tedious. One thing was in Joey's favor: his age. His tissues were healthy and would heal well, despite the damaging effects of surgery. After six months, all the procedures had been done. After placement of the artificial urinary sphincter, we have to leave the device in a deactivated stage for the healing to take place and for the pain to dissipate. The moment of truth came after four weeks of anxious waiting. Would the device work? Could Joey be dry again? All these thoughts were going through my mind, and I am sure through his and his wife's mind, as I walked into the examining room to activate the continence device.

I made a special prayer: please, God, give Joey a new life.

I squeezed the pump to activate the system. There was a squish sound, and the switch was on. I made Joey stand up and cough. Not a drop of urine leaked out.

The joy we all felt in the room was immeasurable. Joey hugged me tight and kept crying, "Oh my God, I can't believe it." All three of us were crying tears of joy. The following week I took out his other catheter, and Joey could urinate like a normal person with full control.

Joey still comes once a year for his checkup. He has taken up many hobbies that he always wanted to do. Painting on canvas was one of them. In November 2018, he gave me one of his paintings, which he said he had done especially for me. It is a forest scene with a beautiful waterfall and spring all around. It was a true expression of his feelings, and I will treasure this painting that hangs in my office in Joey's memory.

Sometimes things look worse than they are

As a very busy urologist, I got to see many patients with bladder cancer, both men and women, in both early and late stages. It is well documented that 50 percent of these cancers are directly or indirectly related to smoking. Smokers, both men and women, have a three to six times greater chance of developing cancer. It is definitely one of the cancers we bring on ourselves, and therefore it gives us a chance to prevent it by changing our lifestyle. We also know very well that smoking also causes lung cancer, pancreatic cancer, chronic lung disease, heart disease, and many other illnesses. What amazes me most is when I see members of the medical profession smoke. How can you be an advocate and an example for something you do not practice yourself?

Bladder cancer is the fourth most common cancer in men. The American Cancer Society estimates that in 2019 alone, 80,470 new cases will be diagnosed, and 17,670 will succumb and die from it. Nine out of ten cases are diagnosed after the age of fifty, and one out of three are invasive disease, with 5 percent having already progressed to widespread metastasis.

Surprisingly, bladder cancer is twice as common in white races. Factory workers exposed to dyes and chemicals, and truck drivers inhaling diesel exhaust, are known to have a higher incidence.

A great amount of progress has been made in the early diagnosis of this cancer with a urine test looking for cancer cells and tumor markers in the urine and blood. Surgical removal through the cystoscope is curative in superficial bladder cancers, but in those that are invasive, the complete removal of the bladder gives the best long-term outcomes. Bladder cancers also have a great tendency to come back, and a vigilant follow-up is necessary.

Mr. S was referred to me by another urologist in town. The patient had been passing large clots of blood in his urine. A CT scan of the abdomen and pelvis had revealed that he had a very large bladder mass practically filling up the whole cavity of the bladder. The mass was also causing obstruction to the drainage from the kidneys, but there was no evidence of the disease going anywhere else. The bladder biopsies had confirmed a low-grade non-invasive cancer. The patient had been specifically sent for me to do the major surgery of removing the whole bladder and creating a urinary channel using a loop of the small intestine to drain the urine into a bag attached to the abdominal wall. The patient and his family were already mentally prepared for this major surgery.

It has always been my practice before performing any major surgery to do a final assessment of the whole situation. I explain it to the patient by saying that I need a road map before embarking on the journey. With Mr. S, I wanted to do the same: take a comprehensive look at the bladder. There was some reluctance from both the patient and the family as they figured enough testing had been done. "Now let's get the bladder out and be done," they said. But I insisted, as I did not want to deviate from a tried and true principle.

The cystoscopy was done under general anesthesia, and what it revealed knocked my socks off. Although the mass was completely filling the bladder, it arose from a small stalk, which was the source of the blood supply. There was no other attachment anywhere in the bladder wall. I took a few bladder biopsies and then, using the laser, I cut the small stem, thereby cutting off the blood supply to the whole mass. Increasing the power of the laser, I started vaporizing the big mass. The tissue just turned into vapor, and within fifty minutes, the entire bladder mass was gone. I took some pictures of the inside of the bladder to show that the rest of the bladder was absolutely normal. Coming out of the operating room, I sat down with the family in the waiting room. "The bladder tumor is gone," I said. "In my book he is cured. We do not need to remove the bladder." Initially what I was saying did not make any sense, but when the findings and the procedure were explained to them in detail, they were absolutely dumbfounded. They could not thank me enough for taking a look in the bladder rather than jumping in to remove it based on someone else's findings.

A few lessons were learned. As a surgeon, you have to do your own evaluation and build your own roadmap. I reaffirmed my belief in following principles and not wavering under pressure from the patient and his family. Good principles and practices always lead to the best possible outcome.

How the bladder impacts our lives

Emily was twenty-three years old. She had a great job as a therapist in a physical therapy center. She had just married her high school sweetheart, and life was great — except for one thing: her bladder.

In the last year or so, she had developed extreme urgency and had to run to the bathroom frequently. She cut down on her coffee and gave up drinking any kind of pop. This helped for a short time, but the symptoms continued to worsen. She saw her family physician, who gave her several courses of antibiotic, with no improvement other than the placebo effect. Finally she was referred to a urologist, who had her kidneys and bladder evaluated by ultrasound. The results came back normal. When he looked in with the cystoscope, he discovered that she had a small-capacity bladder, and also that the inner lining of the bladder had been severely damaged by a condition called interstitial cystitis, or IC. He started her on the full dose of a medication called Elmiron, which she had been taking for over six months. There was hardly any improvement.

Frustrations were building up. At work, she had to excuse herself every fifteen minutes to go to the bathroom during the physical therapy sessions, and a few of the clients reported her to the manager. Relations at home had deteriorated too. The frequency and urgency were annoying, and any attempt at sexual activity was painful. When she talked to other family members, her sister had heard from one of her friends that there was a urologist who was using laser for the prostate. Emily made an appointment to see me, and her mother accompanied her. When I asked her how she was feeling, she went on for twenty minutes with her complaints and unhappiness and ended sobbing, saying, "Dr. Hai, I don't want to live anymore." That was a strong statement from someone in her mid-twenties. Before I could say anything, she started again: "Can you use your laser on my bladder?" I explained to her that the GreenLight laser had been developed for vaporizing the prostate in men who had obstruction, and that there was no indication for it to be used in the bladder.

That day I talked to her about other treatment options, but the idea she had put in my mind lingered: "Why not?" The FDA had okayed it for use on all soft tissues of the body.

Whenever someone tells me "You cannot do it," I say, "Tell me why not." I like to hear a reason supported by evidence. It reminded me of the time I wanted to perform the GreenLight prostate laser surgery in the office and everyone, including Annette, who knew the necessary requirements, said, "We can't do it here." I insisted that they give genuine reasons. When we looked at each one of them, they were all manageable in the office. We complied with all the OSHA, HIPPA, and other pertinent regulations, and indeed we performed the first GreenLight laser surgery in our office.

I did some more research and concluded that, although there had been no specific studies on the subject, lasers could be used in the bladder. We just had to be extremely careful and evaluate the outcomes both subjectively and objectively.

Emily returned two weeks later for her follow-up. I sat down with her, her husband, and her mother, and had a frank discussion. I stressed emphatically that I had not read any literature on the use of lasers for IC, nor had I ever used it for that diagnosis. The procedure would be experimental. On the other hand, I had a lot of experience with the use of the laser, and I felt that if we could clean out the damaged inner layer of the bladder and help a healthy lining grow back with the help of medication, it might work. In addition, while Emily was under anesthesia, I could stretch the bladder with fluids, thereby increasing her bladder capacity. The idea appealed to them, and Emily was desperate to try anything to get out of her misery.

The procedure was performed in our office operating room, under anesthesia. It took about twenty minutes. Using the laser at a very low power, I superficially vaporized the whole inner lining of the bladder, and then stretched the bladder to nearly three times her normal waking capacity. We gave her some strong pain medication before waking her up. I was ready to hear her shrieking and crying in pain. To my surprise, Emily woke up as calm as ever and looked at me. "Dr. Hai, my pain is gone," she said. "This is magic." I myself could not believe it. The laser had again done a phenomenal job. We sent her home on Elmiron, which provides healthy material to reform the lining, and some pain medication.

The recovery took a few weeks, but Emily was soon back at work. We had to repeat the procedure twice over fifteen years, but she lives a fairly normal life with her husband and three children. We have used the new technique in a large number of IC patients successfully and have changed the lives of many who had lost hope of ever living a normal life with IC. By the same token, I learned to listen to my patients and try to make sense out of what they tell me.

CHAPTER 11

Prostate Cases

Miseries of prostate cancer

In the late 1970s, the diagnosis and treatment of prostate cancer was still in its early development. Most patients were diagnosed too late, when the disease had gone too far and spread throughout the body.

Jacob was a seventy-five-year-old man who was brought to the ER in a moribund state, totally unresponsive to voice commands. He looked dehydrated and emaciated and appeared to be on his last few breaths. The ER physician had started an intravenous line and was giving IV fluids. Jacob's wife, who had accompanied him, had told the admitting nurse that he had recently been diagnosed with extensive prostate cancer that had spread all over his body. He had been severely nauseated and, for the last two days, had been throwing up constantly. All his lab results were off the chart and confirmed total kidney failure. The patient was admitted to the ICU and showed very few signs of improvement. The admitting physician had arranged a consultation with me as a courtesy, simply because the patient's diagnosis stated prostate cancer.

It was late evening when I finally got to see Jacob. As I flipped through his medical chart, it was obvious that he had extensive prostate cancer that had spread widely to all his bones and was totally blocking the kidney tubes, leading to complete renal failure. The patient was still unresponsive. His wife and two children were at the bedside. The only question they asked me was, "How soon do you think we should plan for his funeral?"

I pulled them outside the room and said, "Statistically, he may have a day or two to live, but when he will die, only God knows." At that point his son asked me, "Can anything be done?" I asked them to meet with me the following morning.

That night, I sat and reviewed some of the great work done by Dr. Charles Huggins on prostate cancer. Huggins was born in Halifax, Canada, in 1901. After his BA degree, he joined Harvard University and received an MD degree at the age of twenty-two. He then completed his internship and surgical residency at the University of Michigan. At the age of thirty-one, he became a professor of surgery at the University of Chicago. His classic paper on the effect of castration and androgen deprivation in metastatic prostate cancer was published in *Cancer Research* in April 1941. For the next forty-five years, the treatment of prostate cancer involved his strategy. In 1966, when he was awarded the Nobel Prize for Physiology and Medicine, he made the humble remark, "A cancer worker utters the mariner's prayer: 'Oh Lord, Thy sea is so vast and my bark is so small.'"

One of his students, Paul Talalay, has appropriately said, "Humanity owes Charles Huggins deep gratitude. Since cancer of the prostate constitutes one of the most common cancers of man, the untold benefits and relief of suffering which his treatment brought to many older men can hardly be overemphasized. His work also heralded an era of rational chemotherapy for cancer." Huggins later did a lot of work with breast cancer too. A banner behind his research bench simply said: "Discovery is our business." I truly believe in Huggins's work, and his statement: "Research has been my pleasure as well as my job. There is nothing which matches the thrill of discovery."

The next morning, I met with Jacob's family. His condition had remained the same. Based on Dr. Huggins's work, I offered to do the simple procedure of removing both his testicles under local anesthesia in the ICU. It seemed like a drastic measure, but its benefits could be dramatic, as Dr. Huggins had shown. The family agreed, as they felt there was nothing to lose. Jacob was on his last legs. With the help of the nursing staff, I successfully performed the procedure in fifteen minutes. The patient barely felt anything.

The castration procedure produced a miraculous effect. The following evening, Jacob opened his eyes and his mental haziness began to clear. A few days later, he was sitting in a chair, being fed a bowl of cereal. My joy knew no bounds, and of course, the family was overwhelmed with happiness. A miracle had happened in front of our eyes. Two weeks later, Jacob was walking in the corridor with the nurse's help, and I discharged him to a nursing home for physical therapy. A month later, I repeated all his blood tests and the bone scan, and to my utter surprise, the labs were getting normal and his bony metastases were gone.

A month later, he came back for his follow-up. He had no complaints and a long list of "Can I do this?" questions. I okayed everything. He had always wanted to see Chicago and visit his brother in California. Jacob booked many senior citizens' group tours with Greyhound, and his wife was having a tough time keeping up with him. He wrote a beautiful letter to me, saying how grateful he was for giving him a new life. In my heart I knew God had performed a miracle, and that I was simply an instrument in His work. For many years I kept Jacob's letter on my desk, to raise my spirits when I felt down. It was worth more than a million-dollar check.

I had lost touch with Jacob and thought he must be doing well. Three years later, I received a call from the ER. Jacob was back, in the same state as I had seen him initially. This time the disease had come back with a vengeance. A few days in the ICU, and Jacob was gone forever. I was sad, yet happy that he had had three beautiful years to enjoy life and fulfill his dreams.

Stanley and his prostate cancer

Stanley was in his late fifties. He was referred to me in 2002 for an elevated blood level of PSA. Taking in his history, I asked, "What kind of work do you do?"

"I don't work anymore," he replied. "My parents came as immigrants from Poland after the Second World War. They were so poor we couldn't even afford underwear, and I promised myself that I would not live like that." Stanley started working at the Ford assembly plant from the age of sixteen. He saved all his money and invested in an old house in Dearborn, which he renovated and sold for a big profit. He kept doing this, working all the time that he was off from his job, and within twenty years, he had saved enough to buy an athletic club in town. With good management and hard work, money started rolling in. He purchased another athletic club in the neighboring town and, by the age of fifty-five, had built a real estate empire: four athletic clubs in Michigan, two golf courses in Las Vegas and the Bahamas, and a solid portfolio in the stock market. He never married and had no family after his parents passed away.

After a complete evaluation, I advised Stanley to have a needle biopsy of the prostate under ultrasound guidance. Lo and behold, the prostate biopsy came back as extensive high-grade prostate cancer. The CT scans confirmed that there was no spread of the disease beyond the prostate at this point. If we could remove his prostate by surgery, there was an excellent chance of a complete cure. I sat down with Stanley and explained the surgical procedure and the whole recovery process. He would be cured of the cancer and be totally functional in three to four weeks. He agreed, and we scheduled the procedure at the hospital the following week.

Two days later, Stanley came to the office and asked to talk to me. "How are you doing, Stanley?" I asked. "Pretty much the same," he replied. "But something urgent has come up, and I have decided to postpone the surgery for a few weeks and wrap up my business completely before having the procedure done." He explained that he was under a lot of stress and wanted to sell all his properties, especially the golf clubs in the Bahamas and Las Vegas and the four athletic clubs in Michigan. I expressed my deep concern that it might take more than a few weeks, and that the window of opportunity to get a complete cure from prostate cancer might be lost. Stanley assured me that whatever happened, he would be back in three weeks.

Nearly four months went by, and we never heard from Stanley. Whenever the office tried to call him, the recording said that he was not available and please leave a message. We even sent a registered letter to his home address. It was returned by the post office.

One evening six months later, while I was having dinner with my family, the emergency room called. Stanley had been brought in by an older lady who said she was a live-in friend. He was extremely dehydrated and disoriented and looked emaciated. His electrolytes and other labs also looked bad. I asked the ER physician to get a stat CT scan of the abdomen and pelvis as well as a bone scan. A few hours later when I came to see him, I hardly recognized him. He had lost a lot of weight and barely recognized me. On reviewing the imaging studies, it was obvious that the prostate cancer had spread all over, including the bones. I admitted him to the intermediate care unit to correct his dehydration and electrolyte imbalance. The next morning, he was more lucid, and I could make some sensible conversation. I had to give him the bad news that he was no longer a candidate for surgery and that it would be impossible to expect a complete cure. We would still give him palliative treatment with hormones and get him stronger for other forms of treatment. For a few days he improved, and the older lady stayed with him in the room. Stanley had sold some of his properties, but there was still much to be done. He told me that he had no close family other than his live-in friend. He wanted to leave some money for her, and the rest of his enormous wealth should go to charity. He did not trust anyone and wanted me to become the executor of his estate. I was not ready to take up such a huge responsibility, and I suggested that an attorney quickly prepare his will. That afternoon, a nurse called to let me know that Stanley was getting mentally confused again. After seeing the patients in the office, I went to see him. He still recognized me, but just kept saying repeatedly: "Doc! It's time for the vultures." I ordered a head CT scan, which showed that the cancer had spread to the brain. By morning, Stanley was in a coma. His friend just sat in the corner of the room and sobbed.

That evening when I returned to see him, there was a crowd of people outside his room, all claiming some relationship to him. I had never seen any of them before. The old lady was nowhere to be seen. Suddenly it made sense. The vultures Stanley had talked about had arrived, and the battle for his estate was about to begin.

The next morning, Stanley passed away. His wealth and riches had taken away his chances to survive prostate cancer. His own hard-earned money became the biggest hurdle to his survival. And now all these people, who had had nothing to do with him during his life and illness, were going to fight for his wealth and squander it. Stanley's life taught me a few good lessons: all the riches in the world cannot buy you good health, and make sure you document your will and commit to charity while you can.

Rudy, the great traveler and photographer

I had been performing the GreenLight laser procedure for prostate obstruction for a few years. Word was out that it gives great outcomes, and we were getting enquiring phone calls from all over the country. Patients who could not urinate or had failed other procedures were wanting to know if the laser procedure could help them.

A woman called from northern Michigan to say that her husband had gone into urinary retention a few months back. He had been living with a Foley catheter and was told by the urologist that his bladder was so damaged that he would never be able to urinate on his own again. I talked to the couple on the phone. Rudy was sixty-seven years old and had just retired from factory work. The couple were both in good health and had saved money to travel after retirement. But the urinary problem had put a kink in their whole plan.

They made an appointment and came down to the office for further evaluation and discussion — a very nice, cultured, and respectable couple. I developed a great liking for them. The next day we did the usual testing with blood test, prostate ultrasound, a urine flow study, and a quick telescopic look inside the bladder, which is called a cystoscopy. The outcomes were very clear: he had a fairly large prostate, with no sign of cancer. The bladder had been severely damaged with long years of obstruction from the prostate, to a point that it had developed large weak spots called diverticuli. I could relieve the prostate obstruction with the laser procedure, but there was no guarantee that the bladder would work and he would be able to urinate on his own. They understood the problem and agreed to have the bladder obstruction relieved first by the laser procedure.

Two weeks later, they came back for the scheduled laser surgery, which was done in our office under intravenous sedation. The procedure went very well, but the next day, when the Foley catheter was removed, Rudy could not urinate on his own. We had to reinsert the catheter, which was disappointing both for them and for me. The next procedure would be more involved, as I would have to do open surgery and repair his bladder. The date for it was set two months away, to give time for the prostate to heal.

Rudy and his wife drove down the night before, so he would be well rested. This time the procedure had to be done under general anesthesia. Once he was asleep, I opened up and trimmed all the parts where the muscle had been severely damaged. Then, using the remaining healthier bladder wall, I rebuilt the bladder like a double-breasted jacket, thereby reinforcing the weak areas. It made his bladder much smaller, but more functional. He returned home the next day to recover and returned two weeks later. The moment of truth came when we filled the bladder and took the catheter out.

Rudy voided his bladder completely. He and his wife were beside themselves with happiness, and so was I. Rudy was urinating on his own, after being dependent on a catheter for two years. Tears of joy kept flowing from their eyes. A new life had begun, and they could now look forward to all the dreams that had been shattered before.

They both loved wild animals and the forests, and they booked their first safari to Africa. Since then they have done nearly ten safaris, including Tanzania, Kenya, South Africa, India, and Nepal. Rudy became a serious and gifted wild-life photographer. On the ten-year follow up to his bladder surgery, in 2018, the couple presented me with a big album of the most fascinating wildlife pictures I have ever seen, as good as *National Geographic*, if not better.

Flatline EKG: "Oh shit!"

It was 1992, the early days of laparoscopic surgery. Annette and I had taken several courses to learn it and had been doing practice exercises. I still remember her using a mirror to get a better perspective on learning the techniques.

Cathy was one of the nurse anesthetists who had worked with us for a few years at the hospital. Her father, who was in his late sixties, had been diagnosed with aggressive prostate cancer. He was otherwise in very good health. After examining him and looking through all his test results, I suggested to Cathy and her dad that the best way to deal with this issue was to remove the whole prostate, thereby getting rid of the cancer.

Previously we had been doing open surgical removal of the prostate through a big incision, but now we could do it through laparoscopy. This technique is much less invasive, and the recovery in turn is less painful and quicker. The outcomes, however, are pretty much the same. After the patient is placed under anesthesia, we introduce a small needle into the peritoneal cavity and fill it with gas. This creates a large working space and also decreases the bleeding because of the pressure. We then make several small openings in the abdominal wall, called ports. The ports are then used to position a camera and other instruments as needed. The whole surgery is done looking at a magnified image on a TV screen. At the end of the procedure, the gas is let out and the ports are closed with sutures. The patient is able to get up and walk around within a few hours, and can be discharged and sent home in a day or two.

Cathy's dad and her family were all in favor of performing the prostate surgery laparoscopically. We scheduled the surgery at the hospital, and Cathy requested one of her very dear friends, Linda, to give her dad the anesthesia for the surgery. That morning, the patient was brought to the operating room. Linda expeditiously put him under anesthesia. Everything was stable. Annette and I prepared and draped him, ready for the procedure. Once we got the okay from Linda, I introduced the needle into the abdominal cavity and hooked it up to the gas supply.

The abdomen began to distend as expected, and we were waiting to get to the right intra-abdominal pressure when Linda suddenly shouted, "*Oh shit!*" I immediately looked at the monitor, and the EKG recording showed a straight line, which meant his heart had totally stopped. I urgently disconnected the gas tubing and started to let the gas out. As the pressure went down, within a minute, his heart started beating again and the EKG tracing was back to normal. We all took a big sigh of relief. Just the thought that Cathy's dad had died on the operating table was horrifying and nauseated me.

Annette and I both looked up at Linda, and I said, "Linda, you have to say something more specific than 'oh shit!' when things of this magnitude happen. That term does not cut it." Linda was very sorry, and we resumed the procedure. The gas tubing was hooked back up, and the intra-abdominal pressure started rising. My eyes were glued to the EKG monitor. In five minutes, the pressure was getting up to the needed level, and it happened again: his EKG went flat-line. Based on our previous experience, I knew exactly what to do. As I started releasing the pressure, his heart returned to its normal rhythm.

I immediately decided that he was not a candidate for laparoscopic surgery, and we switched to the open surgical removal of the prostate. Thank God everything went very well. After two hours of surgery, I stepped out to the waiting room and told the whole story to the family. At the end, I told them that he was doing absolutely fine and that we looked forward to a normal recovery.

In life, we do not know what will hit us next, but we have to be prepared to face it and change our course and plans as required. Rigidity and arrogance result in disasters.

The physician from California

My office was getting calls from all over the United States and even other countries, from patients suffering as a result of prostate enlargement. Some of them were very interested in the new technology, others had heard a lot of negatives about the old roto-rooter procedure, and a few had been told that they were not candidates for any surgical procedure because of their medical condition. The office maintained a special list of these calls, and I would try to get back to them individually and answer all their questions about the laser procedure. Many of them, after talking to me, decided to come to our center to have their evaluation and the laser surgical procedure.

Because of the high demand, we had developed a GreenLight PVP package that included medical literature on prostate enlargement, a small booklet with details of the procedure and risks involved, a video of the procedure, and general information about the airport, hotels, and restaurants. It also had a personal letter about the tests we would do, referral and insurance information, and the email and phone number of the person who would schedule the appointments and procedures. Once the patient expressed interest, the package would be mailed to him, and after reviewing it, they would call and schedule their visit. Because very few urologists were doing the GreenLight procedure, we were sometimes overwhelmed by these calls. We started seeing six to ten patients every month who were coming from other areas.

Word got around quickly. A well-known physician who is a health guru and publishes a health newsletter was very happy with the outcomes of the patients he had referred to me. In his publication, he wrote that if you were not getting satisfactory results with herbal and medications, you should call Dr. Hai's office. He even gave my phone number. Patients typically would come to the office on Tuesday afternoons when I would talk to them and do any simple test needed. The next morning, they would have the laser procedure in our ambulatory surgical center and go back to their hotel. The following morning, after a follow-up visit, they could head home. Thank God we had great results and received nothing but good reviews from the patients about their whole experience. They also told their friends and relatives, creating a domino effect.

A physician called from California. He had read the reviews of the success of this procedure and, knowing that I had the greatest experience, called wanting to talk to me. The following morning I called him back. He had a million and one questions, and I answered them all to his satisfaction. He called the office back and made an appointment to have a consultation and then proceed with the surgery.

A few weeks later he arrived, a tall and extremely anxious sixty-five-year-old gentleman. He had a thick file of all his medical records. It took me an hour to look through it. Indeed, he had an enlarged prostate causing obstruction to the flow of his urine. There was no evidence of cancer. I looked in his bladder with the cystoscope, and it confirmed the opinion I had formed. We sat down again to discuss the surgical procedure and all the possible complications that could happen. By the same token, I also told him that we had great success without any complications in a very large number of patients on whom we had performed the GreenLight laser procedure. I also told him that, because it was not cancerous, he could live with the symptoms and I could help him with some medications. After much deliberation, he said he wanted to have the procedure done.

The following morning, I met him in the surgical center, went over the plan, and asked him if he had any other questions or concerns. He sounded determined to go ahead. But as I walked away, my inner voice said, "I don't trust this guy." I now wish I had listened to it. The surgery went extremely well and at the end, as is routine, I placed a catheter to drain his bladder. He was well sedated when he was taken to the recovery room next door. The anesthetist was still trying to wake him up. A few minutes had passed when he suddenly opened his eyes, totally confused, and shouted, "What the hell is going on?"

As the words came out of his mouth, his hand reached down and, with all his fury, he pulled the catheter out with its balloon fully inflated. A stream of pure blood started pouring out of his urine passage. There was absolute panic. Luckily, I was in the recovery room talking to another patient. I ran down to his bed and asked the nurse to get me another catheter right away. Within minutes I had the catheter in him, with the balloon inflated to stop the bleeding. It slowed down considerably but did not stop. My mind was racing. He had probably ripped an artery in his urethra and would not stop bleeding until we stopped it surgically. Instantly I called 911 to get the ambulance to take him to the emergency room at the hospital, only four miles away, where we could immediately replace the lost blood with transfusion, and then take him to surgery and fix the problem.

By this time he was fully awake, and I explained what he had done to himself. Within a few minutes, the ambulance came and he was on his way to the hospital. I had to cancel all my other surgeries scheduled for that day and quickly head to the hospital. He was just being wheeled in when I got to the ER. We drew blood to get matched packed red blood cells for transfusion, and started rapidly giving intravenous fluids to maintain his blood pressure, which had gone down very low. I also called the operating room to set up for the emergency surgery. The blood bank sent four units of blood within ten minutes, and we quickly transfused it. His blood pressure and heart rate settled down. He was still bleeding a lot, and I knew the window of opportunity was small to stop the bleeding right away.

I personally wheeled his stretcher to the operating room. The thought kept crossing my mind: "Doctor from California dies immediately after his prostate surgery by Dr. Hai." What a tragedy it would be! The anesthetist and the OR staff were all ready, and within a few minutes, I had the cystoscope up his urethra. What I saw took my breath away. The balloon of the catheter had ripped through the wall of the prostate and urethra, creating a long, deep valley, and several arteries were pumping out pure blood. The bleeding was obscuring my vision too. I got control of myself and, using the cauterization device, started clogging each blood vessel. The bleeding started to slow down, and within a few minutes, I had totally stopped the bleeding. The tear was bad and would take weeks to heal, but my only concern at this point was to save his life. I put in another catheter, and the drainage from the bladder was clear light pink. We transfused another four units of blood, and by the time he came to the recovery room, he was totally stable. We restrained both his arms: I could not survive another episode of what had happened. I stayed with the patient for the next couple of hours in the ICU, making sure he was not bleeding anymore and that his blood pressure remained stable.

By the time I got home that evening, it was 9:00 p.m. I was physically and emotionally exhausted. I had a few quick bites for dinner and headed back to the hospital. There was an inherent fear hanging around me that if, for any reason, he started bleeding again, I would lose him. But he stayed absolutely stable and fell into a deep sleep. Around 1:30 a.m., I told the nurse taking care of him that I was going home but that, if anything happened, she must call me right away. All night I could not sleep and lay in bed analyzing what had happened and how God had protected me. Just the thought of what could have happened was nauseating.

The next morning, I got to the hospital around 6:00 a.m. and went straight to the ICU. I looked through all the notes from the night shift, and nothing had changed. The California doctor was wide awake and looking normal. The urine draining in the catheter bag was clear light pink. As I walked up to him, he smiled and said, "Thank you for saving my life." I sat down and calmly explained to him how he had pulled out the catheter, causing severe damage and profuse bleeding. He kept saying, "I am so sorry." I told him that I would like him to stay a couple more days under observation, and then he could fly back with the catheter. I even suggested that his wife should fly out to Michigan and accompany him on his way back. His answer was, "She is too busy."

The next few days were uneventful. There was no more bleeding, and his urine was perfectly clear. All his lab results were back to normal. The morning he was due to leave, I explained the follow-up process in detail. He said he did not feel comfortable flying back alone and that, if I could arrange a doctor to go with him, he would pay $5,000. Nobody was available on such short notice. My last resort was to ask my wife Annette, who was a qualified urology nurse, to accompany him. She said, "Honey! I have a busy day planned, with meetings and lots of thing I have to finish today." I explained to her my dilemma, and after much persuasion, she agreed.

Annette had to call several people to reschedule her meetings. The California doctor was very happy with the arrangement and asked that she book her ticket in first class to be close to him, in case an emergency happened. He would pay for the ticket plus the $5,000 he had agreed to. I packed all emergency supplies that might be needed and personally drove him and Annette to the airport. I made a special prayer: "Dear God, please get him home safe and make the journey easy for Annette." She had to reach Los Angeles, call for an ambulance to take him straight from the airplane to a hospital where a bed had been arranged for him, and then fly right back to

Michigan. Five hours later, I got a call from Annette that the trip had been uneventful, that he was taken by ambulance straight to the hospital, and that she was getting ready to get on the plane to come back. "I owe you big time, honey," I said. "Thank you, thank you, thank you."

For the next few days, I would call and talk to the urologist who was taking care of him in California. The recovery went smoothly, and he was discharged from the hospital after three days of observation. Two weeks later, the catheter was removed and, to my utter surprise, he urinated with a good stream and full control. I had been seriously thinking that his control mechanism would be permanently damaged from the extensive injury. He called back several times, thanking me for saving his life, doing a successful surgery, and sending Annette to escort him. He also promised to send a check for the $5000 and the airfare.

A few weeks went by, and I did not hear from him. I presumed that all was well and that he must have gotten busy with his practice. A week later, I received a registered letter from him, which I thought would be the check for Annette. To my utter surprise, the long letter stated that the anesthetist and I were extremely incompetent and had nearly killed him. He was sending a letter to the Michigan department of medical licensing and the Board of Medicine, requesting that they take away the licenses of both me and the anesthetist. He was sending another letter to the hospital board, to suspend my privileges for improper and callous patient care. I was totally shocked. The anesthetist called, and we sat looking at each other, pondering at the false accusations this patient had made to cover his own fault in pulling the catheter.

Sure enough, a few weeks later, we got letters from all three organizations requesting all medical records pertaining to the California doctor and a copy of the allegations that had been made against us. We both contacted our professional liability companies and sent them copies of all the letters we had received. We were advised to send the medical records and take no further action. Thank God the medical records were written in detail by the recovery room nurse, the anesthetist, and me.

They all told the same story: the true story as it had happened.

After a few weeks, I received letters again from the three organizations with which the California doctor had filed allegations against me. I had to face several committees in person, which was stressful and a big waste of my time. A few weeks later, we got letters of determination from all three organizations that the allegations were baseless and that the care we had provided was above and beyond what any other physician would have provided in the circumstances. Truth had once more prevailed against falsehood. For the next two years, I kept all the records and documentation, anticipating that his next move would be to file a medico-legal suit against me. It never happened, but neither did Annette get her check for $5,000 plus the return first-class airfare she had paid.

Even today, whenever I am ready to operate on a physician or a VIP of any kind, the memory of the California doctor comes to haunt me. I reason with myself with reassurance that, as long as I honestly do my job well, there should be nothing to fear. Just because of one crazy patient, we should not get paranoid and treat everyone differently.

In 2017, I had to perform the GreenLight laser on a ninety-two-year-old gentleman from California who happened to be a friend of my father back in India. His daughter, son-in-law, and the family have all been very close friends. My anxiety level was very high, and I constantly prayed for a successful surgery. My prayers were answered, and the outcomes were even better than I had expected. It gave a big boost to my faith and prayer.

As surgeons, we deal with all kinds of personalities. Fortunately, the majority of patients are very understanding and thankful for what we do for them. Every human being is uniquely built and therefore the outcomes of a surgical procedure cannot always be predicted or guaranteed. We put up our best efforts, and then pray for the best results. On the same token, we have to be extremely tolerant and compassionate with everyone, never losing our cool.

PART THREE

Professional Issues

CHAPTER 12

The Burnout Dilemma

The Merriam-Webster dictionary defines burnout as "exhaustion of physical or emotional strength, or motivation, usually as a result of prolonged stress or frustration." *Psychology Today* states that "burnout is not a simple result of long hours. The cynicism, depression, and lethargy of burnout can occur when you are not in control of how you carry out your job, when you are working toward goals that do not resonate with you, and when you lack support." The telltale signs include chronic fatigue, insomnia, lack of concentration, anxiety, depression, anger, and even physical symptoms like chest pain, headache, and abdominal pain.

For more than twenty years, I was a solo urology practitioner with a very busy practice. The very first day in practice, my wise financial advisor and accountant told me, "As long as you are able, available, and amicable, you will be successful, and money will follow." That was indeed very true. From the very beginning, I decided that I would try to balance my professional life with family life and community work. During my residency, both in Boston and in Michigan, I had seen quite a few very busy physicians go through burnout, divorce, and addictions. It was very scary.

To protect myself from burnout, I put a few measures in place. First, I blocked off the calendar for a week to ten days every quarter, which I would take off from work and spend with my family. I had played tennis in school and I got back to it, joining the local athletic club and a league. Most mornings I would see my kids before school, and in the evening spend quality time with them before they went to bed, helping them with their homework as they got busier. I tried to attend most of their sports activities. My daughter Ayesha played lacrosse, and their team at Detroit Country Day School (DCDS) won the state championship. My son Yusuf was on the varsity basketball team at DCDS, and they were state champions, too. As much as possible, I would drive out to be at their practices and games.

My practice grew enormously, however, and life became hectic. I was the busiest surgeon in the hospital for over ten years, trying to take care of as many patients and surgeries as physically possible. I was appointed to many committees in the hospital and was busy bringing new technologies and equipment to the surgery department.

I remember the day very clearly when it happened. I had started surgery at 7:30 a.m. and had a long day in the OR. Around 2:00 p.m., I arrived to an office full of patients. I finished in the office at 7:00 p.m. and rushed back to the hospital for the monthly executive committee meeting. Finished at 8:45, I got in the car, changed into my tennis gear, and drove to the athletic club for a league tennis match, which I lost. I returned home around 10:30 p.m. to find the whole household asleep. After finishing my daily prayers, I sat down with a cup of herbal tea, reviewing the day gone by and preparing for the day to come. Finally, I got to the bedroom and changed to get into bed. On my pillow was a sheet of lined paper. Scribbled on it, in my son's handwriting, was this:

School is opening in three days and we need school supplies. When will you have time:

> September 3_____ AM/PM
> September 4_____AM/PM
> September 5_____AM/PM

Signed Yusuf

Reading Yusuf's note felt like a hard slap across my face. I had been postponing shopping for school supplies all summer, because other urgent things kept coming up. It was a shame that my son had to make an appointment to see me. I cried bitterly and promised to bring a change in my life.

Next morning, I was in the hospital administrator's office and wrote resignation letters to three of the five committees I was on. At the office, I asked my secretary Bev for the schedule book and drew a line below 5:00 p.m. every day. On my way home, I stopped at the tennis club and signed out of the tennis league. Here I was shedding responsibilities, and yet I felt a sense of accomplishment! The accomplishment was that I was rescuing myself, and I knew it. When I got home, the kids were waiting, and we went shopping for the long-awaited school supplies.

Since then, I have made it a point to plan vacations well in advance. Even though my wife and I have traveled to sixty-three countries, and more than once to some of them, we always go away now and then, for even a long weekend to be husband and wife, since we worked together. A few days breaks up the monotony of the treacherous daily work routine. I always come back refreshed, happy, and feeling healthy. Traveling opens the hearts and minds of the whole family. New adventures are always exciting, but there is some benefit too in going back to a location that brings you peace and familiarity. Some of us need extreme vacations like scuba diving, mountain climbing, and heli-skiing, but these also increase the risk of major injuries. Sometimes there may be opportunities to mix work with play.

Dr. Sherrie Bourg Carter, PsyD, addressed burnout in an April 2011 article in *Psychology Today*. "Because of the nature of our work, psychologists observe a lot of sad moments in human life," she writes, "but some of the saddest moments I have witnessed in my career have been watching bright lights grow dimmer and dimmer until they eventually burn out." She calls burnout "a cunning thief that robs the world of its best and its brightest by feeding on their energy, enthusiasm, and passion, transforming these positive qualities into exhaustion, frustration and disillusionment." Thank God burnout is not a terminal condition. Once it is recognized and remedied with lifestyle changes, the individual can once again rediscover and become a positive force and shine brightly.

For all busy professionals who take their jobs seriously, there is a potential to get exhausted to the point of burnout. It is the nature of the beast. In the twelfth State of the Specialty survey reported in the *Urology Times* of December 2017, a random 252 urologists and urology residents were asked: "Are you burned out?" The results were astonishing: 41 percent said yes, 32 percent were heading in that direction, and only 27 percent answered no. When asked what factors influenced their decision on when to retire, number one was burnout, reported by 64 percent. Major factors leading to burnout were not time spent in direct patient care, but factors resulting from increasing government regulations, dealing with practice administration, and entering medical data. Declining reimbursement has led to greater workload even to maintain the same income. According a Medscape report of 2019, the incidence of occupational burnout in the general population is 28 percent, overall physician burnout is 44 percent, and urologists have the highest rate at 54 percent.

It is important to remember that, however motivated or successful you are, you cannot ignore the basic maintenance of your body, which includes sleeping, eating, drinking fluids, and of course deep breathing. It helps greatly to have a handle on time management, which regulates your life. It is much easier now with the use of our cell phones and electronic gadgets.

Learn to say *no*. You have to set priorities: you cannot do everything. What I have learned is that there are important things that you and you alone can do best, but there are many tasks that can be designated to those you trust or to your subordinates. Of course, they need follow-up and sometimes close supervision. Bring in the positive in whatever you do. Positive people have a lot of energy, and their energy and enthusiasm lift the spirits of those around them. Remember the things that brought relaxation to you when you had the time. To me, these include reading or listening to poetry or literature, and sometimes music. To some it might be watching mindless

TV shows, gardening, or practicing golf in the backyard. You must designate time for such things, despite the guilt you may feel about not reading your professional journals.

Just as you exercise your mind, your body needs a workout. Working all day is not exercise. Exercise has to be a physical act that increases your heart rate and maintains it for a period of time. The level and type of exercise will vary with age and health conditions. Even a few minutes of meditation or yoga sets the pace and mood for the day. The Department of Health and Human Services recommendations for exercise are either seventy-five minutes of vigorous or a hundred and fifty minutes of more sedentary exercise every week.

The American College of Cardiology strongly recommends reducing sedentary behavior and increasing moderate exercises with five- to ten-minute bouts of severe exercise. Many studies have confirmed the role of exercise in reducing the incidence of high blood pressure, heart disease, and stroke.

Dr. Swensen leads the organizational team in charge of restoring physicians' engagement and joy in work at the Mayo Clinic. He has developed Mayo Clinic's five-pillar anti-burnout remedy. He believes that, besides help from administration and leadership in removing "the pebbles in the shoes," building camaraderie goes a long way. At the end, it falls mostly on the individual physician. He or she needs to acquire and practice healthy habits for his or her own wellbeing. The factors that make a difference are diet, exercise, laughter, gratitude, forgiveness, meditation, and sleep.

Wayne M. Sotile, PhD, founder of the Center for Physician Resilience in Davidson, North Carolina, has treated over twelve thousand physicians for burnout over the last thirty years. He believes that the key is resiliency: the ability to get through difficult times and come out stronger. The main factors are to re-think, re-frame, and re-engage, so that the physician can remain motivated and find meaning in his or her work and personal life journey.

A group at the Mayo Clinic showed that, if you can provide 20 percent of time to a physician to engage in meaningful activity, other than one's main profession, it can alleviate burnout by almost half (Arch Intern Med 2009; 169:900-5). Every individual physician will have a different meaningful activity, whether it be teaching, research, process improvement, or community service. Help from mentors and faculty goes a long way.

Since burnout does not happen overnight, it is unrealistic to expect it to go away quickly. Integration of positive changes into your routine is the best way to see improvements. Recovery requires a planned approach, including maintenance. Here are some steps suggested by Dr. Sherrie Carter:

- Take an inventory and make a list of all the situations that cause you to feel stressed, anxious, worried, frustrated, and helpless. Add to it as things come to your mind.
- Next, to each item on the list, write down ways to modify the situation to reduce its stress.
- Just say *no* to new commitments and responsibilities while you are recovering, unless they are of utmost importance.
- Delegate as many things as possible, with the understanding that it may not be done quickly and equal to your standards.
- Take breaks between projects to give your mind and body a chance to recover.
- Control your devices by turning them off as much as possible. Technology can hijack your life.
- Socialize outside your professional group. This can provide fresh perspectives, stimulate new ideas, and help you discover new resources.
- Resist the urge to take work home, and if you do so, put a limit on the time you spend.
- Reinforce effort, not outcome. Even the best players do not hit a home run every time they step up to bat.

- Consider joining a support group that is not necessarily a therapeutic group. Sometimes this can be a few casual friends getting together to vent and share ideas.
- In general, rediscover your passion with a new self-awareness. It might mean redefining your role at work or home or both. Redistribute the load you're carrying, even if it means finding a new passion that will offer more balance so you can enjoy life as you once did.

Giving the 2019 commencement address at the University of Michigan Medical School, my very dear friend, Dr. Abdul El-Sayed, former Executive Director of the Detroit Health Department, made a very appropriate remark.

"If Hippocrates had to deal with Electronic Medical Records (EMR), he'd probably have picked a different profession or he'd have changed the oath to 'First do no harm unless it's breaking the damn computer'."

Life has always been very busy for me, and I always took on more than I could handle. There were many a time when I was exhausted and ran out of steam, but by God's grace, I never went into burnout. Let me share with you some of the methods I used.

Good health *is* your greatest wealth. Money, fame, power, possessions are no good if you do not have your health. All illnesses lead to depression. Besides, becoming unhealthy is most of the time our own doing. In the process, you not only hurt yourself, you hurt all your loved ones and well-wishers. You become a burden on society, not to mention the loss of health-care dollars. It is true that many of the cancers that afflict us are a product of our own doing. Results of recent studies reported by David Nield (2017) state that 40 percent of cancer deaths are preventable with lifestyle changes like exercising more, drinking less, cutting out smoking, and eating a healthy diet.

Plan your time off and vacations well in advance; otherwise they may be perpetually postponed. Take a break at least once every three months, even if it is only a long weekend. Once the plan is finalized, block those dates off on your calendar, and let your office do the same. Last-minute plans can be expensive and bring a lot of grief to your office staff, patients, and co-workers.

A recent comprehensive report, "A crisis in health care: A call to action on physician burnout," is the outcome of a partnership among the Massachusetts Medical Society, Massachusetts Health and Hospital Association, Harvard T.H. Chan School of Public Health, and Harvard Global Health Institute. They believe that physician burnout is a public health crisis. This has been echoed by the major medical journals and the lay press, as it brings with it a severe impact on the well-being of the American public. The day-to-day demands of the physician's work too often diverge from, and indeed contradict, their mission to provide high-quality care.

It is interesting to note that burnout is more common among physicians than among other US workers. This is because of mounting obstacles to patient care, which contribute to emotional fatigue, depersonalization, and loss of enthusiasm. The condition affects a wide range of physicians, from medical students to senior practitioners.

Physician burnout began growing rampant in the 1990s, when electronic health records (EHR) were introduced and later mandated. EHR provides a means to ensure legible documents, easy workflow, and patient safety, but they also make the doctor's day more robotic and dehumanized. The process takes away a lot from the art of clinical practice and the sacred and warm physician-patient relationship. The 2009 American Reinvestment and Recovery Act (RRA) and the 2010 Affordable Care Act (ACA) brought new attention to quality improvement and the value of physician reporting and accountability. The current era was transformed on the basis of rewards, punishment, and pay for performance.

In 2016, in the magazine *Health Affairs*, CEOs of ten major health systems declared physician burnout to be a public health crisis. In 2017, recognizing that burnout is endemic and affects patient outcomes, several other organizations including the Institute of Healthcare Improvement (IHI) and the National Academy of Medicine have come out with papers with such titles as "Framework for Improving Joy at work" and "Action Collaborative on Clinician Well-being and Resilience." The American Medical Association has raised this banner and is urging Congress, hospitals, and health plans to recognize the coming crisis as an early warning sign of a dysfunction that is becoming an epidemic in the health-care system of our country. Medscape surveyed more than fifteen thousand physicians from twenty-nine specialties and published the "National Physician Burnout, Depression & Suicide Report 2019." The online survey found an overall physician burnout rate of 44 percent. My specialty, urology, was among the highest at 54 percent.

I can understand why. As a busy practicing urologist, I have studied and even experienced the main factors leading to burnout. As we all know, there is a great shortage of physicians. The US Department of Health and Human Services has predicted a shortage of up to ninety thousand physicians by the year 2025. Most of us are overworked, trying to catch up with the demands of our patients. When I calculated my work hours, the number came to more than seventy hours per week. I know some of my partners in our fifty-member urology group who are up to eighty hours per week — twice the workload of an average forty-hour employee.

In the Medscape survey, almost 60 percent of respondents cited "too many bureaucratic tasks," such as charting and paperwork, as the leading cause of burnout. When asked how they personally cope with burnout, almost 50 percent of the respondents chose exercise, 43 percent said they talk with their family or close friends, but unfortunately 42 percent said they isolate themselves from others, while 32 percent eat junk food and 23 percent drink alcohol.

Many physician and hospital organizations are beginning to realize the gravity of physician burnout and its impact. Efforts to replace lost physicians comes at a steep cost to employers. One estimate of the lost revenue per full-time-equivalent physician is $900,000 and the cost of recruiting and replacing a physician can range from $500,000 to $1 million.

Patients do not like to be treated by a physician going through burnout, and evidence further suggests that it leads to increasing medical errors. Health-care leaders have expanded the requisites for health care to what is referred to as a "Quadruple Aim," whose four components include improved patient care, better outcomes, lower costs, and the newly added "clinician wellness."

The AMA has realized that the well-being of an organization is a reflection of the wellbeing and satisfaction of its membership. It has studied the issues causing and fueling physician burnout, including working hours, advances in technology, and government regulations. They have established the AMA Education Hub, which offers educational resources and continuing medical education (CME) on professional well-being. The AMA's STEPS Forward platform offers innovative strategies that allow physicians and their staff to thrive in the current health-care environment. To guide the executive leadership team, there are strategies for "Creating the Organizational Foundation for Joy in Medicine."

The Massachusetts Medical Society/Harvard study, mentioned above, strongly recommends that addressing the burnout crisis will require action by all stakeholders impacting physician practice, including systemic and institutional reforms to mitigate the prevalence of burnout. In their opinion, physician wellness or self-care strategies such as exercise, meditation, and yoga should be deployed only as a complement to broader interventions. First, they recommend that physician institutions, including medical associations, hospitals, and licensing bodies, should proactively support mental health and burnout challenges faced by physicians. Second, EHR should be made more user friendly by decreasing the regulatory and payer requirements. Simpler application programs need to be introduced to make it easier to customize the workflow. Finally, they recommend the appointment of an executive-level chief wellness officer (CWO) at every major health-care organization. There is strong evidence to indicate that effective leadership is one of the most impactful interventions for addressing burnout. Stanford Medicine has not only appointed a CWO but also offers courses out of their WellMD Center. Kaiser Permanente has done this too. The survey concludes, "If left unaddressed, the worsening crisis threatens to undermine the very provision of care, as well as eroding the mental health of physicians across the country."

At the end of the day, it is our life and our family that are most affected by the burnout syndrome, and we as individuals need to take charge of preventing it. By including daily exercises, meditation, healthy eating, spending time with the family, doing community work, and taking vacations, I have stayed ahead of the game. It was not easy to do, and many times I have had to overcome my ego and desire and say no to a project I would have loved to do. You only live once, and there are no do-overs in life.

Despite working very hard with long hours in the operating room and the office, I have always maintained my sanity. To me, the most important thing is the attitude of the physician. I love what I do. Time spent in the operating room has always been a challenge and an adventure. How can I do the procedure better and get even better results? Surgery is more an art than a science, and a good artist, whether a musician, an actor, a painter, or a photographer, is always striving to improve his or her performance. That is what gives you a sense of accomplishment. I never hurry through surgery, because every additional minute spent pays dividends in the recovery period. It always feels better to look at a nicely closed incision, and it heals better too. Sometimes I have had to face anger and grief from patients and their families for the delay, but once I explain to them my philosophy of keeping focus and not worrying about time, they are very appreciative.

I was so privileged that my wife Annette and I worked together through surgery and the office. She was indeed a great help with everything, making it easy to take the right decisions.

Some surgeons hate to be in the office, seeing patients, because they have to face different problems and personalities. Fortunately, I love the time spent in the office. I enjoy meeting people, following up with long-term patients or meeting new ones. To me it has been like a family reunion every day. Yes, there are times when you have to deal with difficult and demanding patients and their families, but that is rare. I believe the saying: "If you love what you do, you never work a single day in your life." Between seeing patients, Annette and I would constantly chat with each other, and if time permitted, we would eat a salad or have a cup of tea for lunch. Talking to someone you love and trust is the best stress reliever.

Over the years, I have developed a system to relieve stress and steer clear of burnout. Every morning I get up early and go down to the basement, which is quiet and serene. After doing my morning prayers, I meditate for fifteen to twenty minutes, connecting with my Creator. This sets my day in the right perspective. Then I either get on the treadmill for thirty minutes or jump in the exercise pool for a similar workout. This is the time no one can take away from me.

In the evening, Annette and I always have dinner together, however late or early it may be. We then sit back with a cup of espresso and watch the news. This itself is a great way to unwind after a long day at work. The next few hours I would devote to my non-medical work. Having been involved with several non-profit organizations, there was always lots to do, and this has provided a great diversion from the practice of medicine. And we both have a good habit of reading in bed for half an hour before going to sleep. Most of the time for me this is either a car magazine, a medical journal, or Urdu poetry. Annette catches up with Food Network, Bon Appetit, or a Sudoku puzzle. And a good night's sleep gets us ready for the next day.

CHAPTER 13

The Opioid Crisis

Although I had encountered many drug abusers during my residency training, my first personal experience with drug abuse occurred in 1998. I had a colleague, also a close friend, who presented at the ER with severe right kidney pain. Imaging studies confirmed it to be a small stone passing from the kidney to the bladder. I saw him right away, and he was given an injection of morphine, which relieved the pain instantly. But the pain persisted overnight, and he was given repeated shots to keep him comfortable. The next morning a repeat X-ray confirmed that the stone had not moved and was impacted, causing significant obstruction to the kidney. After discussing the pros and cons of the planned procedure, I took him down to the operating room. He was placed under general anesthesia, and I was able to remove the stone easily. While he was still under anesthesia, I did another X-ray with contrast material, to confirm that indeed there were no other stones and the channel was clear, with the kidney draining normally. Post-operatively his pain subsided, but he was still requesting and receiving morphine injections every four hours.

The following morning when I came to see him, he complained that his pain was still intense and he needed the morphine shots every four hours. His eyes were glossy, and he was very demanding in his demeanor, quite unlike his personality. We repeated the X-ray again, and it was reported to be normal. I thought we would give him another day of rest before sending him home in the morning.

The next morning, reviewing his medical records, I noticed that he had been asking for the morphine shot every four hours around the clock. When I went to see him, he was sound asleep. I woke him up, and immediately he started complaining of intense pain and demanding a morphine shot, although he had just received one two hours earlier. Facts started connecting in my mind. Here was an intelligent young physician, and this was the beginning of his addiction. I immediately changed my stance and told him that I would be discharging him home on strong oral pain medications. He objected strongly, but I prevailed.

He demanded that I write him a prescription for twenty oxycodone pills, and I insisted on ten, explaining that since the problem had been resolved, he should be back to normal within a day or so. The next morning, I was in clinic seeing patients, and the receptionist came to tell me that the same physician had called. He had been very rude and nasty on the phone and demanded that I call him a prescription for twenty more pills. I called him back and requested that he go to the radiology department at the hospital. I had called in for him to have an urgent kidney X-ray. Two hours later, the radiologist from the hospital called to inform me that the X-ray was absolutely normal. At this point, I had to take a firm stand. I called the physician back and told him that his imaging study was totally negative, and I was not calling in any more pills. Infuriated, he hung up on me.

A month later, I saw him in the doctors' lounge. He came up to me and sincerely apologized for his past behavior. He had to be admitted to a drug rehab facility for two weeks and had just been discharged to come back to work. I learned my lesson, and from that day onward, I have never written a prescription for an opioid pain reliever.

There are several facts we have to understand in this business. First, pain is part and parcel of illness, disease, and recovery from surgery. We wrongly tell our patients that we will guarantee total pain control, especially after a surgical procedure. We fail to understand that pain is an integral part of the recovery system. Pain has a purpose, which is to restrict excessive activity and protect the part of the body involved during the healing process. Our role should be to keep the pain within tolerable limits. If, by using very strong pain medications, we completely suppress the pain, patients will sometimes do things that will harm or delay the healing process.

Recently I read an interesting letter in *The New York Times* from a middle-aged American woman who was living with her husband and family in Germany for work. She had been having some major gynecological problems and was seen by a gynecologist. The doctor advised her to have a laparoscopic hysterectomy, removal of the enlarged uterus, at the local hospital. The procedure was performed successfully in the morning, and she was getting ready to be discharged later that afternoon. The surgeon sat down with her and her husband and explained the post-operative care. The only prescription he wrote was for Tylenol pills. The patient went ballistic and demanded that she be given some strong narcotic medications. She knew the pain after a major surgery like hers would be intolerable. Very calmly, the surgeon explained to her: "Madam, please calm down and listen to me. Yes, there will be a fair amount of pain, and the Tylenol will relieve some of it to a certain comfort level. Nature has a purpose for pain. It is a reminder for you to restrict your activities and make you rest. Narcotics have many unnecessary side effects, like slowing the bowels, constipation, nausea, urinary retention, etc., which can delay your healing process. Try to walk around in your home and let the body settle down. Do not baby yourself lying down and resting too much."

With much dissatisfaction, the lady returned home. The first few days the pain was moderate in intensity, but the Tylenol kept it under control. She pushed herself to get up and walk. By the third day, she was feeling fairly comfortable. A couple of weeks later, when she went for her post-surgery visit, she thanked the doctor for his good advice.

There is no arguing that each of us has a different threshold of pain tolerance, but I believe there is no pain that cannot be controlled by medicines and means other than the use of opioids. And if the pain is really that bad, something active needs to be done about it. The only exclusion is a terminally ill cancer patient, whom you cannot deny pain relief. In the last twenty years of my practice, I successfully proved the point. Over the years, I acquired the knack of detecting which patients are drug seekers and come to see me primarily to get opioid drugs. I refused to accept them in my practice.

The major problem, in my opinion, is that physicians do not take the time to think about the devastating effects of opioids before writing a prescription. It is much easier to write the script than to take a few minutes and explain why the patient is having pain and how he can alleviate it. And when they do write it, the quantities are much more than needed. The medication sits in the house and sometimes gets in the hands of others seeking the drug. In all my years of practice, I can remember only two patients who returned the opioid pills to the nursing staff, saying they did not like their effects.

It is interesting to note that in the twenty years from 1991 to 2011, the number of prescriptions for opioid medication has substantially increased, from 76 million to over 200 million. In tandem with this rise, there has been a significant increase in hospital visits and deaths associated with opioid overdose. By government statistics alone, thirty thousand deaths were caused by opioid overuse in 2015. Since then the numbers have continued to grow exponentially, and the Centers for Disease Control and Prevention estimate drug overdose deaths in 2017 to have been in the range of seventy-two thousand. Another study, recently reported in the Annals of Internal Medicine, was done by the CDC's Annual National Ambulatory Medical Survey, which reviewed nearly thirty-two thousand patient visits for the decade between 2006 and 2015. The study showed that 60 percent of the patients were treated for pain diagnosed by a physician, 5 percent for pain linked with cancer, but 30 percent had no documentation that they were suffering from pain. It is a sad fact that half of deaths due to drug overdose are related to prescription drugs.

Additionally, it has been estimated that, in 2013 alone, the cost of opioid use, abuse, and overdose came close to $80 billion. With the current population of the United States estimated to be 325 million, there is no question in anyone's mind that the opioid crisis is a national epidemic. In 2017, researchers announced that US life expectancy was down for a second year, the first two-year decline since the early 1960s, when flu deaths were likely to blame. The current culprit is the opioid overdose epidemic.

The signs and symptoms of opioid abuse can be categorized by the patient's physical state. It could be as mild as just a craving for the drug, to withdrawal state, and eventually to a state of intoxication even leading to death. The specific reasons behind the ongoing opioid epidemic remain frustratingly murky, but new research points to one previously hidden psychological trigger: social isolation.

Great work has been done by Dr. Michael Englesbe, professor of surgery at the University of Michigan in Ann Arbor. He is also the co-director of the Michigan Opioid Prescribing and Engagement Network. Leading the Michigan initiative to tailor acute care prescribing, he believes that prescriptions can be cut to minimize opioid exposure. According to his studies, about 90 percent of surgical patients are opioid-naïve, and of those, about 6 percent may become new, persistent opioid users. Referring to these patients in an address to the American College of Surgeons Quality and Safety conference in 2018, Dr. Englesbe said, "This is a very vulnerable population where their operation can lead to life-changing events way beyond their surgical outcomes. We have to really worry about them. It's hard to identify who they are, and I think minimizing exposure to opioids is the best we have at this point." According to a research letter recently published in the *Journal of the American Medical Association* (JAMA) Surgery, with the help of evidence-based prescribing guidelines, Dr. Englesbe and his colleagues were able to reduce prescription size by 63 percent, with no increase in refills and no change in pain score.

The government and the Federation of State Medical Boards (FSMB) have updated their guidelines on the use of opioids in the treatment of chronic pain, with new policies underscoring the need for physicians to be proactive in helping to turn the tide of the epidemic. The current guidelines recommend comprehensive treatment with pharmacological agents as well as psychosocial therapy.

Death rates from synthetic opioids other than methadone increased 72 percent in the period from 2014 to 2015. With increasing education and legislation, opioid prescribing trends have shown a slowing of the increase in deaths from opioid abuse and misuse, based on a CDC report at the end of 2016. It is encouraging to know, from the AMA's Opioids Task Force 2018 progress report, that the total number of opioid prescriptions has gone down from its peak of nearly 252 million in 2013 to 196 million in 2017. But in my opinion, we still have a lot of work to do in this field.

The remedy will need all parties involved and billions of dollars in support. Societal norms need to be reestablished about the modality of pain, its tolerance, factors that influence it, and the uses and harmful effects of medications. The pharmacies producing opioids need to be regulated. Physicians need to be reeducated in pain control, restricting the use of opioids, and writing very limited quantities when they're actually needed. Dr. Englesbe's work at the University of Michigan has adequately proven this. State and federal authorities need to rewrite the laws and regulations with increasing penalties and punishments associated with abuse. Medical societies and organization should champion such efforts, before opioids erode our whole society. Unfortunately, this affliction is increasingly affecting our younger generation. And then there is the whole enormous problem of street drugs and non-pharmaceutical products.

I strongly believe that our religious organizations, moral and ethical societies, and civil leadership have a major role to play in helping us out of this crisis.

In a sermon delivered in June 1966, the Reverend Dr. Martin Luther King Jr. talked about the dynamic dance between Good Friday and Easter, between death and resurrection, between despair and hope: "The church must tell men that Good Friday is as much a fact of life as Easter; failure is as much a fact of life as success; disappointment is as much a fact of life as fulfillment. God didn't promise us that we would avoid trials and tribulations but that if you have faith in God, that God has the power to give you a kind of inner equilibrium through your pain."

The ball is in the court of medical researchers to address the opioid crisis. We need to understand pain better: What causes it, why it is a part of our nature, and how we might block it at the nerve ending without the perception of pain in the brain. A large amount of research is being done in this field, which will bring valuable contributions to pain management. Working as a team, physicians, pharmaceutical companies, government agencies, and society as a whole can bring an end to this crisis.

CHAPTER 14

The Business of Medical Practice

I was in the second year of my solo practice when one of the senior cardiologists, Dr. N, stopped me in the hospital corridor and told me to meet him in his office after work. Not knowing what he had in mind, I was a little scared, but still I showed up in his office that evening. He told me that he had purchased the vacant land across from my current office and was planning to build a new medical office building. He wanted me to be a 25 percent partner in the construction. The idea sounded great, but I had no money or resources to offer. I talked to a few of the physicians I trusted. They were all very skeptical, and two of them said the same thing: "Don't get into any business deal with Dr. N. He will take all your money and will give you nothing in return. And his wife is even more unscrupulous."

Dr. N had given me some plans that looked good, but did I want to get into a project with him and his wife, knowing the reputation they had in dealings with others. I talked to my accountant, Larry Brown, who was great with numbers and whom I trusted fully. Larry was all in favor of me investing in my own office building. He worked out the numbers, and came up with the idea that if I owned half the building and charged rent to my corporation, it would pay the monthly mortgage and taxes, and in ten years, I would own 50 percent of the building free and clear. The important thing was to have legal documents clearly spelling out the details of the deal. Over the next few weeks we met the builder, who happened to be an extremely nice Indian gentleman and looked very honest and trustworthy.

After evaluating the whole scenario, I met with Dr. N and his wife and told them that I was agreeable to the plan, on one condition: we would be equal partners, each with 50 percent equity. After much deliberation, they agreed. We finalized the plans, had all documents legally prepared, and got an okay from the bank for the construction money. When the time came to sign the papers, I was really nervous and made a prayer for God's guidance.

Within a few weeks, the foundation had been dug and the construction started. Every day after work, I would stop to check the progress, and a great excitement started to develop in me. This was truly my first business venture. I could imagine my own office with a nice big desk, artwork on the walls, and a tall-back chair on wheels. My secretary, Bev, had designed her office for maximum efficiency. We envisioned three examining rooms, two bathrooms, a large front office, a lab, and storage areas. The front entrance led to a small foyer that opened into a large common waiting area that we would share with Dr. N. I included a back-door entrance into my office, to avoid the embarrassment of walking through a room full of patients when I was running late. The parking lot in front would be adequate for a large number of cars. It all looked so big and fulfilling.

With a few hiccups, the office building was completed. All the carpets, furniture, and artwork we had selected matched beautifully. The open house introduced many doctors, nurses, and patients. The number of patients increased rapidly, and we had to hire another medical assistant to handle the extra load. Dr. N and his wife took charge of all the financial responsibilities of depositing the rent checks and paying the mortgage and other building expenses. Then, a couple of years later, I asked Mrs. N to show me the books on the office building. After several requests, she reluctantly gave them to me. When I started reviewing the bills and checks written, I realized that there were several bills that had been paid but had no relevance to the office building. I made a list of them and questioned both Dr. and Mrs. N about it. They were very embarrassed and explained that by mistake they had been paying some of the home bills through the office check book. I politely asked them to refund the amount I had added up, back into the office account. Going forward, I also took charge of the deposit and bill payment process to make sure it was done right.

As we were growing fast in our practice, there was a great need for a clinical person to help me, especially with taking patient histories and procedures like cystoscopy and vasectomy, which were taking too much of my time. I mentioned my need to the OR supervisor at Annapolis Hospital. She informed me that Annette Clement, a highly skilled nurse, who had been working at the hospital, would not be returning there. I had known Annette since 1979, when she started working as a graduate nurse in the ICU at Annapolis Hospital. She had then transferred to be a scrub nurse in the operating room. For nearly ten years, we had performed many surgeries together. She was well known among her colleagues as the smartest and most dedicated nurse in the OR. Her inquisitiveness to learn more and understand the reasoning behind each procedure had turned her into an excellent scrub nurse. She had taken a new job as head nurse in the OR at the Westland Medical Center (formerly Wayne County General Hospital). After a year she had moved again, and now was working part time at Garden City Hospital, down the street from our office.

I got her phone number and called her. "I hear you are not working full time these days. That's not fair when I am doing double duty," I said, joking. "Why don't you come and work in our office. We desperately need some clinical help." She seemed a bit skeptical. "Well, I've never worked in a medical office, and I have no idea how it will work out," she replied. "We can only find out if you give it a try," I insisted.

A week later, she visited the office, had a look around, and decided to work for a month on a trial basis, starting in January 1990. She liked the work, as it appealed to her creative nature, and we agreed on the salary and terms.

From the beginning, Bev had run the office very efficiently. When Bev retired, Sue took over as the office manager. Sue was making all the bank deposits. I barely had time to look over the finances. My mistake. The practice had grown so much that at times there was standing room only in the waiting room. Since all the billing was being done on the computer, it became easier for me to check the money coming in. I just had to print the correct column from the ledger and it would tell me how much should have been deposited. In December 1992, Larry Brown, our CPA, came to the office to balance the books and rectify the bank deposits. He printed all the reports from the computer and clearly showed me that there was embezzlement going on. Someone had pocketed over $25,000. We confronted Sue, and she outright admitted that she had been stealing cash and checks written by the patients. Her excuse was that she needed the money at home. I was extremely hurt. "Why didn't you ask me for it? I would have given it to you," I said in a sad, soft tone. She had no answer. We had to fire her instantly.

I had never done this before, and it took me weeks to get over the bad feeling. I also decided not to pursue any legal action — what was gone was gone. I learned a big lesson: you cannot blindly trust anybody. At the end of the day, it is your practice, your business, and your money. Going forward, I asked Annette to take over some of the financial management of the office.

Our urology practice was growing by leaps and bounds. We changed the name from Mahmood A. Hai, MD, PC to Affiliates in Urology and, with the help of a professional company, developed new logos and signs. Annette set up the procedure room based on all her OR experience. When the patient came for their appointment, Annette would see them, record the chief complaint, and take a history of present illness, past history, allergies, and other relevant information. She would apply her clinical acumen so that, most of the time, I would have a provisional diagnosis even before I saw or talked to the patient. I would then walk in, confirm the facts, make a working diagnosis, and establish a plan that we both agreed to. All the patients loved Annette because of her personal and compassionate approach. My productivity nearly doubled, as I had more time to see patients.

After a few years, I began to notice that Annette was getting bored with the office work. It was not totally fulfilling her passion for surgery. Knowing that she was a certified OR nurse (CNOR), I came up with a bright idea: "Why don't you come to the OR at Annapolis Hospital in the morning and assist me with the major surgeries, then go to the office from there?" She liked the idea, and I got the necessary privileges approved for her. This really reignited her enthusiasm. A year later, she took a special course to be a Registered Nurse First Assistant (RNFA) in surgery. This gave her the ability to replace the second surgeon in major cases. Now the operating room time became very efficient. We would start the surgery together, I would do the major part, and I would then leave her to finish the case while I did a quick case independently. The patients soon began to appreciate their beautiful incisions, as Annette was a better seamstress than me.

During this phase, I had taken on many administrative responsibilities at the hospital. I became a member of the executive committee, then chairman of the credential committee and OR committee, and finally chief of the surgery department. The administrative work and the meetings were overwhelming.

I had been looking to add another urologist to the practice, and interviewed a few doctors. Most of them were concerned about how much money they would make. How many weeks of vacation? How many night calls? There was no concern about patient care, and it was absolutely frustrating. Then, in September 1998, came Dr. Muzammil Ahmed, an enthusiastic young man who had grown up in our community and had just finished his urology residency at the University of Michigan. I had known his family for many years. Just one meeting, and I knew he was the right person. He brought a new life to the practice, and after twenty years, I was now no longer on call 24/7. Very soon, I realized that Muzammil was not only hardworking but honest and respectable, with a sincere desire to do the best for the patients. He was also a quick learner and was well liked by the office staff and everyone in the hospital. We signed a one-year salaried contract. Muzammil was heaven sent.

A year later, I met with my accountant and financial advisor and told them that I wanted my new associate to become a full partner. "But how can you do that, Dr. Hai?" they demanded. "He is just a young urologist starting out, and you have put in over twenty years to build this practice." "The practice of medicine is like another marriage," I replied, "and if you don't treat your partner equally, the relationship will fall apart. He is working hard, and I will continue to work hard, and we will share equally what we bring home." There were no arguments after that. The document was drawn up by our attorney.

By now Annette had fully taken over the management of the office, in addition to her clinical responsibilities. With all three of us working very hard, the waiting room was packed and there were no more parking spaces. We had two options: either to expand the current office, or move to a new one. Larry Brown's prediction had come true. The current office building was totally paid off, and we owned 50 percent of the building free and clear. Larry had always said that, as a professional, your first investment should be your house and your second investment should be your office. This advice has served me well financially.

In 2000, we hired a commercial real estate agent who was very experienced in our geographical area. "Don't you worry, Dr. Hai, we will find the best office for you," he said, and the search began. Every week we would spend hours looking at different office buildings, but none satisfied all our needs. At this point, we had decided that we would build an office operating room and bring many of the simpler surgeries, including the GreenLight laser, out of the hospital. The ideal office building came on the market in early 2001. It was less than two miles from our current office and was better located on a major street, Cherry Hill Road in Westland. The building had an interesting history. It belonged to the Spizak family. They had owned the land since the 1930s and originally lived in a large tent with a candy shop in front. Then they had built a three-bedroom home for the family. One of their kids graduated from college and became an accountant. His business did well, and the family built a large two-story office attached but not connected to the house. At one time, it was the largest accountant's office in Michigan. Business flourished until Mr. Spizak developed lung cancer. His wife tried to run the accounting business, but she was diagnosed with colon cancer a few years later, and they had to put the building on the market. Some of the staff in the office believe Mr. Spizak's spirit still lurks around on quiet evenings.

We were all very impressed by the building. It was solidly built and, with some major modifications, would serve us well. The lower level would be the office and the upper level would become the operating rooms. Negotiations went on, and we were able to purchase the whole 6,500-square-foot building for a bargain price. One of our friends was in the commercial construction business, and we requested his opinion about remodeling the whole building to our needs. He inspected the building and said, "Mahmood, it is very simple. I will have my bulldozers come this week and level up everything. Then we can build you a brand-new building exactly the way you want it." I was appalled. "There is nothing wrong with this building," I insisted. "Let us use our talent and creativity to make it right for our use." That was the end of the conversation, and the plan to remodel was on its way. I learned that, to run a successful medical practice, you also have to be an engineer.

A massive renovation plan was developed, with input from everyone in the practice. Some walls had to be taken down to connect the old house with the office, and all windows, carpet, and flooring had to be replaced. After much deliberation, the blueprints were finalized and approved by the City of Westland. Once the remodeling project started, Annette and I realized that it needed close supervision, and Annette decided to take on another big responsibility. She had to wear a new hat for six months, this time the hard hat of a construction supervisor. As planned, the ground floor was converted into the urology office, with examining rooms, offices, conference room, front desk, waiting room, kitchen, and bathrooms. On the upper floor I wanted two large operating rooms and a procedure room. The plan in my mind was to make this a teaching center for GreenLight laser and other urologic procedures. There was great resistance from everyone, including the engineers, but I was not ready to take no for an answer. "Tell me why we cannot," I said.

"We will need all OR standards, clean air circulation, HEPA filters, temperature and humidity control and all that," came the excuse.

"Let's find out exactly what we need and fulfill all the requirements," I insisted. It took many hours of planning and work, and most of it fell in Annette's lap. On December 11, 2002, the City of Westland did its final inspection and issued us the Certificate of Occupancy. All our hard work paid off, and when the construction work was finished, it was one of the first complete office surgery centers in the country. We were all delighted and felt a great sense of accomplishment.

We needed to hire more nurses and office staff. Fortunately, we acquired another gem. One of the OR nurses, Shirley Elrod, had decided to retire from Annapolis Hospital at the age of sixty-five. We had all known Shirley and had worked with her for years at the hospital. She was admired by everyone for her hard work and integrity. I approached Shirley and asked if she could help us set up the new operating rooms, even if she wanted to work part time. There were two reasons she agreed to do so, she explained. "First, I would love to work with you, Dr. Ahmed, and Annette. And second, I have decided that whatever I earn, will help pay tuition for my grandchildren to go to a parochial school." We were then joined by two great anesthesiologists Dr. Alhadi and Dr. Johnson. Our team was now complete, and we were ready to make Affiliates in Urology truly a center for excellence.

I clearly remember the day we did our first surgery, as it happened to be Wednesday, December 4, 2002, my birthday. A few months earlier, I had been giving a talk on the laser procedure in Fort Myers, Florida. An older gentleman sitting in the back was listening to me very intently. At the end of the talk, he came up to me and introduced himself. "I am Dr. Perry Hudson, a retired urologist," he said.

"Of course, I know you," I said. "You're the famous urologist who developed radical perineal prostatectomy and has written several books and papers about it."

"Dr. Hai," he said, "I have read all about your work. I have seen the videos of your GreenLight procedure, and tonight you have confirmed everything I have read. I am now ready to hand over my prostate to you to be taken care of." On further questioning, it came to light that he had a very large prostate that had been causing urinary retention for more than six months. He had been self-catheterizing to drain the urine. When I told him about our new office surgery center, he insisted on being its first patient. Later, when I thought about it, there were two aspects of that plan: If everything went well, it would be the best advertisement for office-based GreenLight laser surgery. But if, God forbid, something went wrong, the news would spread like wildfire.

Dr. Hudson and his wife came to the office on December 3. We went over all the pros and cons of the procedure in great detail, and I again offered to do the surgery in the hospital, if they so desired. "Dr. Hai, I want to be your first guinea pig," he said, laughing loudly. The next morning, everyone was sweating bullets, making sure everything was checked and re-checked.

By God's grace, the procedure went as well as it could have. After the procedure, the Hudsons went back to their hotel near the Detroit airport, and the next morning they came back for their post-op check-up. His urine was absolutely clear, and I filled his bladder with water and took the catheter out. He went into the bathroom and came out all smiles. "I peed like a champ, Dr. Hai, thank you."

Then Mrs. Hudson spoke. "Dr. Hai, he really tested your procedure last night," she said.

Worried as to what had happened, I asked, "And what did he do?"

"He wanted to have pizza for dinner, and we called the pizza shop down the street, but they refused to deliver the pizza because of the snowstorm last night."

"You should have called me and I would have got it for him. Anyway, what did you do?" I asked anxiously.

"You won't believe it, but against my wishes he got dressed and walked through the snowstorm, picked up the pizza, and walked back to the hotel."

I looked at Dr. Hudson. He was smiling like a mischievous child, and I couldn't stop my laughter either. "You really wanted to test me, didn't you?" I said with a sigh. After sincerely thanking me, the Hudsons took the flight home that afternoon. The GreenLight procedure had passed the acid test.

Six months later, I met Dr. Hudson at our annual urology conference. He was telling all the urologists about the success of the GreenLight surgery and added, "I had phenomenal results with the GreenLight procedure, and if you continue to do the old TURP procedure for BPH, you are doing a disservice to your patients."

Starting with this great success, a whole new era began. We got started on planned training for urologists in the new GreenLight laser procedure. They started coming from all around the country and even from overseas, accompanied by their company representatives. We would meet in the conference room downstairs and give them a complete didactic course, and then they would come upstairs and observe the surgery on patients and actually learn how to do it. The urology world was lit up with GreenLight.

Things were working out well on the office side too. Annette had decided that, if she was going to run the office, she wanted to do everything par excellence. She attended several conferences, including the two-day Professional Management Symposium at the annual urology meetings. Based on all the government rules and regulations, she wrote the Employee Handbook, clinical and business policies and procedures, and a complete Compliance Manual. She was totally overwhelmed and inundated with everything. I could see the frustrations building up. One day she sat down with me, and said, "Mahmood, we have to make a decision. There are three different things I am doing, but I can only do two things well, and you have to choose between office manager, clinical supervisor, and wife/homemaker." I thought for a few minutes, and the answer was very clear to me. "Honey," I said, "just make one of the other nurses in charge of the clinical work, and focus on the other two." She got up and hugged me, saying, "I feel so relieved."

Affiliates in Urology grew tremendously over the following years, not only in size but also in quality. In 2003, Charlie, one of our twin sons, joined the OR team and became an expert with the laser machine. After working for us for a few years, he was recruited by a mobile laser company that helped teach the use of the GreenLight laser to many urologists around the Midwest. On May 1, 2007, another wonderful thing happened when Dr. Vijay Kotha joined the practice. He had been well trained in upstate New York and wanted to move close to our area, where his wife had grown up. From the time I first interviewed him, I knew he was a no-nonsense kind of guy who was genuinely concerned about patient care. A year later, we made him an equal partner too. Adding another feather to our cap, the American Urological Association declared us to be one of the best-managed urology offices in the country. We were asked to give a three-hour course on office surgical management, with special reference to GreenLight, at the annual meeting in 2009. Thanks to its great success and demand, we delivered the course for the next three years.

Our second twin son, Matt, had gone to culinary school and had worked as a chef in Chicago for a few years. It was very demanding work, and after suffering a bad case of professional burnout, he returned home. He joined our management staff in June 2008 and worked under Annette's tutelage. Even the least doubt of nepotism was ruled out very soon when Annette wrote him up the second time he was fifteen minutes late to work. Everyone put on their best performance and felt ownership in a truly democratic fashion. Annette had repeatedly reminded them, "I never want anyone to be rude or uncompassionate to the patients. They are here not by choice, but because of illness. Remember, your paycheck comes from them."

Our monthly office meeting was held in the waiting room and was a level playing field for everyone. We had made it very clear that all functions had to be above board, and that if anyone saw anything illegal or unethical it was to be brought up right away and dealt with correctly. Backbiting was strictly prohibited. If you had an issue with another employee, we advised them to deal with it face to face. In one of the meetings, an allegation was made against me that I had called the office informing them that I was running late and would be in the office in half an hour, but had not shown up for an hour. The front desk secretary looked at me. "Dr. Hai, because of your being late, two patients were very angry, and one of them even called me a liar." I had to give a reasonable explanation: "I was running out of the hospital that afternoon when the ER called to tell me that a patient was bleeding profusely and I must see him right away. It took me half an hour to put in a catheter, stop the bleeding, and explain everything to the family." I sincerely apologized. "I am very sorry," I said. "I should have called you again and let you know. It won't happen again."

For many years, I had been asking the hospital administration to open a new ambulatory surgical center across from the hospital, where patients who were in good general health could come, have their procedures done, and go home to recover. This was a trend all around the country, in every surgical specialty. A group of ten busy surgeons like me wanted this project to be a joint venture. The hospital administrators paid no heed, so we, the surgeons, got together and started looking at alternatives. "Dr. Hai, you have already established operating rooms in your office and are doing many of your surgeries there," one of them remarked. "Can't we just expand the facility into an ambulatory surgery center?"

"Yes, we can," I replied. "But there are many different requirements that need to be fulfilled. Firstly, in Michigan you have to show the need for an ambulatory surgical center (ASC), and then the state issues a certificate of need (CON). Secondly, there are very stringent building and functioning rules and regulations that have to be implemented. I am not saying it cannot be done, but it will take a lot of work."

We all agreed to proceed with it. Interestingly, a few weeks later I received a call from a gentleman in California who had built an ASC there and offered to help us do the same in Michigan. A week later their team, two entrepreneurs named Ted and Stu flew in, and Annette and I met them for lunch at the Andiamo restaurant in Livonia. The meeting went well, and they seemed to know what to do. Together we inspected our current building, and they were very eager to take on the project. After our preliminary talks and meeting with our surgeon group, the surgical center of our dreams seemed achievable. And then the big negative came from Annette. "I just don't trust these guys," she remarked. I said, "On their next visit, let's introduce them to our accountant and financial advisor and see what they think."

Two weeks later, the two men came back with a plan. They would help us get the CON, raise funds from shareholders, plan and oversee the construction complying with all the requirements, hire the staff, and get the center going. For all their work, they would own 25 percent of the partnership and we, the surgeons, would own 75 percent. I liked the idea but, as we had decided, I arranged for them to meet with our accountant and financial advisor. Amazingly, both of them said exactly what Annette had said: "These guys are not trustworthy, and they will take you and your whole group for a ride." I was reminded of my early dealings with Dr. N and his wife. I had been warned about them, yet I was able to have a successful business deal with them.

I sat down with Annette and the surgeon group, and said, "I understand all of your concerns, but it's my belief that you can do business with all kinds of people, as long as you have everything written and signed on paper." And that is exactly what we did. I had the attorney prepare all the documents in detail, with defaults built in, and everyone signed it. Key Bank agreed to give the loan, on the condition that we transfer all our banking to them, which we did, and the loan was approved. Ted and Stu worked very hard over the next few months. We got the CON from the state, and the remodeling and construction of our office started. The plan was to extend and build the ASC on the second floor, with its own entrance and elevator from the back of the building. We also got the name of the ASC approved as the "Surgical Institute of Michigan," or SIM for short. The building turned out to be a showcase piece for anyone wanting to build an ambulatory surgical center. Despite our initial fears about Ted and Stu, the plans went through. It reaffirmed to me that, as long as you are honest in your dealings and have full documentation, you can have a successful business dealing with anyone.

With everyone's hard work and efforts, SIM opened its doors on July 20, 2010. Charlie, our son, came back and worked with a dedicated team, setting up the entire surgical center. Because he had been involved with all the equipment installation, we put him in charge of all building issues and also designated him as the laser officer, based on his long experience. All the surgeons started doing cases at SIM and took pride in the quality of service they could provide, which had sometimes been substandard at the hospital. Each member of the staff knew that they were not only responsible but also answerable for what they did. The patients were delighted to receive the personal care that they had missed in the hospital environment. Our satisfaction surveys ran in the high ninetieth percentile. We got full certification from the federal government, the state, and the ambulatory surgical agencies. With all the hard work, honest dealings, and selection of the right people, we had achieved another landmark.

While all this was going on, in early 2009, our three-man urology group was approached by Dr. Don Moylan. He was the head of the group called "Comprehensive Urology," about a dozen urologists who practiced at the well-known Beaumont Hospital in Royal Oak. "Dr. Hai, we have heard a lot of good things about you and your group," he said. "We would like to get together and see if you guys can join our group." This was quite an honor for us, as Beaumont Hospital was among the top fifty hospitals in the country and the urology department had a great reputation. I immediately remembered their radio ad to patients: "Do you have a Beaumont doctor?" as if you would die if you did not have one. Now here was the opportunity to become one. I consulted Dr. Ahmed and Dr. Kotha, which led to a few meetings and many documents and legal agreements. In July 2009, we became a part of the Comprehensive Urology group — *Beaumont doctors* indeed.

There are pros and cons to joining a large group or corporation. No doubt you lose the individuality of the medical practice, and everyone in the group has to work under uniform rules and regulations. But by the same token, you are not wasting so much time in administrative duties and you can focus on what you went to school for and do best: practicing medicine. Immediately after joining Comprehensive Urology, we realized that our mindset had to change. We were no longer independent, all decisions had to be made by committees, and consensus would prevail. Sometimes a group decision is not to your liking, but so long as it doesn't go against your moral or ethical values, you can agree and abide by it. The merger proved to me that as long as you work hard, are honest and professionally competent, your reputation will grow and you will be recognized. It was a great achievement for our small urology group.

The other big advantage of joining a group of fifty specialists was that now we had subspecialists in our group. For the patient, it was a win-win situation: we could refer them to the urologist in the group who was most experienced in what the patient needed, and the receiving urologist in turn continued to get better at what he did best. A lot of my colleagues felt that I was very good with the GreenLight laser and could do the surgery very efficiently in difficult cases. I had less experience with robotic surgery and would refer those patients to Dr. Ahmed, who was a wizard at it. Complicated kidney stone cases went to Dr. Kotha, who was excellent in treating stones.

We have to learn to respect each other as equals. Only then does true partnership work. As I have said, it's like a marriage. As professionals, we have to control our egos at all times. Problems occur when professionals become too big for their britches and develop a God complex, like Alec Baldwin in the 1993 movie *Malice*. Patients love physicians who are humble and down to earth and speak using language they can understand. It always gave me great pleasure to meet patients and their families in Walmart or Trader Joe's while shopping.

The decade of 2005 to 2015 was an era of travelling and teaching laser surgery around the world. Patients came from all over the United States, and some came from abroad. The big advantage of being in a large group was that coverage was always available to my patients, even while I was away, and I did not feel guilty. They were always in good hands. They also understood that the travelling was part of my commitment to spreading the knowledge and experience I had gained. The major issue was, when I returned from a trip, I had to make up for lost time, seeing more patients and spending longer hours in the operating room and the office. There were times when I would fly to a foreign country, get off the plane, and be taken straight to the operating room to start my teaching assignment. And there were times I would fly back on a seventeen-hour flight, get off the plane, and come straight to the office and start seeing patients. Because I loved what I did, it never felt like a burden. At the end of the day, your state of the mind and willpower can overcome fatigue and physical tiredness.

Ted and Stu had been flying back and forth from California nearly every month to make sure the Surgical Institute of Michigan was running in high gear. Every month, we would review patient care as well as quality and financial issues. They had opened a few other centers in the Midwest, and the long flights and time away from home were wearing them out. I suggested that they find another good management company, which would buy their shares and run the surgical center. After a long search, they contacted a company called Surgical Management Professionals (SMP), headquartered in Sioux

Falls, South Dakota. It was a physician-owned company that managed more than twenty surgical centers around the country, a reputable group that ran its business efficiently and ethically. We had several intense preliminary meetings; serious discussions began in March 2013. Since I was the executive director and president of the board, I put my executive hat and concluded the deal amicably. SMP wanted majority ownership in SIM, and by diluting some of the physician shares, we were able to give them 51 percent ownership in the business. Attorneys from both sides worked hard to get all the documents ready. The papers were finally signed in June 2013, and a new era began for SIM.

In the fall of 2013, I was approached by the leadership at American Medical Systems (AMS) to review the progress of GreenLight laser. They had just finished an important prospective study, called the Goliath study, with a large group of European urologists from eight different countries, but to convince American urologists, we needed data from the United States. I flew in to their headquarters in Minnetonka, Minnesota, for two days and discussed a plan for a multi-center retrospective study based on US data. I was selected to be the principal investigator (PI), to work with five major urology centers in the United States and Canada. The five urologists selected were Dr. Ricardo Gonzales from the Methodist Hospital, Texas Medical Center; Dr. Greg Eure from Virginia Medical Center; Dr. Lewis Krietman from Atlanta; Dr. Kevin Zorn from the University of Montreal Hospital Center (part of McGill University in Canada); and myself from the Surgical Institute of Michigan.

I met with representatives from each center and the supporting team from AMS, and the scope and timeline of the study were established. We decided to review data from one thousand patients, two hundred from each center, and obtain their data for three years in a retrospective fashion. We had to obtain consent from each patient and from the Internal Review Board (IRB) of each institution. This part was an overwhelming task. The data collection process then started and, as the PI for the study, I had to spend a great deal of time making sure there were no inaccuracies. After months of hard work, the study was completed and approved by all the IRBs. Then started the analytical process to get the final results. All our hard work paid off when the outcomes of the study confirmed that indeed the GreenLight Laser was the new gold standard for the treatment of obstruction caused by the prostate. In 2014 alone, I gave lectures and surgical demonstrations in India, Colombia, Indonesia, Tanzania, and China. All through 2015, the data from this large retrospective GreenLight study was presented by our group at different meetings in the United States and around the globe. GreenLight laser was shining out like a beacon in the urology world.

An interesting string of episodes happened in November 2015. I was invited to give a talk on the outcomes of the multi-center retrospective study on GreenLight laser. The meeting was at the Ritz Carlton on Amelia Island in Florida. After a long day in surgery and in the office, I flew from Detroit and arrived at the airport in Jacksonville around 9:30 p.m. A few of my Comprehensive Urology partners were on the same flight. I had rented a car, and we all got in with our luggage and started driving. There was pouring rain with thunderstorms and lightning, leading to poor visibility. Normally it is less than a one-hour drive to Amelia Island, but it took us over two hours. When I got there, I signed in at the registration desk, went straight up to my room, and was fast asleep by midnight.

My talk was at 8:00 a.m. I got up refreshed, showered, and dressed. Breakfast was set up next to the meeting room, and I grabbed a croissant, some fruit, and a cup of coffee, and walked into the conference. Within half an hour, I was called to give my presentation, which went very well. A flurry of questions followed, and I was out by 9:00 a.m. I had committed to give a talk at the LXVI Congreso Nacional De La Sociedad Mexicana de Urologia (Mexican Urology Congress) in Cancun, Mexico, the following day. The valet pulled up the rented car and loaded my luggage, and I was off to the airport. The flight from Jacksonville was at noon, and I could not afford to miss it. I flew through Atlanta and landed in Cancun late in the evening. A dinner meeting had been set up with a group of South American urologists at 9:00 p.m. With extensive questions and answers, the get-together ended around midnight. It had been another long day, and I needed a good night's rest to be ready for another challenging day.

The next day was full of meetings and presentations, including an hour-long presentation in the main conference hall packed with over thousand delegates. There were headsets available for both English and Spanish translations, for whoever needed them. I opted for a set that would translate the Spanish questions into English for me to answer. The spontaneous and accurate translation was amazing. I was surprised and greatly humbled to receive a standing ovation at the end of my presentation. That night I took a red-eye flight back to Detroit, again through Atlanta. Luckily, when I got home at 7:00 a.m., it was Saturday morning, and I could catch up on my sleep.

A few months went by, and one day while I was seeing patients in the office, Trish, the office manager, said, "Dr. Hai, a package got delivered for you. Did you order something from Amazon?"

"No, I can't recall ordering anything, but please go ahead and open it anyway." We found a letter in the package from the American Urological Association (AUA) and an engraved wooden plaque with a relief of an older gentleman with circular glasses. Reading the letter, it all became clear. The day after I left Amelia Island, an AUA committee had judged my talk the best presentation at the annual meeting. The wooden plaque had a large bronze bust relief of a renowned urologist, Dr. Edwin L. Thirby, and the award was presented in his honor. It was for my talk on the safety and effectiveness of the GreenLight laser. It brought tears to my eyes. The most meaningful form of recognition is the one that comes from your own peers. I felt honored yet humbled.

In December 2016, I turned seventy. I met with the CEO of our Comprehensive Urology group, Dr. Donald Moylan, and asked him to change my status to Senior Urologist. "We don't have anything documented for that designation," Don said. "Suppose you write the details, and we will present it to the board for approval. I know you'll be fair." It was nice to be told that I had a good reputation with the group. There were three things of importance to me: working four days a week, three months' vacation every year, and no night or weekend calls. The board unanimously approved it, and I continued to work hard, remain productive, and stay up to date with the practice of urology until the day of my retirement, February 28, 2019.

At the insistence of my surgical colleagues, I still serve as the executive director of the Surgical Institute of Michigan. Indeed, I am currently negotiating a new deal that will reinforce the work done at the institute, further improving its long-term overall stability. As one of the founders of SIM, I want to do all I can to ensure that this legacy of good work will continue serving patients for many years to come. Even as I am writing this chapter, I am working on a complete re-structuring of SIM to give it long-term financial stability so that the quality of care remains at the highest standards. Every new and existing surgeon is strictly evaluated before getting privileges to do surgery at SIM.

Medical business is like any other business. The principles remain the same whether you take a Franklin Covey course or a course in leadership. They all talk about honesty, truthfulness, strategic planning, avoiding back-biting, etc. What I have learnt is that they are all very important, but your biggest investment is in people. You have to build trust every day, and that leads to your reputation. It takes years to build it and sometime minutes to destroy it. The character of a company or an organization always starts from the top and trickles down to the frontline. Those who are opportunists and waiver in their basic moral values always fail in the long run. We need to be firm in our dealings and yet not lose the virtues of kindness and compassion. It is always good to consult and incorporate the opinions of those who are involved in the project for it to be successful. Think with an open mind and sometimes out of the box, and remember your ideas may not be the best all the time. Whatever you agree to, document it because verbal commitments are sometimes forgotten or misunderstood. But if you say something, live up to it; that is what will build your reputation. Have a clear vision, and pursue it with passion.

CHAPTER 15

The Medico-Legal Dilemma

In 1997, after nearly nineteen years in my urology practice, I was hit with my first lawsuit. A gentleman came to the front desk at the office and told the secretary that he had an envelope that had to be hand delivered personally to me. I met him in my office, and he gave a sealed envelope, stating that it was a summons from the court, and left immediately.

Anxious to know what it was, I immediately pulled out the document. The papers filed were from an attorney who was representing a forty-five-year-old patient I had seen for the first time a few months before. Let us call him Alfred. He presented with the typical symptoms of acute inflammation of the prostate gland, a condition called acute prostatitis. He was having burning with marked urgency and frequency of urination, associated with a deep perineal pain in the rectal area. On physical examination, we found his prostate was swollen and extremely tender. The urine sample showed the presence of bacteria. I explained to him the findings and my rationale for making the diagnosis. Looking at his medical records, I confirmed that he had no known allergies. In those days, the best treatment was to give the patient a month of antibiotics, and I prescribed a sulfa drug that has great effectiveness in the prostate gland. The patient agreed, and I called in the medication to his pharmacy.

Two days later, while I was seeing patients in the office, the receptionist told me that Alfred was on the phone and wanted to talk to me. "Doc!" he cried. "I've had a very severe reaction to the medication you prescribed.

I've broken out with large blisters all over my body and I'm itching all over." I advised him to stop the medication and urgently go to the ER at the hospital. They would give him an injection of Benadryl to counter the reaction immediately and then send him home on a short course of steroids to reverse the allergic reaction.

On his way back from the ER, the patient stopped at our office. My wife Annette, who at that time worked as a nurse in the office, saw him briefly. He had a few small red spots on his skin, which he claimed were itching. She assured him that the medication given in the ER would take care of the problem and made a complete note of his office visit. We never saw Alfred again in the office.

The notice of the lawsuit from his attorney took me by surprise. I immediately called the medical liability insurance company that I had been paying large premiums to every year. The lady who answered was very reassuring and said, "Doctor, don't worry. We will assign an attorney who will help you fight this case. This is not anything unusual, and besides, most of these cases settle out of court." I was so upset and angry that I could not concentrate on work that day.

Once I received the letter, life suddenly changed. I began constantly questioning myself: Had I done something wrong? Was I a bad physician? I couldn't sleep at night, and I felt tired even before leaving for work. Every patient I saw prompted a question in my mind: will he or she sue me?

A week later, I met the attorney who was appointed by the insurance company. Her name was Cathy, and she appeared very competent and respectable. We reviewed the patient's medical records together, which at that time were just a few pages of paper in a Manila folder. The patient had answered all the initial questions in his own handwriting. To the question "Are you allergic to any medications?" he had clearly written "No known allergies." The attorney felt very confident that the suit would be dropped or would be settled for a nominal amount within the limits of my coverage. To a certain extent, this lowered my anxiety.

Nearly six months passed, and I did not hear from anyone. Then Cathy called and asked for a time that we could meet and discuss recent developments. We met a few days later, and she said the plaintiff's attorney had called her and wanted to settle the case for $100,000. The insurance company was negotiating with them and had offered to settle for $25,000. Not knowing the intricacies of this business, I innocently asked Cathy, "But why should we pay anything? You know I have done nothing wrong." She explained that the insurance company looks at all aspects of the case: attorney fees, cost of preparing to fight the case in court, my time away from the practice, and the "unknown," in case we had to go to trial, knowing that a jury in Wayne County could award the patient a huge amount. She also explained that, if we did settle, there would be no acceptance of negligence on my part.

I looked out the window for a few minutes and ran the whole scenario in my mind. Cathy was expecting me to say yes to the plan and let the insurance company negotiate to a lower number. It would all be settled, and I could continue my life and practice. But the inner voice of my conscience said, "No! You have done nothing wrong, and you have to stand up for the truth." I told Cathy exactly what I felt and said I would fight this case to the bitter end, whatever the consequences. So I also had to sign a paper stating that, in case the judgment came back for more than $100,000, the insurance company would cover only the $100,000 and I would have to pay the balance from my pocket. The agent from the insurance company also tried to scare me by saying the judgment could be a million dollars. But I had made up my mind.

The wedding of our eldest son, Yusuf, had been set for the end of July 1999. Cathy called to let me know that the court had set up the trial date in mid-July and the case could go on for one to two weeks. She again offered to settle the case without going to court, but I was firm in my decision. The night before the trial date, the plaintiff's lawyer called Cathy and offered to settle at $50,000. She called to see if I had changed my mind. Again, I refused. I had already blocked off my office and surgery schedule for two weeks.

Appearing in court was a totally new experience for both Annette and me, and we were both extremely nervous. The first two days were spent in jury selection. Annette had also been named in the suit, and she was put on the stand first and asked all kinds of questions including embarrassing personal ones to try to discredit the evidence provided by her and her notes. I was also asked insinuating questions, to show the jury that I was incompetent and unreliable. I had decided to stick to the truth, and it was easy to describe everything as it had happened.

On the fourth day, the patient was put on the stand. His attorney started to show pictures of the patient's whole body. It was full of large blisters and raw weeping skin all over. The jury no doubt would be extremely sympathetic to the sufferings of this patient.

Both Annette and I were shocked looking at the pictures. The patient had been seen in the ER, and the ER physician and nurses had mentioned nothing about these skin conditions in their notes. Annette had seen the patient immediately after the ER visit, and she could swear there was nothing like it. Cathy and we were totally perplexed. At the end of the day, I asked Cathy to get copies of all the photographs of the patient that had been presented in the court.

That evening, after dinner and some rest, we laid down all the pictures on our dining table and started looking carefully at them. The front and back of Alfred's chest, both arms, and even parts of his abdomen were severely affected. But as we looked closely, a light bulb came on. In one picture taken from the side, showing his arms, the upper part of the chest showed normal skin. In another picture from the front, where he was pointing to a chest lesion, the skin of the hand and arm was normal. As we looked more closely, the truth emerged. The patient had pasted these pictures of severely inflamed skin lesions onto his body while having photographs taken; a few pieces had fallen off, exposing his normal skin. We immediately called Cathy, who just could not believe it. The next morning, we met with Cathy one hour before court started so she could also see how the patient had camouflaged his skin.

Once the jury were in their box, Cathy asked the judge if she could review the pictures in the courtroom. She then exposed the whole fraud. Everyone present in the court was flabbergasted. How could anybody bring such false evidence? The judge was furious and came out with a severe judgment against the patient and his lawyer. She not only discharged all the charges against us, but also reprimanded the patient and made him sign an affidavit that he would never sue a doctor again. The plaintiff's attorney's license was suspended for supporting such a frivolous lawsuit. Truth had prevailed against falsehood, and our faith in the judicial system was reinforced.

We later found out that the patient had sued two other doctors before me, and that both had settled out of court to avoid the hassle of losing time from their busy practice. This had encouraged the patient to try a third time to collect an easy bounty.

Needless to say, a heavy burden had been lifted from our shoulders. The wedding went very well, and we were relaxed and enjoyed it. A week later, we returned to the office feeling rejuvenated.

*

I had first met Dr. B in 1984, a few years after beginning my practice. Born and raised in Uruguay, he had finished his medical school there and came to the United States for his residency in internal medicine. He then joined a group of internists who took care of patients at Annapolis hospital where I was working. Dr. B was a thorough clinician and a perfect gentleman. He spoke English with a strong Spanish accent. All his patients loved him. The two of us worked well together and admired each other's clinical abilities. Very soon, Dr. B began referring all his urology cases to me, and I would send him any patient who needed a good internist. We also had great communication, which is extremely important in coordinating a patient's medical care.

One morning, we were both making rounds in the hospital when Dr. B called me. He had admitted an older gentleman, two days earlier, with heavy bleeding in his urine. Jim had been a patient of his for many years. Further testing and X-rays confirmed a right-sided kidney mass. We met in the patient's room with his family. Dr. B introduced me as an excellent urologist that he recommended to treat the patient's kidney issue. Jim happily agreed, and Dr. B left me with the patient. After going through the history, I examined him. As usual, there was no other finding, as the kidney is usually not palpable because it sits within the rib cage. I suggested a needle biopsy of the kidney under X-ray guidance. The pathology result confirmed that it was kidney cancer. Because of the large size of the mass, I advised a complete removal of the right kidney. The surgery went very well, and Jim was discharged and sent home within five days. I saw him several times in the office for post-operative follow-up. He recovered well and had no complaints. I advised him to go back to Dr. B for his routine medical care and control of high blood pressure.

A few months later when the patient came back for his six-month follow-up, he and his wife were delighted with his recovery and grateful for the care Dr. B and I had given. He had one wish: Dr. B and I take him out to lunch one day. I reluctantly agreed, because it was very difficult to get out in the middle of office or on a surgery day. Besides, I was never in the habit of having lunch. It broke up the whole day and cost me precious time. Usually a salad, fruit, or nutrition bar on the go between patients kept me going until the end of the day when I would have a good dinner at home.

Although it was an unusual request — and we are always advised to keep professional and personal relationships at arm's length — Dr. B and I talked on the phone and blocked off an hour out of the office to have lunch with this gentleman. We chose a nice restaurant that would be quick and close by. When we got to the restaurant, our common patient, Jim, was already there waiting. We sat down, and the waitress came to take the orders. Dr. B and I opted for a lunch salad, while Jim ordered a full meal, a double cheeseburger with fries, a large chocolate milkshake to start, and an apple pie a la mode to end the meal. We watched him eat rather voraciously, while we talked about the weather and the traffic. When we were done, the waitress came with the bill. I took it and offered to pay for it with my credit card. Jim made a wry remark: "You should pay it anyways. You guys make so much money." We were already running late, and I did not want to get into a heated debate. I let the comment slide, and we all left at the same time.

Three months passed, and one day, when I arrived at the office after morning surgery, the receptionist told me there was a gentleman waiting to see me. I called him into the conference room, and he immediately handed me an envelope and a paper receipt to sign. "I'm sorry, doc, but this is from the court." I signed the paper, and before I knew he was gone. The envelope contained a letter of intent from Jim's attorney. He was suing me for "loss of sexual function following the kidney surgery." I almost lost my balance. The waiting room was full of patients, and I quickly put the envelope away on my desk to worry about it later.

The following day, I came to the office an hour early to review Jim's chart. I looked up the first consultation I had done on him in the hospital before the surgery. It was my practice to go into details about the patient's history, to make sure nothing is missed. On that day I had specifically asked Jim, "Do you have any sexual problems?" I had noted his reply verbatim: "I am seventy-three Doc, and I have not had an erection for over five years. My wife has no interest in sexual intercourse, and so it is a done deal." I made a copy of that page. It was the best evidence, in his own words. His claim that he had "loss of sexual function following the kidney surgery" was totally baseless.

I called the malpractice insurance company. They requested a copy of the letter of intent and said that an attorney would be assigned to the case and they would get in touch with me soon. I made a personal request to see if Cathy, the attorney who had helped me with the previous case, was available.

Cathy called the next day and came into the office the following week, and we talked in detail about the whole case. I told her all that had happened with this patient and showed her the sentence he had spoken at his first consultation. Cathy was very happy that I had documented it in the medical records. The following week, she met with Jim's attorney and showed him that it was well documented that Jim had erection problems long before the kidney surgery. The litigation was promptly dropped, and I sighed with relief. Following this, Cathy and her husband became good friends, and we went out for dinner several times.

Unfortunately, there is a false perception in society that doctors make a lot of easy money, and if you sue them, it is easy to settle for a decent amount.

*

Annette's mother had been living alone in a house in Chagrin Falls, Ohio, following the death of her husband. We were always concerned about her health and welfare, and after much persuasion, in 2014, we were able to convince her to sell her house and move into a condominium near us in Canton, Michigan. We finally found one to her liking, and an offer was made and accepted. Her own house in Ohio had been on the market for a few months, and her purchase of the new place was dependent on the sale. We had talked to a few banks for a possible bridge loan to make the transactions happen. In this regard, we were dealing with the vice president of a local bank, a portly middle-aged gentleman named Charles. One morning, Annette and I met with him to finalize the bridge loan. The documents required us to be the co-sponsor for the transaction, and Charles needed all our financial information, which we duly provided.

Charles knew that I was a urologist, and one day he called to say that he was having a lot of urinary problems. He had seen several urologists before and even had surgery with no improvement. I asked him to make an appointment, as a patient, to discuss everything in detail, and I advised him to bring any previous medical records he had. A week later, after reviewing all the information and examining him, I ordered several tests.

The results confirmed that Charles had an enlarged prostate that was causing obstruction to his urinary flow, which in return was causing repeated prostate infection. He had been on many courses of antibiotics and had even had a surgical procedure on his prostate. All this had led to extensive scar formation in the prostate and the neck of the bladder, known as bladder neck contracture.

Bladder neck contractures are not common, but when they do occur, they tend to be recurrent. I explained all this to Charles and his wife and told him that I could undo the blockage by vaporizing the scar tissue surgically, but the chances of it coming back were very high. With this understanding, we did the procedure at our ambulatory surgical center. The following day, when his urinary catheter was removed, he could urinate with a forceful stream. Charles and his wife were extremely delighted with the outcome.

For the next few months, his urinary problems were totally resolved. But six months later, Charles called the office. His stream was gradually slowing down again. I advised him to have a flow test, and said I would also take a look with the scope to see what was happening in the prostate-bladder neck area.

When we looked in, we saw that the scar tissue was coming back to block the bladder neck. This time we not only vaporized all the scar tissue but also gave the patient a course of oral steroids to decrease the chance of scar formation. Unfortunately, the disease condition continued to recur several times over the next few years. I even suggested to Charles and his wife that he should get a second opinion from either the University of Michigan or Wayne State University, but they felt very confident with me.

This time, as a preventive measure, I also taught him to catheterize himself once daily with a clean catheter. This helped immensely by breaking the cycle of recurrent obstruction to the urinary flow. Charles was delighted, and we did not see him again for over a year.

Then, one morning, Charles called the office informing me that he had developed a bad urinary tract infection that had gone up to his right kidney, and that he had been admitted in another hospital under the care of another urologist. I called him back and assured him of a good recovery. After a week of antibiotics and a few minor procedures, he had been discharged and was doing well at home.

Another uneventful year passed by, and I received a letter of intent from a downtown Detroit attorney representing Charles. The accusation was that during surgery I had caused damage to his urinary system, which led to the severe kidney infection.

Many years had gone by since the last lawsuit, and I had changed malpractice insurance companies. A new attorney was appointed to this case. He and I went through all the medical records, and there was no evidence of any injury or negligence on my part. My attorney set up a deposition of Charles in his office. I was present in the room that day. Charles would not even look me in the eye. Maybe he was ashamed of the fact that I had always treated him well and he had betrayed me with a lawsuit. During the deposition, one fact came up. When Charles had gone to the other hospital with the bad kidney infection, he was told by the urology resident that Dr. Hai must have caused some damage, which led to this severe infection. Charles believed it unquestioningly.

During my deposition, the plaintiff's attorney asked me what I thought was the reason for Charles's bad infection. I clearly explained to everyone present that the infection had been caused by Charles self-catheterizing himself every day. If he did not clean the catheter, he most likely introduced bacteria into the bladder, from where they spread all the way into the kidney. There was never any evidence of damage done during surgery.

After this there was not much value to the case, and it was settled for a nominal amount. My attorney strongly felt that, since Charles knew all the details of my finances, he thought he could get some easy money with a lawsuit. I have heard it said that you have a much better chance of hitting the jackpot by filing a lawsuit in Wayne County, Michigan, than by playing poker in the casino.

*

I recall another malpractice story that did not involve me directly, but was related to a patient I had performed surgery on. A sixty-five-year-old patient had been admitted through the ER in acute urinary retention. The routine workup showed that he had a very large prostate obstructing the urinary passage. This was in the early eighties when we had no medications for prostate enlargement. The only way to deal with large prostates was to do open surgical removal of the gland. I discussed the procedure with the patient and his family, and they all agreed that we should proceed as planned. The patient was in excellent health, and the procedure had a very low risk factor. For any major surgery, the best form of anesthesia involves placement of a tube in the throat by the anesthesiologist, to assure good lung ventilation throughout the procedure.

At this time, there were two very good anesthesiologists in the hospital, both of Chinese origin. Their last names were exactly the same, and the first name of the older one started with "H" and the younger one with "Y." In the OR, they were fondly called "Honey Wu" and "Yummy Wu." My patient received anesthesia from Honey Wu. The surgery went perfectly well, and the patient was discharged home after four days. On the one-month and six-month follow-up visits in the office, there were no major complaints.

A year later, I was waiting in the surgeons' lounge for my next case when Honey Wu approached me. He told me that he had been sued by this patient of mine. The complaint was "damage to the vocal cords during anesthesia."

The document stated that, since the day of the surgery, the patient's voice had turned hoarse and was getting worse. There was a testimony from an ENT specialist that the cause was the passage of the endotracheal tube under anesthesia. Honey asked me to talk to his attorney and see if I could be of any help.

The next day, I called the defense attorney and asked him to set up a deposition for me. I told him I would provide strong evidence in support of the defendant, Honey Wu. After the date and time were set up, the plaintiff's attorney called me, very angrily saying, "Why are you sticking your neck out in this case? Your name is not even on the defendants' list. We can really get you in trouble." I said nothing and hung up.

The day of the video deposition arrived, and everything was set up in our conference room. With my right hand up, the court reporter swore me in to tell "the truth, the whole truth, and nothing but the truth." Then the plaintiff's attorney started questioning me about my credentials and clinical experience.

"You have no training or clinical experience as an ENT specialist — is that correct, Dr. Hai?"

"Yes," I replied.

"What qualifications do you have to give a deposition in this case?"

"Well, it was my patient; I did the surgery and then followed the patient for six months," I answered.

"What else, doctor?"

"And I have basic common sense."

That sentence threw him into a rage. He literally shouted at me, "And what does that have to do with the case at hand?"

"It has a lot to do with it," I replied calmly. "If you will kindly let me, I can explain it to you."

"Go ahead," he shouted back.

I took a deep breath and started talking. "First, I saw this patient and talked to him when he was admitted to the hospital, and he answered all my questions. Next, I talked to him about his test results and explained the surgical procedure, and he asked questions. Then he talked to me in the operating room just before the surgery. Following the surgery, I saw him in the recovery room, and he asked me how the surgery went. Over the next three days, I talked to him on my rounds, and then I saw him at the one-month follow-up and finally at the six-month follow-up. *His voice never changed,*" I said with great emphasis.

There was pin-drop silence in the room.

"Besides," I continued, "he talked to the nurses before the surgery and after the surgery for three days, and nobody noted anything about a change in his voice. He never complained to anybody about his voice or throat pain. How could everybody miss it?"

The plaintiff's attorney just shook his head. He had nothing to say after that.

The defense attorney said, "Thank you, Dr. Hai. I have no questions." That was the end of the video deposition. The defendant's attorney used it in court, and the jury gave their judgment in favor of Dr. Honey Wu, the anesthesiologist.

We need to build the courage to speak the truth. Staying silent is not good enough.

Unfortunately, we are seeing this in every sphere of our society. The bad people and the wrong-doers shout with loud voices, and the good people keep silent. The old proverb is so true: "The squeaky wheel gets the grease."

Often, I have thought about how frivolous malpractice lawsuits are filed against physicians and surgeons, and many are settled because the doctor does not want to take time to fight the case or for other financial reasons. We in the United States have become a very litigious society. So often we hear unbelievable stories. On a bitter wintry day, a lady slips on a small patch of ice in the parking lot and sues the Target store, or a thief breaking into a house fractures his wrist and sues the owner of the house. Do we not have common sense and some social responsibilities? You turn on the TV, and law firms are soliciting you to file lawsuits! The cost of doing business has gone up enormously because of liability insurance.

Medical malpractice is defined by the American Board of Professional Liability Attorneys. It occurs when a health-care-providing facility, doctor, or other health-care provider, through a negligent act or omission, causes injury to a patient. The negligence might be the result of errors in diagnosis, treatment, after care, or health management. To prove it, several factors have to be present: a doctor-patient relationship, negligence by the doctor causing injury, which in turn leads to specific damages, failure to diagnose, improper treatment, and failure to warn a patient of known risks.

Most lawsuits start on an emotional basis: loss or suffering of a loved one, or anger and mistrust of the treating physician. Some lawsuits are provoked by another family member, medical personnel, or a law firm advertisement, and sometimes it is purely lust for easy money. By the same token, I totally agree that, if indeed there was negligence or a missed diagnosis, justice demands that there should be fair compensation for the one who suffered.

But medical liability lawsuits are rampant. Medscape, a national industry-wide organization, did a survey of over four thousand physicians from more than twenty-five specialties and published a report in November 2017. More than half of the physicians surveyed had been sued, and most of those more than once. A lawyer friend once jokingly told me, "If you've never been in a medical lawsuit, you're probably not seeing enough patients."

One third of medical lawsuits are alleged to be related to childbirth and surgery and another third to misdiagnosis or failure to diagnose, while the remaining are due to medication errors, delayed treatment, or anesthesia. Among surgeons and OB/GYNs, 85 percent have been sued, while those practicing orthopedics, urology, or ENT are in the seventy-fifth percentile. As a result of this, physicians' liability insurance premiums have been skyrocketing ridiculously. In New York, the average annual premium for OB/GYNs was $195,900, for surgery $141,600, compared to only $37,800 for internists. This could account for nearly half of a physician's annual earnings, from which they also must pay overhead, taxes, and other expenses. Many good physicians have moved away from areas where reckless judgments have been given, including Wayne County, Michigan.

Most lawsuits filed against physicians are frivolous. The Medscape statistics show that, in only 2 percent of medical malpractice lawsuits, the jury or the judge declared a verdict in favor of the plaintiff. The time spent by the defending physician can average from six to forty hours, of which 20 percent is spent in court. Forty percent of lawsuits drag on from three to five years before a resolution is reached. The amount of humiliation, mental agony, and stress to the involved physician can be insurmountable, besides which there is no compensation even if they win the case.

I believe we have to stand up and tell the truth. It needs courage and sacrifice of time and effort. The battle against falsehood has to be fought at all levels. By the same token, I strongly believe that, if the doctor is at fault, he should be strongly punished, penalized, reprimanded and, if necessary, lose his license to practice, as you will read in the chapter on bad doctors.

In 2004, the US Congressional Budget Office found that malpractice costs 2 percent of total health care spending. The National Data Bank shows that fewer than 5 percent of physicians are responsible for more than 50 percent of malpractice suits, and it costs their insurers nearly $21 billion in damages paid to patients. It would behoove us as a community to join hands with good citizen organizations, medical societies, and state medical boards to identify these negligent or incompetent physicians and take their licenses away.

Over the last few years of my career, I signed up as an expert medical witness in four medical malpractice cases involving urologists. Before taking up each case, I thoroughly reviewed the medical records to make sure there was indeed no negligence committed by the physician. Then I tried to analyze the precise cause of the injury, to satisfy myself that there was no malpractice in the case. If I found that there was negligence or injury caused by the physician, I would let the defendant's attorney know the facts and I would not take up the case. In every case, I would seek the truth and bring the facts to light.

In 2017, I attended a two-day seminar on how to be a good expert witness. Here is what I learned. First and foremost, you have to tell the truth. You need to have a good knowledge base of the subject in question and extensive clinical experience in that field. It is also important to familiarize yourself with the medico-legal process. Finally, you need to have a calm demeanor and be able to communicate medical information in a clear and understandable fashion. The four cases on which I have served as expert witness were in the states of Indiana, New York, Michigan, and Florida, and thank God the jury gave their verdict in favor of the defending physician in every case.

Other lessons I have learned include the importance of always communicating with patients and their families in clear and simple terms, to create good rapport with them. I look my patients in the eye and tell them the truth, however harsh it may be. Then I give them hope with alternative methods of treatment and guide them in making the right decision. This has often been made easier when I think, *What would I do if it were my own aunt or uncle or nephew?* It is also always more useful to make the patient and his family a part of the decision-making. I also document in detail the whole conversation and have them sign the consent for the procedure we agree on, with all the possible common risks and complications that might happen.

On the day of surgery, I briefly go over the highlights again, to refresh their memory and answer any questions the patient or the family might have. During the procedure, I take pictures and videos to document the facts. A picture is worth a thousand words. After the procedure, I see them back in the recovery room with their family, show them the pictures, and again answer all their questions and concerns. Frivolous lawsuits will still happen, but if the truth is correctly documented, their outcomes will be in the physician's favor.

As a society, we need to identify the bad apples — physicians who are incompetent or negligent. Frivolous lawsuits should be penalized as well. It would help if a panel of physicians and attorneys screens the cases for their merit before they are filed. Negligence happens when physicians are burned out or exhausted, and these situations must be identified and avoided. Patients need to be educated and taught to understand that physicians are their partners and well-wishers in good health.

CHAPTER 16

And There Are Bad Doctors Too

"The only thing necessary for the triumph of evil is for good people to do nothing."

—*Irish Statesman Sir Edmund Burke*

Dr. K was a surgeon I came to know when I first started practice at Annapolis hospital in Wayne, Michigan. He was probably in his early sixties, tall and thin, with very few hairs left on his crown. No one knew much about him. From what I was told, he had been the chief of surgery in a small hospital in northern Michigan. When the hospital closed, he moved down to Wayne, Michigan, and bought a very small house right across from Annapolis hospital. He had decided not to open his own office, but merely to assist other surgeons during surgery. He was a great help, especially if you had to perform emergency surgery in the middle of the night. Dr. K was always available, and wanted to be called. It was the early eighties then, and insurance companies were paying a 20 percent fee to the surgical assistant. It was by no means a great income, but definitely adequate to make a living.

Dr. K was a very interesting personality. He lived in surgical scrubs all the time, ate leftover food from patient trays, and showered daily in the surgeons' lounge. He would hardly talk to anyone, and one thing I remember is that he called every nurse Agnes. Everyone tried to be nice and kind to him, but the favor was never reciprocated. I had a soft spot for him, because I knew how lonely and forlorn he was.

One day, I was walking in from the parking lot and saw that Dr. K had a flat tire in his big old Chevy and was standing helplessly in the freezing cold. It was snowing heavily. I felt sorry for the old man. I asked him for his car keys and told him to go inside. It took me about half an hour to take the flat tire off and put the spare on and clean the piled snow on the car. By the time I got done, my whole body was freezing. I went in and gave Dr. K his car keys and told him that everything was all set. With a totally emotionless face, he looked at me. "But why did you do it?" he asked. "Because I'm a lot younger than you," I replied. We never talked about it again.

A few years later, Dr. K very innocently asked me, "Dr. Hai, I am really having a tough time making ends meet. Do you think if I moved to a small city in India I could survive with what I get from Social Security?" Not knowing the details of his finances, I gave a very generic answer: "All I can tell you is that your dollar will go a long way, as food and living are much cheaper there." The conversation ended as we were called to start our scheduled surgery. After the surgery, Dr. K picked up his billing sheet and left.

Over the years, in summer when I would drive past his home near the hospital, I would see Dr. K sitting on his porch, or putting laundry on the clothesline, or doing some gardening. His house was in really bad shape, and the yard was poorly taken care of. Sometimes I would see a skinny old African American lady sitting with him. On a few occasions, when I was not in a big hurry, I even thought of stopping and asking Dr. K if there was anything I could help him with. But I never did.

Years went by, and life went on. One late summer morning, we were all busy in the operating room, and word got around that Dr. K's house had been raided by the cops and there was a lot of activity going on there. After I finished my list of surgeries, I changed into street clothes and walked to the edge of the grass lawn that separated the hospital property from Dr. K's house across the street. Nearly half of the hospital staff was there, and all kinds of rumors and conjectures were being discussed. Nobody really knew what was happening. Soon we saw three cops bringing Dr. K out of the house in handcuffs and putting him in a police car. I wondered what the old man could have done to get arrested. The sirens went on, and the police car left with Dr. K in the back. What happened next was also amazing. Nearly a hundred big, full garbage bags were brought and loaded in the other cars. Within fifteen minutes, the whole place was cleared and quiet again. No one had any concrete information on what had happened.

The next day, the local newspapers had the full story. It was totally unbelievable. The police had received an anonymous tip that Dr. K was writing fraudulent prescriptions and disability letters for factory workers and collecting cash from them. The FBI got involved and sent its undercover agents to confirm the tip. Now and then, Dr. K would simply park his car in a factory parking lot and send word out that you could buy a prescription from him for any drug you wanted. If you wanted time off for medical disability, you could get that too, for cash. On another score, Dr. K had not filed his tax returns for many years. So, on October 26, 1982, the local police, the FBI, and the IRS had all teamed up and done a joint raid.

Most surprising of all was what they found in Dr. K's little home. According to the court records of the US District Court in Michigan: "The execution of the warrant seized, among other items, three bundles of cash, approximately eleven cardboard boxes of cash, a sterilizer or autoclave full of cash, and a green metal box containing an undetermined amount of money in the form of Krugerrands, Canadian and English gold coins, and miscellaneous silver all belonging to Kieffer." According to undocumented sources, the total amount was close to three million dollars.

Some of the hospital staff who saw him leave claimed that Dr. K was still smiling and muttering that they had only got half of his stash; the rest was in a hidden location. The Michigan Department of Treasury filed a levy of $298,638.86 against Dr. K, and the Internal Revenue Service determined that $1,289,198 was owed in personal taxes for the period between 1969 and

1982. He was also charged with writing prescriptions of Talwin (pentazocine) for non-medical purposes, in violation of state and federal law.

Why would a man with so much money be struggling day to day and doing illegal things? Annette and I have pondered on this question, and our only answer is that Dr. K was mentally deranged.

Nobody saw Dr. K for many years thereafter. Then, one cold and blustery day, Annette and I were at a bank ATM in Wayne. We saw Dr. K on a bicycle, going from dumpster to dumpster, collecting pop bottles and cans to get refund money. I felt great pity in my heart for Dr. K. Unfortunately, his mental illness was by then beyond repair. If the mind is not in a state of equilibrium, nothing else in life matters.

Medicine has its heroes and scoundrels. The rascals invariably show more consistency in their misdeeds. Some are outright predators, engaging in assaults on women or children. Others engage in lucrative unconscionable care, giving significance to diseases not present, purely for financial benefits. While these doctors are more profiteers than predators, the evil is in the unneeded care, especially when there are risks involved. Then there are a few who do things beyond their competence purely for financial reasons. And there is a very small group that are involved in non-consensual human experimentation, which is unethical and illegal too.

Unfortunately, medical schools and residency programs produce and train capable people, though not always ethical physicians. I have often said that you have to be a good human being before you can be a good doctor. The white coat gives you a lot of privileges, but also many responsibilities. If physicians are not ethical, they can turn into monsters.

Human beings who continuously engage in wrongful acts, in the long run, kill their conscience, the inner voice that tells us to be righteous. If a thief steals only once, in all likelihood he will never be caught. Unfortunately, greed and lust make them do bad things again and again, and that is how they get caught. When Annette used to teach coding and reimbursement courses, she would say, "If you do something fraudulent or unethical, the question is not 'Will you be caught?' but yet more likely, 'When will you be caught?'"

One of the most infamous examples of a physician who became a monstrous predator is Dr. Larry Nassar. Nassar was born in 1963 in Farmington Hills, Michigan, about ten miles from where I live. In 1986, he began working with the USA Gymnastics national team as an athletic trainer. He graduated as a doctor of osteopathic medicine from Michigan State University (MSU) in 1993, and completed a fellowship in sports medicine in 1997. He was soon appointed as an assistant professor in the Department of Family and Community Medicine at MSU. From 1996 to 2014, he was the national medical coordinator for USA Gymnastics.

In August 2016, Rachael Denhollander, a gymnast who had become a lawyer, was the first to file a complaint against Nassar at the MSU police department and the university, alleging that she had been sexually assaulted by Dr. Nassar when she was a fifteen-year-old gymnast seeking treatment for low-back pain. Hundreds of other women then came forward with similar allegations. Many lawsuits were filed against Nassar, Michigan State University, the US Olympic Committee, and USA Gymnastics. Well-known gymnasts including McKayla Maroney, Aly Raisman, Gabby Douglas, and Simone Biles came out with similar allegations. By January 31, 2018, the BBC News reported that Dr. Nassar had abused 265 girls.

In July 2017, Nassar was sentenced to sixty years in federal prison after pleading guilty to child pornography charges. On January 24, 2018, he was sentenced from 40 to 165 years in Michigan state prison and, on February 5, 2018, for many additional years for numerous charges of sexual assault. In the aftermath of Nassar's conviction, the entire eighteen-member board of USA Gymnastics resigned, as did both the president and the athletic director of MSU. Michigan State University agreed to pay $500 million to 332 alleged victims of Nassar in a lawsuit settlement — the largest amount ever paid by a university to settle a sexual abuse case. It still horrifies many that a criminal was sheltered for sixteen years just because truth was suppressed by a group of high-ranking officials. They are all equally to blame for being a party to all of Nasser's heinous crimes.

We always have to remember: no one is above the law, whether he is the powerful president or the lowly janitor. Justice must be served to all and at all costs. Sometimes criminals get false protection because of their rank and file, but all those who protect them become a party to the crime.

Our judiciary system is good, but sometimes it takes a long time and reminds us of an old dictum: "Justice delayed is justice denied."

Another black sheep was Dr. Farid Fata, a hematologist/oncologist who ran seven cancer centers in suburban Detroit. Rather than using his medical degree to save human lives, this monster callously violated his patients' trust as he used false cancer diagnoses and unwarranted dangerous treatments as tools to steal millions of dollars from Medicare, even stooping to profit from the last days of some patients' lives. Fata's horrifying acts did far worse than defraud government health-care programs; he breached the most basic and important principle of the medical profession: "First, do no harm."

I came to know of Dr. Fata through my financial advisor, who was also managing the doctor's investments. He had shown no wrong behavior with the advisor, just mentioning that his medical practice was doing well. Later, when the whole story came out, the financial advisor and his company went through a major audit costing him thousands of dollars. The good news was that the company came out of the audit without fault.

Dr. Fata lied to his patients and their families about their health and intentionally put their lives at risk. In fact, some of those patients he was entrusted to care for likely died because of his lies. In court, Dr. Fata — whom I hate to even call a doctor — admitted to prescribing and administering unnecessary aggressive chemotherapy, intravenous iron, and other infusion therapies to patients in order to increase his billings to Medicare and other insurance companies. He also admitted to soliciting kickbacks from hospices and other nursing homes in exchange for referring patients to those facilities.

Many brave individuals impacted by Fata's criminal acts had the strength to come forward, express their experience of pain and suffering, and collaborate with law enforcement and prosecutors to ensure that his despicable actions were brought to an end. In September 2014, he pleaded guilty to thirteen counts of health-care fraud, one count of conspiracy to pay or receive kickbacks, and two counts of money laundering. US District Judge Paul D. Borman of the Eastern District of Michigan sentenced him to forty-five years in prison and ordered him to forfeit $17.6 million.

I feel ashamed even to bring up the story of Dr. Joseph Osterling. Unfortunately, he happens to be one of the most brilliant urologists I have ever known. Osterling graduated from the Columbia University College of Physicians and Surgeons in 1982. He then completed the prestigious John Hopkins University surgery and urology residency program, ranked by *U.S. News & World Report* among the top ten schools for urology in the country.

Upon completion of his training, Joe joined the staff at the prestigious Mayo Clinic in Minnesota, another famous center for urology. He became world-renowned for discovering the prostate cancer tumor marker, prostate specific antigen (PSA), and conducted extensive research in defining the role of PSA in the diagnosis and treatment of prostate cancer. By now, he had authored hundreds of peer-reviewed scientific papers and was appointed editor-in-chief of the leading journal *Urology*.

In 1994, at the young age of thirty-eight, he was appointed head of the urology department and director of the Prostate Institute at the University of Michigan in Ann Arbor. There was hardly any published paper on prostate cancer that did not have his name at the top. Besides his fame in clinical research, he developed a sterling reputation as a surgeon and one of the pioneers in the specialized nerve-sparing prostatectomy for prostate cancer. Friends and admirers in the prostate cancer community praised him as a man who spent hours of his personal time answering calls from doctors and patients far and wide, trying to help them through the maze of treatment decisions. Along with all this, he lectured at numerous universities nationwide and had traveled to more than seventy-five countries, teaching urologists the latest advancements in the diagnosis and management of diseases related to the urinary tract.

Annette and I attended many of his lectures and incorporated much of his knowledge and techniques into our urology practice. As a person, Joe was very friendly and gregarious. One Saturday afternoon, after finishing his talk, Joe sat with us at our lunch table. I remember Annette telling him about her love for gardening and yard work. Joe smiled and said, "That reminds me, I have to go home and mow my lawn."

In the early spring of 1997, rumors started floating around that Joe was in some kind of trouble. No one knew the exact details. In July, all hell broke loose for Dr. Joseph Osterling. The University of Michigan medical school interim dean, Lorris Betz, sent a letter to the university president, Dr. Bollinger, identifying charges against Dr. Osterling in four areas:

> "(1) unapproved and excessive, outside employment in violation of written University and Medical school requirements; (2) undisclosed conflicts of interest resulting from dealings with pharmaceutical companies and other non-University entities; (3) personal profits derived from University resources or efforts; and (4) multiple billing of expenses and falsification of related records. . . . The conclusion I have reached is that Dr. Osterling's conduct is so egregious and inconsistent with standards expected of faculty of the University of Michigan that termination proceedings must be implemented against him."

The medical school cooperated with the Department of Public Safety's criminal investigation. A few months later, Lisa Baker, associate vice president for University Relations, stated: "The criminal proceedings appear to be nearing a conclusion, and the University must now act. The evidence uncovered to date strongly indicates that Dr. Osterling has engaged in a pattern of misconduct that the University will not tolerate. The University also is considering separate legal action to recover amounts it believes is owed to it by Dr. Osterling." The university also forwarded copies of its investigation materials to the Michigan Department of Consumer and Industry Services, which was responsible for considering disciplinary action against Dr. Osterling.

I personally spoke to some of the residents who had trained under him. Joe would make them do personal domestic chores, like taking his laundry to the dry cleaner or giving his wife a ride home from the airport. Even the pharmaceutical representatives still talk about his immorality and lust for money. I even heard that he was building a palatial house and wanted everything to be paid off, leaving no amount to be mortgaged.

While earning a salary of close to $400,000 a year, Joe had accepted extra money from companies whose products he was testing in clinical trial. He was found guilty of taking money under false pretenses and charged with a felony. He was made to resign from his university job and his editorship of *Urology*. Further, he was sentenced by Washtenaw County circuit judge, Melinda Morris, to a year of probation and community service. The Michigan State Board of Medicine suspended his license. He was also ordered to repay the University of Michigan over $100,000. The following year, the American Board of Urology revoked his board certification and discredited a lot of his clinical research work. Dr. Joseph Osterling had quickly climbed the ladder of achievement and fame, and now he had lost everything at the age of forty-one. His case gained international attention as an example of physician conflict-of-interest issues and how lust and greed may lead astray even the smartest among us.

Dr. Osterling's tawdry woes actually continued for another two decades, culminating with another suspension of his medical license and $100,000 fine following a December 2016 arrest on seven felony counts of overprescribing

Schedule II controlled substances in clinics in Saginaw and Mount Pleasant. The charges involved the operation of a so-called "pill mill," with drugs including hydrocodone, methadone, oxycodone, and amphetamines being prescribed for patients.

His story is a very sad one of a brilliant young physician who could have respectably obtained name and fame, honor and respect, with lawful money coming from all directions, but whose demons of lust and greed devoured everything.

I first came to know of Dr. Aria Sabit in 2011 when he applied for surgical privileges at the Surgical Institute of Michigan (SIM) in Westland, Michigan, where I was the executive director and president of the board. He had filled in the routine application and submitted documentation of his medical credentials. The medical director, who was also the chairman of SIM's credential committee, had thoroughly reviewed all the documents, and due process was followed. Dr. Sabit had been practicing at the Community Memorial Hospital in Ventura, California, for eighteen months, and had recently moved to Michigan with his family. He had obtained privileges to do surgery in a few hospitals in Detroit and its suburbs. When asked why he had left California, he said that his success had led to peer jealousy. We checked the National Data Bank for physicians, and there were no allegations or medico-legal cases filed against him at that time. The letter from the Community Memorial Hospital administrator stated the only negative was that he had missed some important meetings. As the executive director and board president, I had to sign in favor of the credential committee's recommendation.

A few months later, as I was walking through the recovery room at SIM, I saw a new face in surgical scrubs. As it was my habit, I walked up to the person and introduced myself. He said that he was Dr. Sabit, a neurosurgeon, who had recently joined the staff and was doing a few small surgeries. We went our separate ways, and I have never seen or talked to him again since then.

In June 2012, it came to light that, while practicing in California in 2010, Dr. Sabit had invested $5,000 in a physician-owned distributorship, Apex Medical Technologies, that supplied screws, plates, rods, and other pieces of spinal instrumentation. He then persuaded the hospital to buy the products for him to use in spine surgery. Dr. Sabit then went on a spree of unnecessary surgeries as well as legitimate ones, in which he overloaded patients with hardware from Apex. According to court records, he received illegal kickbacks of almost $440,000. Prosecutors described some of the operations as "plain butchery." During the eighteen months that he practiced in California, 71 percent of his patients were unexpectedly readmitted to the hospital. Many of them developed infections, and several even died from complications. The hospital temporarily suspended his privileges, explaining that it was necessary to "protect the life and well-being of patients." Unfortunately, none of this had been documented in his physician personnel file, nor had it been reported to the National Data Bank at the time SIM checked his credentials. In early 2011, when Dr. Sabit realized that his career in California was going up in flames, he abruptly moved to Michigan and obtained privileges in several hospitals, including SIM.

In Michigan, as the second chapter of fraud unfolded, he hit upon a new scheme. He started pursuing patients to undergo spinal fusion surgery unnecessarily. He claimed to have used extensive metal instrumentation during surgery, and then he fraudulently billed for it. FBI Special Agent Peter Hayes later reported that "subsequently, after continuing pain, all patients received second opinions from other doctors stating that no such spinal fusion had been performed and there was no evidence of any screw, or any medical device in the spinal column of the patient." Diagnostic imaging revealed that Dr. Sabit had never installed the hardware and had not performed spinal fusion. The Department of Justice later stated in a news release that he had fraudulently billed more than $33 million and had collected more than $11 million from Medicare, Medicaid, and private insurers for services he never performed. Prosecutors argued that

Sabit used his deceitful funds to finance his two-million-dollar mansion in Bloomfield Hills and even hid $600,000 of the embezzled money in his children's bank accounts.

On November 24, 2014, Dr. Sabit, age thirty-nine, was hauled into court unshaven and disheveled, wearing jeans and a white T-shirt. He was refused release on bond by US District Judge Paul Borman, for fear that he might flee the country. Judge Borman heard many tearful pleas from former patients, some of whom entered the court with canes or in wheelchairs. One of the victims very eloquently said, "I have faith that our system will eventually get him, and hopefully, he will get the time he greatly deserves."

Dr. Sabit composed his own plea for mercy, not only for himself but also for his wife and three children. In a court filing in November 2016, he described how he had survived persecution as a Jew in Afghanistan, sold bubble gum and cigarettes in a refugee camp in Pakistan, went hungry as an immigrant in Virginia, and finally won a college scholarship that led to medical school. "I came from absolutely nothing to become a neurosurgeon and squandered the opportunity," Dr Sabit said. "I do not deny my guilt."

On January 9, 2017, in a federal district court in Detroit, Dr. Sabit admitted to unnecessary as well as fake operations and illegal distribution of controlled substances. He was sentenced to a prison term of nearly twenty years. Prosecutors said they wanted a sentence that would make other physicians think twice about following in his footsteps.

Thank God he did only a few surgeries at our center SIM. One of his surgical victims did file a malpractice suit that included SIM in the allegations. In the fall of 2018, I had to appear in court to testify that, when SIM granted privileges to Dr. Sabit in early 2011, there were absolutely no documentations or allegations against him.

Thus ended another story where lust and greed turned a young neurosurgeon into a monster, who destroyed the lives of many innocent people. I truly believe that the punishment he is getting in this world is nothing compared to the eternal hellfire that is awaiting him in eternity.

PART FOUR:

Personal and Professional Reflections

CHAPTER 17

Working with Different Organizations

9/11 & the formation of Interfaith Community Outreach (ICO)

Sometimes, calamities bring us together.

On Tuesday, September 11, 2001, my day began in the usual fashion. I got up at 5:30 a.m., did my morning prayers and meditation, and worked out on the treadmill for thirty minutes. Then I showered and got dressed to go to the office. Annette's mother and stepfather were visiting from Ohio and had stayed the night with us. We sat down to a quick breakfast with them, since I had to be at the office by eight thirty. They planned to go back home that day. After saying goodbye to them, I gave Annette our routine hug and kiss and said, "I'll see you in the office later, honey."

It was a beautiful clear, sunny late summer day as I drove to the office. The traffic was not bad and, within twenty-five minutes, I was at my desk and had turned on my computer to look at my new emails since last night. At nine, I walked into Exam Room #1 to start with the first patient. As I was saying hello to the patient, my cell phone rang. It was Annette. "Did you see what's happening in New York? We're under attack! Turn the TV on to ABC News." It was Annette's routine to watch *Good Morning America*. She was on the ABC channel with Charles Gibson and Diane Sawyer, and at eight fifty-one, they suddenly switched gears. Something terrible had happened at the World Trade Center in New York. Everyone watching could see a commercial plane crashing into the second tower and going into flames at 9:01 a.m.

All our staff and patients quickly gathered in the waiting room, where we had a big-screen TV. We could not believe what our eyes were seeing and our ears were hearing. We stayed glued to the TV for the next hour, at which point I told the office manager to cancel the office for today and call the patients and reschedule their appointments. When the news hit home, we could not hold our tears. I could not imagine thinking of anything else at this time, let alone seeing patients and making life decisions. Annette called back again, sobbing on the phone. "Honey! Please come home as soon as you can. I'm in a state of shock." I changed quickly, and was home within half an hour.

When I got home, Annette and I hugged and cried for a few minutes to give an outlet to our emotions. It seemed like the end of the world was coming. Never in our wildest dreams could we have imagined anything like this happening. We called our children and advised them to come home immediately.

The next few days were miserable, as we watched the whole calamity unfold in front of our eyes. Our tears flowed, food was tasteless, and our sleep was fragmented, with fearful dreams. For two days, we were stuck at home, hooked on the television news. Whenever I looked at Annette, she was in a daze, trying to comprehend what had happened. On Friday afternoon, I told her to turn off the TV, sit, and talk with me. I began with a prayer for the three thousand innocent human beings who had fallen victim to these monsters, the thousands who had been injured, and especially for the three hundred and forty-three members of the Fire Department of New York who had sacrificed their lives saving others. Then, in a soft and remorseful tone, I said, "Honey, it is indeed the greatest tragedy that has happened in our lifetime. We cannot change what is past, but we can work hard to make the future better." I continued: "This is not the end of the world. Life has to go on. Let's try to think how to make the future of our people and country better."

The horrific events of September 11 were indeed an eye-opener for the entire world. That one day changed the lives and thinking of millions of people. First came the shock, then the grief, and then intense anger at these criminals who stole our nation's peace and harmony. It was something we had never anticipated. Those who did it in the name of religion were devoid of any element of faith. No religion teaches violence or approves the killing of innocent people. It took days to overcome the shock, weeks to figure out who those murderers were, months to plan the response — and it will take years to repair the loss. It is even difficult to comprehend the disaster that was wrought. There was loss of lives that can never be replaced; loss of property, which will take years to rebuild; and then there was loss of trust and faith. Our society broke into fragments, like a beautiful piece of crystal falling off its pedestal. Divisions were sown between religions, parties, groups, and even families. The faith of many, especially the young, was shaken. "Why does God let this happen?" One of my biggest concerns was the breakup of the Abrahamic family: Christians, Jews, and Muslims. Then there were the Buddhists, Hindus, Sikhs, and people of other faiths. Everyone had been shaken up. The repair had to be started, and soon.

I was invited to give talks to different religious groups. Down the street from where we live is a Catholic church, the Resurrection Church of Canton. Father Richard Perfetto, the priest in charge, invited me to give a homily one Sunday on Islam and its basic tenets.

I talked about faith in the one God, whether we call Him God, Jehovah, Allah, or Yeshua. It is interesting to note that all Arabic speaking people, whether they be Muslim, Jew, or Christian, refer to God as Allah. I showed the link leading from Adam to Noah, Abraham, Moses, Jesus, and Muhammad. I also pointed out how all of God's messengers had come with the same message of love, kindness, honor, justice, and condemnation of hate, cruelty, and falsehood in every form. Then I read the translation of a few passages from the chapter on Mary, the mother of Jesus Christ, in the Quran:

And mention, O Mohammed, in the book, the story of Mary, when she withdrew from her family to a place toward the east. And she took, in seclusion from them, a screen. Then we sent to her Our Angel, Gabriel, and he presented himself to her as a well-proportioned man. She said, "Indeed, I seek refuge in the Most Merciful from you, so leave me, if you should be fearing God." He said, "I am only the messenger of your Lord to give you news of a pure boy." She said, "How can I have a boy while no man has touched me and I have not been unchaste?"

He said, "Thus it will be: your Lord says, 'It is easy for Me, and We will make him a sign to the people and a mercy from Us. And it is a matter already decreed.'"

And a few lines later, when Jesus spoke from the cradle: "Indeed, I am the servant of God. He has given me the Scripture and made me a prophet. And He made me blessed wherever I am and has enjoined upon me prayer and charity as long as I remain alive. And peace is on me the day I was born and the day I will die and the day I am raised alive."

A lot of people asked me, "Are you sure these passages are from the Quran and not the Bible?" and I showed them the original book. There were many questions asked, and I answered them to the best of my abilities.

In the spring of 2009, Annette and I invited Father Perfetto to our home to have tea with us. We talked for a few hours about Canton and its cosmopolitan community of ninety thousand residents. There are several churches representing different Christian denominations, as well as synagogues, mosques, Hindu temples, Sikh gurudwaras, and other places of worship. Father Perfetto suddenly looked at me. "Dr. Hai. Tell me, why did you invite me here today?"

It was the moment I had been waiting for. "You know we come from different faith traditions," I said. "We follow our scriptures and perform our rituals, but there is a common thread of humanity which we are all a part of, and together we have a great responsibility of doing good, support-ing what is right, and condemning what is wrong. Annette and I would like to start an interfaith organization which would collectively fulfill those responsibilities."

Father Perfetto, Annette, and I sketched out a plan to start an interfaith organization that would have representatives and volunteers from all the different congregations. It would even include those who had no religious affiliation. The purpose was very simple: "To know and accept each other as members of the human society and do good for humanity."

At our second meeting, we invited leaders of all the communities in Canton and Plymouth who wanted to be part of the new group. Unanimously we agreed to call the organization the Interfaith Community Outreach of Plymouth and Canton, ICO for short. There was great enthusiasm and camaraderie among those who attended.

Realizing that Thanksgiving and winter would be coming soon, I suggested that the group do a clothing drive. It would not cost anything, as the work could've been done by all of us voluntarily. Everyone loved the idea, so we got started. Flyers were distributed all around Canton and Plymouth, asking people to go into their closets and pull out clean clothes that were in good condition and had not been used over the years. They needed only to put them in garbage bags and, on the collection day, leave them on their front porch. Our volunteers went around, picked them up, and brought them to the basement of Crescent Academy. Over the next few weeks, we all worked together, sorted the clothes by gender and size, and put them on hangers donated by local dry cleaners. When we finally did a count, lo and behold, we had over thirty-five thousand pieces of clothing, including lots of winter coats and sweaters of all sizes.

We then distributed flyers in food shelters and places of worship, announcing the date for the free give out. It is a day engraved in my memory. Thanksgiving was two weeks away. Many needy people came, some as families, some alone. They could try out the clothes and take whatever they needed. The volunteers passed out empty bags for them to take the clothes away.

One vivid memory has stayed in my mind. A young lady came with two little children, a boy and a girl. The boy was probably five and his sister around seven. They all walked over to the section where the kids' clothes were on racks. The boy started looking through the winter coats. His face was emotionless as he walked through the hanging garments. Suddenly he stopped and his face brightened when he saw a bright blue winter coat with black lapels. "I love this one, Mama," he said loudly. The mother looked at him lovingly and replied, "You have to try it on, honey. It may not fit you." The little boy took the coat off its hanger and eagerly put it on. "Look, Mama, it fits me perfect. I love it." His happiness knew no bounds, and everyone around could see it. His eyes met mine, and I walked up to him and gave him a big hug. "This coat is just for you," I told him. In that moment of joy, I felt that all the time and effort had paid off.

Everyone in the group of volunteers and organizers had similar experiences and felt a great sense of accomplishment. We had all got together and done something selfless with no direct benefit to us. Along the way we had made many friends, and there was more space in our closets for our clothes to breathe. It was the beginning of a very rewarding journey.

Over the next few months, the whole group worked feverishly to set up the website and Facebook page. The emblem was chosen, showing two helping hands with a rising sun in the background. The aims of the organization were defined: promoting diversity, acceptance, and understanding, working together, and building friendships, through community service and education. Our commitment was further defined:

WE BELIEVE:

> That we are called to lift each other up,
> That we are stronger standing together,
> That our differences are our blessings,

That empathy and love reveals the path to peace,

And that justice will prevail

Because each of us is Beloved.

THEREFORE, WE COMMIT TO

Answer intolerance with goodwill,

Live by faith and hope, not fear,

Seek understanding and friendship whenever we can,

Stand with those facing prejudice and injustice,

Meet resistance with resilience,

As we build the community each day.

Since then the Interfaith Community Outreach (ICO) has grown rapidly, with many new members and groups with the same philosophy joining in. Many food drives have been held to support the community food banks and soup kitchens such as the Detroit Rescue Mission, Forgotten Harvest, and Gleaners.

On September 11, 2011, the tenth anniversary of the great tragedy was marked with prayers, talks, and recitation of poems. Township officials, police officers, and community and faith leaders all got together with a commitment to move forward to a better community providing mutual support. Annette wrote a beautiful poem:

"Remembrance of September 11th

Remember that day, the day of explosive black rain,

Remember those lost, their loved ones in pain.

Remember the heroes, the troops who have toiled,

Our American spirit, it will not be spoiled.

Remember to pray to the God up above,

May He grant us strength and patience and love.

May He bond us, unite us, no matter our color or creed,

May He guide and protect us, in our time of need.

Remember that day, just a few years ago,

Our resolve as Americans, to the world we show."

The ICO group has continued over the years with monthly service projects including clothing and food drives, free community health-care clinics, game nights with veterans, and work in homeless shelters. It has also led many walks of support in the face of tragedies occurring in the interfaith communities throughout the country. Religious Diversity Journeys (RDJ) classes have been taught to thousands of students and teachers locally and around southeast Michigan. The youth have been integrated through roller skating, pizza, and movie nights to develop better acceptance and understanding.

The ICO has played an integral role in working with the Canton Township to start the Canton Response to Hate Crimes Coalition. This movement received national recognition for its "Not in Our Town" community program and now has chapters and activities across the nation. It is a national award-winning coalition of local law enforcement, community leaders, and representatives from faith-based organizations, who are committed to raising awareness of hate crimes, bias incidents, and bullying, building safe and inclusive communities for all.

Throughout 2017, the ICO group spent time creating an interfaith quilt that has representation from all faiths and creeds. The quilt demonstrates our bonds of oneness while celebrating our diversity. It proudly hangs at the Canton Public Library, as a true representation of our closely knit yet diverse community.

Team members have played an active role in helping elect and appoint the right candidates for the township boards, committees, school boards, and other important positions. Besides continuing to work on these important aspects of community life, discussions are going on with local government, the police and fire departments, courts, and faith leaders to address problems of mental illness and domestic abuse. The ICO has been recognized for its work by the State of Michigan and has received public testimonies from state representatives.

On October 24, 2018, at its annual awards dinner, the Interfaith Leadership Council of Michigan bestowed its Interfaith Award on the Plymouth-Canton Interfaith Community Outreach group, recognizing its years of work in community service, assisting the poor, and raising awareness against bullying, hate crimes, and bias. The *Canton Observer* stated it well: "The importance of ICO members forming friendships and relationships as well as representing and serving, will strengthen the Plymouth-Canton community far into the future."

On April 28, 2019, we celebrated our Faith Potluck at the Church of Latter-day Saints in Westland. The activity hall was packed with families representing many religions, colors, and creeds. Every one who came brought their best dish with them, and we all had a delicious meal. Pastor Bryan Smith and Anne Marie Graham-Hudak, who have been leading the organization, spoke of the beautiful love of diversity and inclusion. Pat Williams, the current supervisor of Canton Township, and other community leaders also celebrated the occasion with us. On one side of the room, tables were set up and all of us joined in to make bags of necessities for the homeless. The function ended with prayers for peace and understanding with special reference to the recent synagogue shooting in California.

Unity Productions Foundation (UPF)

Annette and I personally became involved with Unity Productions Foundation in the fall of 2000. The organization was conceptualized in late 1999 by its two founders, Michael Wolfe and Alex Kronemer, during an international flight when they were traveling together. In the spring of 2000, UPF was registered as a 501(c)(3) nonprofit corporation. Its mission was "to increase worldwide understanding and tolerance by developing and disseminating balanced, fair and accurate journalistic material regarding the world's cultural and spiritual traditions with a long-term goal to establish a permanent institution that works to create cross-cultural understanding through the media."

Michael Wolfe was a well-known, award-winning poet and writer, who had also been a publisher of poetry and avant-garde prose. He had authored several books, including *One Thousand Roads to Mecca*, *The Hadj*, and *Taking Back Islam: American Muslim Reclaim Their Faith*, which won a 2003 Wilbur Award. He had also been involved with TV since 1997 when he wrote and reported the Emmy Award-nominated ABC Friday News Special *Nightline on Hajj* with Ted Koppel, in April 1997.

Alex Kronemer was a journalist with a master's degree in theology from Harvard Divinity School. He was a national speaker who had appeared and participated in numerous TV programs, including CNN's first year of live coverage of the Hajj. In 2000, when I first met him, he was serving as a special appointee in the State Department's office of Human Rights and International Religious Freedom under Secretary Madeleine Albright. He was also a founding staff member of the United States Institute of Peace.

Alex called me one day in October 2000, saying he had heard about my philanthropic inclinations and that he wanted to meet Annette and me for dinner during his visit to Michigan. It was a beautiful fall day. We picked him up from the Hyatt Regency in Dearborn and drove a mile to Big Fish, a well-known Joe Muir seafood restaurant. The hostess sat us at an outdoor table for alfresco dining. The food was excellent, and what was supposed to be a two-hour dinner meeting ended up as a five-hour open-ended discussion of many world issues. Alex told us about UPF and the plans for its first movie, still in the early stages. We promised to help to the best of our ability. Funds were needed for their first production, and Alex asked me point blank: "So, Dr. Hai, how much do you think you can raise for us in your community?" Off the top of my head, I said, "A hundred thousand dollars." "That would be great!" Alex responded with a big smile. We dropped him back to the hotel — a new bond of friendship and mutual admiration had begun.

Over the next few months, we communicated through teleconferences, and in June 2001, we met with Michael, Alex, and a few community leaders at our home. Annette had prepared a delicious meal, and the details of the fundraising plans were discussed. The event would be a lavish dinner at the centrally located Hyatt Regency Hotel in Dearborn, and the date was finalized for Saturday, October 13, 2001. Annette and I took charge of the main dinner plans, and other members of the planning committee divided the rest of the work. Formal invitations were sent out, and the RSVP response was very good. We were all getting very excited about the event.

And then, on September 11, all hell broke loose. A few days later, after we had recovered somewhat from the shock, Alex called, very depressed. "We need to cancel the fundraising dinner," he said. "Many other cities which were planning have also cancelled." I was silent for a minute, as my mind processed his words. Finally, I spoke. "No, Alex, we are going to do it," I told him. "The need for the movie is even greater now than it was before."

"Are you sure?" he asked. "What kind of attendance will you get?"

"We are going to go ahead as planned," I assured him with determination. "And my agreement to raise $100,000 stays as it was."

With just a month to go, we all jumped back on the bandwagon with new enthusiasm. The fundraiser had to be a success, and the movie project had to move forward. And instead of a historical documentary on the Prophet Muhammad's life, we switched to a contemporary movie with a new name, *Muhammad: Legacy of a Prophet*. It would depict Muslims living in the United States of America and following the Prophet's teachings in their day-to-day lives. A week before the dinner, we started receiving more calls to buy tickets, and by the day of the event, we were totally sold out.

People came in large numbers, and the hall was packed. After the informal reception, Michael and Alex gave a brief introduction to UPF and the planned movie. A short but impressive clip of the film was shown, followed by a sumptuous dinner. Then the real test came — it was fundraising time. I gave a short motivating speech and started the process.

Both men and women present opened their hearts as the fundraising began. I had been skeptical about the $100,000 that I had promised Alex, but as things progressed, we surpassed our goal. The event went over by an hour, and when I added all the funds collected and pledges made, we had raised close to $ 250,000. I nearly fell out of my chair, and Alex and Michael and the rest of the organizers could not have been happier.

Muhammad: Legacy of a Prophet ended up as a two-hour documentary, and it aired on more than 350 stations of the Public Broadcasting System (PBS) nationwide on December 18, 2002. According to the polls, 5.7 million people watched the program nationwide. It has subsequently been rebroadcast by numerous local PBS stations and internationally through *National Geographic*, and its impact has been extended with the development of an interactive educational PBS website, a community outreach program, and an educational website for teachers.

Both Michael and Alex were working extremely hard, running around the country to promote UPF's great success. I could see burnout coming soon. We put our heads together in a meeting. I said to both of them, "You just cannot keep on at this pace. We have to come up with some long-term plans. You guys are phenomenal at what you do as moviemakers and journalists, and it should be our responsibility to provide you support." Two great ideas came out of that meeting. First, we decided to build a solid financial base. The Pioneer Club, with a yearly contribution of $6,000 and a commitment for a minimum of three years, was started. UPF's annual operating budget at that time was close to $500,000, and if we could get hundred members to sign up, we would collect $600,000 yearly just from the membership. We also created the Underwriters Club, with a donation of $25,000 for those donors who sincerely believed in a particular project. The next idea was to find a director of development who would coordinate all the activities and promote philanthropy in the community. After interviewing several candidates, we hit the jackpot in the spring of 2004. Jawaad Abdur Rahman was an enthusiastic young man who had graduated with a master's degree from the Indiana University School of Public Affairs. He quickly took charge and brought the organization to a new level. Alex and Michael could now focus primarily on their work.

In March 2004, we revisited the vision and mission of UPF. The mission statement now read: "To build a respected foundation, creating high-quality films and media products for broadcast that increase understanding of the world's spiritual and religious traditions."

In April 2004, Alex and Michael both came to Michigan and stayed with us. They had quickly become part of our family. We had several get-to-gethers, and the one at the Grosse Ile Country Club was very successful: we signed up ten new Pioneer Club members. Within the next few months, we had signed up forty-three Pioneer Club members from around the country. Jawaad was on an adrenaline rush.

The next few years were increasingly busy with multiple projects and movies in the making. The products of their hard labor began to materialize. *City of Lights: The Rise and Fall of Muslim Spain* premiered on August 22, 2007, and was rated the number one show for that month by PBS. It was done in collaboration with the renowned documentary film director Rob Gardener and with a grant from the Corporation for Public Broadcasting. The movie showed how it had been possible for Christians, Jews, and Muslims to coexist and thrive together for nearly seven hundred years in Spain and become the starting point of the European Renaissance. The movie won several international television and video awards.

By May 2004, plans were on track for another hallmark movie, *Prince Among Slaves*, with support from the National Endowment for the Humanities. The script was based on a book with the same title by Terry

Alford, who had done extensive research in original documents confirming the story of an African prince caught up in the slave trade in 1788. He worked as a respectable, educated slave for forty years when he was recognized and honorably returned to Africa in 1829 with the help of Secretary of State Henry Clay and President John Quincy Adams. The movie was directed by Bill Duke and Andrea Kalin, among the most respected producers and directors in Hollywood. The voiceover narrator was Mos Def, another well-known actor. The live shoot was done on the banks of the river at Saint Mary's in Maryland. Annette and I visited while the movie was being shot and got a firsthand experience of how movies are made.

Prince Among Slaves was completed in December 2007 and premiered on 350 PBS stations, with an audience of more than six million, on February 4, 2008. It generated eight significant awards, including the Cine Golden Eagle and the Best Documentary of 2007 from the American Black Film Festival. More than seventy media outlets covered it, including *Time* magazine, the Associated Press, the *Los Angeles Times*, and National Public Broadcast. The movie shed light on a part of African-American history that had never really been heard about. A few weeks later, it was screened for a highly select audience at the US Capitol.

With the collaborative effort of many churches and organizations, we arranged to show *Prince Among Slaves* at the Fellowship Chapel in Detroit. Over a thousand tickets were sold, and on the day of the show there was standing room only. It was shown in all the major cities around the country. UPF had made a mark in the media and movie world.

I joined UPF's board of directors, and later was appointed the chairman of the board, following in the footsteps of Safi Qureshey, the co-founder of AST computers and one of Southern California's leading philanthropist. UPF had become a passion for both me and Annette. Alex, Michael, and Jawaad would frequently come to Michigan and stay with us to plan out new strategies. Alex loved to cook in our kitchen with Annette, and we would all be beneficiaries of their creative and delicious dishes. We traveled to different cities for premiers and fundraisers for ongoing projects. UPF added a new dimension to our lives.

Many other projects and movies rolled out of Unity Productions Foundation, depending on what we all felt was the call of the day. An epic journey across nine countries and over 1400 years of history was recorded in *Islamic Art: Mirror of the Invisible World,* narrated by Academy Award-winning actress Susan Sarandon and broadcast on PBS in July 2012. In August 2012, UPF began production of its tenth movie. We believe that a good story may entertain and teach, but a heroic story can change how we see the world. *Enemy of the Reich: The Story of Noor Inayat Khan* depicts the inspiring true saga of a Muslim woman who opposed Hitler, risked her life, and helped launch the French Resistance during World War II. In 1943 in Paris, working as an underground operator in disguise, her Morse code transmissions back to England helped save many innocent people from Nazi aggression and laid the foundations for the secret communications that would eventually contribute to the success of the D-Day invasion. Later captured by the Gestapo, she was deported to the infamous Dachau death camp. On September 14, 1944, she refused to reveal any allied secrets and was savagely beaten and shot. The last word she shouted before she was killed was *"Liberté!"* — the French word for freedom.

Enemy of the Reich was narrated by the famous Hollywood actress Helen Mirren and broadcast in the Fall of 2014, and seen by 2.5 million people on the first night. It has been shown in thirty-five cities and over a thousand classrooms around the world, and has received multiple awards and rave reviews from the *Boston Globe,* the *Washington Post,* the BBC, and NPR.

In June 2019, we took a Viking River cruise that included visits to Auschwitz-Birkenau camp and the Jewish quarters in Prague, Krakow, and Warsaw. It is forever a painful expression of the world's bad conscience. The remains of the Nazi death camp remind us of the darkest moments of human history. It was here between 1940 and 1945 that the Nazis murdered more than one million Jews, as well as tens of thousands of Poles, Slavs, Gypsies, Soviet POWs, and other innocent people.

A more recent movie, *The Sultan and the Saint*, has brought Unity Productions Foundation to a totally new level. It was produced in-house and directed by Alex Kronemer himself, with extensive help from Michael Wolfe, Jawaad, and the whole UPF team. I had read the book by Paul Moses that it was based on, and was also convinced that it would make a great movie. Moses, an accomplished journalist, had extensively reviewed the life of Saint Francis of Assisi and based the book on multiple reliable sources. The story is set in the year 1219, at the height of the bloody religious conflict known as the Crusades. Saint Francis risks his life, walking across enemy lines against the wishes of the Pope, to meet the sultan of Egypt, the Muslim ruler Al-Malik-Al-Kamil. The two men of faith explore and exchange spiritually amidst a battlefield of horror. This remarkable historical encounter took place in the last two years of a terrible and wretched war that had devastated both armies. The final outcome was love, kindness, and peace. Both learned from each other's spirituality and, in their own time, changed enmity into friendship, hate into love, and war into peace.

The movie was mostly shot in the warehouse district of Baltimore. All the sets were built locally. Annette and I had become underwriters for this movie project, and with some other donors, we were invited to see the actual film production. We flew down for a weekend and became a part of moviemaking. While we were intrigued by the whole process, Alex asked us, "We need some extras for the coming scene. Are you guys interested in being part of the movie?" Without hesitating or waiting for Annette's response, I replied, "Of course! We would love to." Annette readily agreed too, and Alex sat with us explaining the scene we were going to be in. It was a pub scene in old Assisi, where I am sitting at a table drinking from a big mug (although in real life I have never had a drop of alcohol). The man sitting next to me has just passed out. Annette is my significant other, sitting across the table and strongly advising me to stop drinking. Right at this moment, everyone in the pub is appalled to see Saint Francis bringing a leper into town.

First, we were sent to a tent, where we changed into the appropriate attire, and then we spent more than an hour with the makeup artist who got us ready for the scene. The scene was shot at least eight times, before the director and the team were satisfied that everything had gone well. During editing, a lot of the footage was trimmed, and we are in the final movie for maybe three seconds. While watching it later, we told our family and friends, "Don't blink, or you'll miss us." It was truly an amazing experience, and we quickly realized how painstaking it is to make movies. Once all the editing had been done, the narration was added, performed by British Academy-Award winning actor Jeremy Irons.

After much thinking, we decided to have the premiere of *The Sultan and the Saint* at a major Franciscan institution. The Kresge Auditorium at Madonna University in Livonia, Michigan, was selected, and the date chosen was Sunday, October 22, 2017. We were extremely delighted to meet Sister Nancy Jamroz, who was leading the Center for Catholic Studies and Interfaith Dialogue. She graciously opened the doors to us, saying, "We at Madonna feel so privileged that you chose our institution to hold this memorable event." On the day, a delicious reception was set up next to the hall. Alex gave an exciting introduction, and then we all watched the movie. Everyone present was full of praise, and the film received a standing ovation. PBS broadcast it nationwide on December 26, 2017. According to reports, over eight million viewers watched it that night, and since then it has been shown hundreds of times around the world.

We arranged to show the movie to a large audience in the Michael Guido Theater at the Ford Community and Performing Arts Center in Dearborn on March 25, 2018. A planning committee was formed that included Sister Nancy, Steve Spreitzer, president and CEO of the Michigan Roundtable for Diversity and Inclusion, Bill Joyner, editor and publisher of *Friday Musings*, Annette and me, and several others. Invitations were sent to the leadership of the Franciscan brothers, Catholic churches, mosques, temples, and many community centers and organizations. With everyone's efforts, on the day of the function, the thousand-seat auditorium was filled to capacity with standing room only. I served as the master of ceremonies, and Michael Wolfe was the main speaker. The event was well organized, and everyone present was overwhelmed by the message of the movie. We were all exhausted but greatly satisfied that the hard work done by the Unity Productions Foundation team had been appreciated by representatives of different religions, cultures, and creeds.

In May 2018, Alex visited Italy, and *The Sultan and the Saint* was premiered in Assisi to celebrate Saint Francis's 800th birthday. It was also shown at the Vatican to many cardinals and high-ranking priests. In November 2018, we had a great opportunity to show it to the Archbishop of Detroit, the Most Reverend Allen H. Vigneron. On December 6, 2018, I was really touched to receive a letter from him saying, "Thank you for your thoughtfulness for sharing with me the movie *The Sultan and the Saint*. Your kindness is greatly appreciated. With heartfelt thanks, and with prayers for you and those you love, I remain" — and personally signed by him.

The movie received over eighteen laurels at film festivals, including the Gold Prize at Germany's World Media Awards, the Award of Excellence at the Communication awards, and the Best Documentary of the Year at the Christian Film Awards. Our excitement and happiness knew no bounds when the National Academy of Television Arts & Sciences nominated it for the News and Documentary Emmy award at their 39th annual gala. The fashionable event was scheduled at the Frederick Rose Hall at the Lincoln Center in New York on October 1, 2018. Alex and Michael called us: "Both of you must come for this occasion." None of us had ever imagined that a movie made by a small organization like Unity Productions Foundation would ever reach such national recognition.

We quickly booked our flight and a room at the Marriott close to the event site in Manhattan. We reached the hotel a few hours before the function. The event was a big gala affair, such as we had always imagined when watching the Oscars. Everyone was dressed for the occasion, and the food at the reception was delicious, served on a large glassed-in balcony overlooking Central Park and skyscrapers. Then came the photo session, and we all had pictures taken like celebrities, rubbing shoulders with many known personalities of the media world. We were then escorted to the main hall. There were the usual speeches and multiple awards to ABC, NBC, PBS, *Dateline, 60 Minutes, Anderson Cooper 360*, and many others. Although we did not win the award, it was an honor just to be in the league of media giants. The whole experience was a lifetime memory.

What I learned from working with Unity Productions Foundation has changed my life. I had an opportunity to appreciate and learn from great people like Alex, Michael, and Jawaad and their commitment to a great cause. My advice to everyone is to get involved in other activities beyond your professional work. It will enhance your knowledge and personality, save you from burnout in your job, and contribute to the betterment of humanity. Join organizations and institutions that you know are honest and devoted to their cause. Become passionate about this work, and contribute to it however you can, with time, money, and emotional support. If your daily work or profession is science-related, choose something in the field of art, or vice versa. I have realized that our lives are more fulfilled when we acquire both science and arts in our lives. This kind of work will give you endless joy and gratification, and a true purpose for our existence in this world.

I will end this chapter with a famous prayer of Saint Francis of Assisi:

"Lord,
Make me an instrument of your peace;
Where there is hatred, let me sow love;
Where there is injury, pardon;
Where there is doubt, faith;

Where there is despair, hope;

Where there is darkness, light;

Where there is sadness, joy;

O Divine Master,

Grant that I may not so much seek to be consoled as to console;

To be understood as to understand;

To be loved as to love.

For it is in giving that we receive.

It is in pardon that we are pardoned.

It is in dying that we are born to eternal life."

CHAPTER 18

Stewardship and Legacy

"When a person dies, his actions come to an end, except in respect to three things that he leaves behind: a continuous charity, beneficial knowledge that helps others and righteous children who pray for them."

—Hadith

The Merriam-Webster dictionary defines stewardship as the careful and responsible conducting, supervising, or managing of something entrusted to one's care. Good examples are the act of making wise use of the natural resources or the responsible management of the staff running an estate.

As human beings, we are the stewards of many things entrusted to us: our health, children and family, wealth and possessions, and all the resources provided to us on this earth. I strongly believe that all the gifts we have in this life are truly not ours but entrusted to us to see how we use or abuse them. Good stewards take care of themselves, are committed to selfless service, practice inclusiveness, embrace innovation and change, and are team players, always ready to give others credit. In essence, stewardship is the basis of good ethics and can be applied to health, environment, nature, economics, property, information, theology, etc. The opposite of this is the attitude that I am much smarter than a lot of other people, I worked very hard for what I have, and I do whatever I please with it. Unfortunately, this is becoming the prevailing frame of mind.

From rags to riches

I sincerely believe that God tests us in many ways. To some, He gives a lot of material blessings like family, power, riches, authority, etc., and then tests us as to how we bring it to use.

The more we are given, the greater is the answerability. That is one of the reasons that Jesus said, "It is easier for a camel to go through a needle's eye than for a rich man to go to heaven. And sometimes He gives and then takes it away." During my own growing up I witnessed this.

There was a very brilliant man from a small village near our home town in India. With his intelligence and hard work, he became the best-known attorney in the entire state. He went to England, and came back as a barrister-at-law, and was later even knighted by the British Empire as Sir Sultan. It was well known that, in any legal case he took on, the judgment would come in his favor. With this kind of magical reputation, his law practice knew no bounds. People were lined up with cash for him to fight their case in court. His riches grew quickly. He built an enormous estate that was called the "Sultan Palace". As children, we would be told that the palace had twenty bedrooms and ten bathrooms, and our pupils would turn big imagining it.

Unfortunately, Sir Sultan, as he was known, did not have any children. He adopted one of his sister's sons and raised him as his own. This young man, growing up with all the affluence, turned out to be an absolute spendthrift. He squandered money as if it had no end. He would go to Europe for months, entertain his friends lavishly, and everything he did had to be done in a grand fashion. While his spending kept increasing, Sir Sultan's income continued to go down as he got older. He started taking loans, using his palace as a collateral.

My father happened to be the personal physician to the family and often made house calls. The tradition with wealthy patients in those days was to slip in the physician's fees in their pockets as they were walking out. The amount depended on the person's status. The very rich would pay in gold and silver coins.

My father told me that one evening he had to make a house call to see Sir Sultan's wife. At the end of the visit, as was customary, his fees were quietly slipped into his pocket. My dad, reaching into his pocket, found not coins but a piece of Lady Sultan's jewelry. He respectfully returned it, saying, "This is your family's honor. Please, keep it and pay me later when you have money."

Debts kept building up, and soon after, the palace had to be auctioned. The old man had to move back to his humble dwellings in the village, and a short time later passed away in grief. We witnessed the story of rags to riches and back to sheer poverty when I was just a boy.

Rags to riches to the pinnacle of philanthropy

> "A strong work ethic and intense desire to make something of his life, led Tom Monaghan from the orphanages of Michigan to the creation of the second-largest pizza chain in the world. His business grew from a single $500 store in Ypsilanti, Michigan, to over 6100 franchised and company-owned stores in 64 countries, with revenue of over one billion dollars."
>
> The Encyclopedia of World Biography, 2010

It was the fall of 1975 when I first met Tom Monaghan in Ypsilanti. I had gone to meet a family who were from Patna, my hometown in India. The young son was in the pizza business and had his own pizza shop, "Faz Pizza," right across from the Eastern Michigan University campus. Although both Tom and Faz were competing for business, they were good friends and had even worked together. Being a Sunday afternoon, the Domino pizza shop was hustling and bustling. There was a whole line of young students waiting to place the fresh pizza in the insulated bag and deliver every order immediately. Tom had started a new campaign: "Delivery in 30 minutes or the pizza is free." We said hello and quickly parted, but from that day onward I have followed Tom Moaghan's life very closely.

Thomas Stephen Monaghan was born on March 25, 1937, in Jackson, Michigan, into an Irish-American family. His father, a truck driver, died of peritonitis on Christmas eve, when Tom was four years old. The family lived in a small farmhouse built by his father. After his death, Monaghan's mother, with meager earnings of $27.50 a week, had great difficulty raising him alone. In 1943, when he turned six, she took him and his younger brother James to an orphanage, Saint Joseph Home for Children, in Jackson. It was run by the Felician Sisters of Livonia. Six years later, in 1949, after completing the nursing degree, she began work at Munson Hospital in Traverse City. She collected the two brothers back from the orphanage and brought them home again.

In 1959, after serving for three years in the Marines, Monaghan received an honorable discharge. On his return, he wanted to become an architect and enrolled at the University of Michigan. To support his college tuition, he and his brother James borrowed $900 and bought a small pizza store called DomiNick's Pizza in the adjacent town of Ypsilanti. When once asked, he said, "I started out in architecture school, and got into the pizza business to pay my way through school. The pizza business was losing so much money, I never got back to architecture."

From then on, working eighteen hours a day, Tom focused exclusively on making the best pizza in the world. He visited nearly three hundred rival pizzerias to understand the business. Then he sat down to create a simple menu with the best dough from high quality flour, expensive cheese, and the highest quality toppings. He also developed the dough trays, the conveyer oven, the non-collapsible corrugated pizza box, the insulated bag for transport, and indeed the best delivery system.

Fourteen months after getting into the pizza business, Tom set up his new store in Mount Pleasant, Michigan. The first order came from the dormitory at Central Michigan University. When Tom arrived on his first delivery, the woman working at the reception desk, Margie, caught his eye. As Monaghan writes in his autobiography *Pizza Tiger*, "After our second date, I gave Margie a heart-shaped pizza for Valentine's Day. It was a big hit with her friends in the dorm. On our third date, I looked into those big blue eyes and realized I was in love." The following year in 1962, they got married. Margie Monaghan worked with Domino's Pizza for decades. They were blessed with four girls.

In 1965, the pizza shop on Cross Street in Ypsilanti, right across from the Eastern Michigan University campus, changed its name to Domino's Pizza. Being a great businessman, Tom sold his first franchise in 1967.

Soon after, a number of challenges came up. A fire destroyed his anchor store in Ypsilanti, as well as the company's office. By 1970, Domino's was in debt over $1.5 million and nearly went bankrupt. By support from local businessmen, he regained control and became profitable again. In September of 1975, a big manufacturer, Domino Sugar, sued for infringement of trademark. Finally, in 1980, the court's decision came in Tom's favor.

Tom Monaghan's next brainwave was to open franchises and deliver to college campuses around the country. By 1978, he had carefully rolled out two hundred stores in college towns, and by 1983, stores started opening in Canada. Domino's expanded rapidly through the 1980s.

With Domino's Pizza doing so well, Tom's interests were diverted. He became a flamboyant spender, fulfilling all his childhood dreams. In 1983, Monaghan was able to purchase the Detroit Tigers baseball franchise from John Fetzer for $53 million. To his great good fortune, in the very first season of his ownership, the Detroit Tigers won the World Series. The jubilation made Tom a statewide hero.

Tom Monaghan got into some big stuff. With his lifelong love for architecture, he became a collector of furniture and artifacts created by the great Frank Lloyd Wright. His collection grew to over three hundred items, valued at over $30 million. He built a ten-thousand-square-foot National Center for the Study of Frank Lloyd Wright, complete with a museum to house his collection.

Later, his interest shifted to antique automobiles. At one point, Monaghan owned more than 250 antique cars, which were displayed in a special museum. I clearly remember him buying a 1932 Bugatti Royale valued at over eight million dollars in an auction. Only six of these cars exist in the world. He also bought the Drummond Island Resort, on the Michigan-Ontario border. At the peak of his buying frenzy, he owned five boats, three planes, and various other companies.

Another calamity befell him in 1990. A woman was injured by a Domino driver, and the case ended in court. The judgment cost Domino's $78 million dollars. The company decided to give up its thirty-minute-delivery guarantee.

In 1992, Monaghan sold the Detroit Tigers baseball franchise to one of his rivals, Mike Ilitch, cofounder of Little Caesars Pizza. He wrote, "It's good to keep the team in the pizza family!"

Although Tom Monaghan had met Pope John Paul in 1987 and had encouraged Catholic executives to spread the faith in their business and personal life, his true metamorphosis occurred in 1998. According to an article published in the *New York Times* on February 14, 1999, a book totally changed the direction of Tom Monaghan's life. After reading C. S. Lewis's book, *Mere Christianity*, Monaghan decided to give up his sin of pride and rededicate himself to God. In his interview he said, "I don't want to take my money when I go, and I don't want to leave it for others. I want to die broke."

In 1998, Monaghan announced his retirement after thirty-eight years with Domino's Pizza, selling 93 percent of the company to Bain Capital of Boston for close to $1 billion. He ceased to be involved in the day-to-day operations of the company, and subsequently dedicated his time and considerable fortune to Catholic causes. He took up the banner "to combat the nation's moral crisis" and also became a champion of the pro-life movement.

Later in a letter, he wrote, "I came into the world penniless and as a Catholic Christian, I know that I cannot take any of it with me, so it has long been my desire to use the material resources that I have been blessed with to help others in the most meaningful ways possible. I am very grateful not only for the resources that I have been blessed with, but the opportunity to use these resources to help others in the best way I know how."

Early in 2002, Monaghan sought to establish the Ave Maria University in Ann Arbor, but it could not be done owing to zoning issues. Eventually, community leaders in Collier County, thirty miles east of Naples, Florida, offered him a large piece of undeveloped land for the university. In June 2004, Governor Jeb Bush signed Ave Maria Stewardship Community District into law. Tom Monaghan donated $250 million to found the university. In February 2006, ground was broken for the new Catholic university and town.

My next-door neighbor in Canton, Michigan, built a home there, and Annette and I visited him a few years back. The most striking structure in Ave Maria Town is the distinctive church, the Oratory, where daily Catholic masses, concerts, and group events are held. Catholicism dominates the landscape with the church, university, parochial school, shops, cafes, and over seven hundred homes. In 2014, the *Ave Herald* stated, "There are people of all faiths and some of no faith living in Ave Maria. Some come because the homes are a good value. Others come to live by a golf course, as many people in Florida do. And yes, some people come because the town is built around a Catholic university and offers a family-friendly environment for people of all religious beliefs."

Whatever the reason, the town is growing. Ave Maria Town was one of the fastest growing communities in Southwest Florida, with 283 new homes built in 2015.

In 2010, Monaghan signed "The Giving Pledge," which is a commitment by the world's wealthiest individuals and families to dedicate the majority of their wealth to giving back to philanthropic causes before or after their deaths. The campaign was started by Microsoft co-founder Bill Gates and his wife Melinda Gates and the investor Warren Buffett. Later many others like Paul Allen, Michael Bloomberg, Richard and Joan Branson, and Mark and Priscilla Zuckerberg joined. As of 2019, there are a total of 190 pledgers adding up to more than $365 billion in charitable gifts. It has become the largest philanthropic fund in the whole world.

A few months back, on January 12, 2019, Annette and I were flying back from Fort Myers to Michigan. By our good luck, we had been upgraded to the first-class cabin. Soon after I sat down, Annette whispered in my ear, "Do you know who is sitting behind you? It's Tom Monaghan." I looked back, and indeed it was Tom. I was seeing him after nearly forty-five years. He still looked very elegant, active, and in good health. I turned around, introduced myself, and reminded him of our meeting in Ypsilanti when I was accompanied by Faz. I told him how I had closely followed his life over the years and what a great example he was for all of us. After we disembarked from the flight, we chatted for a few more minutes and I asked his permission to include his life story in the book I was writing. He gladly agreed.

The Mother Theresa of Michigan

I first met Najah Bazzy and her husband, Ali, in the late nineteen eighties. She was working as a critical-care nurse in the cardiac care unit of Oakwood Hospital in Dearborn, Michigan. We lived nearby in the condo's of Fairlane Woods. One evening they stopped by for coffee and dessert. I presented her with the philanthropic work I was involved in and soon we were building the future of Michigan Educational Council together. Her children went to the Crescent Academy and she and her husband became great advocates for the school.

Her life-changing spark came in 1996 while she was still working as a nurse. She was medically helping an Iraqi refugee family, when she realized that they had absolutely nothing to support life. According to her own words, "when I saw what I saw, it was a pivotal momemt in my life. I could have walked away, which I could not, or do something. That kind of started the entire story."

She started a grassroots organization called Zaman International which ran out of the back of Najah's van. She gave up her six-figure salary in healthcare to start a full-time job of collecting food, clothing and household goods for impoverished families; to break the cycle of poverty. With her extremely hard work and sacrifice over the years, Zaman has grown into a non-profit organization with a two million dollars annual budget, six thousand volunteers and over four hundred supporting businesses. Later she also founded 'Plots for Tots', a non-profit organization that aids grieving, poverty-stricken parents with the burial of their deceased children.

Recently in an interview with the local Observer & Eccentric newspaper, Najah said, it's been an emotional journey. I cry a lot: not because of the pain the people are in, but because of the hope we give them. Seeing them move from pain to hope is what puts me in tears."

In September, 2019, seeing Bazzy's angelic work, the news giant CNN recognized her as one of their twenty "Heroes" chosen out of over forty thousand nominations that they reviewed this year. When I texted her my congratulations, she humbly replied, " truthfully the heroes are 'Zamanitarians' like you who support the project." To me, Najah Bazzy is the Mother Teresa of Michigan.

Although the simple definition of legacy only refers to inheritance, gifts, and endowments, it is much more. The more holistic understanding of legacy is when you share what you have learned, not just what you have earned. It refers to genuinely offering yourself and making a meaningful, lasting, and energizing contribution to humanity by serving a cause greater than your own. It requires that you embrace your uniqueness, passionately immerse in it, so that your gift will be to all and that it will have a life beyond you. In essence, you focus on making a difference in the lives of others by giving back for all the blessings you have received.

In this regard, each one of us can leave a worthwhile legacy as long as we sincerely make the effort.

Learn to give, and you will taste the sweetness of giving. Both Annette and I love giving gifts as much as we can. While children are excited to receive it, even adults are thrilled about it. It brings a different kind of joy. Whenever we travel, we make a gift list and pick up something small for everyone including the whole office staff. It's not the value of the gift but the thought that counts.

Philanthropy in one form or another has been known to exist forever. I agree with the principles of philanthropy, whether achieved conventionally or through current thinking.

The roots of effective altruism (EA) come from the writings of Peter Singer, an Australian moral philosopher and professor of bioethics at Princeton. In his 2009 book *The Life You Can Save*, he argues that people in affluent countries have a moral obligation to save lives and end poverty in developing nations. In an earlier essay he states, "It makes no moral difference whether the person I can help is a neighbor's child ten yards from me or a Bengali whose name I shall never know, ten thousand miles away . . . The moral point of view requires us to look beyond the interests of our own society."

The EA philosophy emphasizes logic and results, and encourages giving where your dollars will do the most proven good, regardless of any emotional attachments to a given cause. The classic example of wrong-headed giving, according to this model, is donating to your alma mater or to an arts institution to get your name plastered on the building. EA's moral pragmatism appeals to many young donors. There are some who are even living frugally to maximize their donations to worthy causes. It is also getting more important to measure the impact of your giving. This can be achieved by assessing the cost per live saved, transparency of reporting, and evidence of impact.

Then there is the old saying, "Charity begins at home." This has a different kind of relevance. When we are part of a family or a community, it behooves us to take care of it — we receive many benefits and we must do the same in return. If each family and each community took care of their own socio-economic problems, there would be no national or international crisis.

As for myself, I believe in both the philosophies, and practically contribute in both ways. As individuals, we need to decide which format serves us best. The important message is to make a commitment and keep giving to a point that it hurts your own wallet. "You have not really given till you give that which you love most" the scripture says. The pleasure you get from selfless giving is beyond comprehension. A plaque hangs in my office that says:

"Doing God's work pays little, but the retirement benefits are out of this world."

If we all work together and open our hearts, we can make a difference, creating a world with food and shelter for all of humanity — a world of compassion and love.

In the last few decades, extensive research has been done in the field of philanthropy. The only school fully devoted to this subject is the Lilley School of Philanthropy affiliated with Indiana University. I feel privileged to be on the advisory board associated with it and have learnt a lot about philanthropy.

It is heartening to know that kindness is trying to make a comeback after being in short supply. USA Today reported on its front page, on October 7th., 2019 " The University of California, Los Angeles has announced a global first: It will use a twenty million dollar alumnus donation to start the UCLA Bedari Kindness Institute, researching ways in which showing kindness benefits people and society alike. --- to be able to roll out tangible results in the form of programs that teach how to better integrate kindness into one's daily life."

Darnell Hunt, dean of social sciences at UCLA said it so well "If we can learn more about the conditions that are conducive to people being empathetic toward others, which is the core of kindness, then maybe we can push for kinder policies from our politicians."

CHAPTER 19

Prostate Cancer and Its Prevention: My Personal Fight Against It

Cancer anywhere in the body starts when cells begin to grow out of control. Scientists believe that we all have a potential for it, but positive factors such as our immune system keep cancer in check.

The prostate, which is present only in males, is a walnut-size solid gland that sits below the bladder, surrounding the first part of the urethra, the tube that drains the bladder. It has a role to play in the reproductive years by helping to liquefy the semen, thereby activating the sperms. But after that, it is nothing more than a nuisance. In every man, the gland enlarges, a process that is called benign prostatic hyperplasia, or BPH for short. If the cells start to grow uncontrollably, it turns into cancer. Unfortunately, prostate cancer does not show many symptoms until the disease has spread to other organs.

Other than skin cancer, prostate cancer is the most common cancer in American men. The American Cancer Society estimates that this year about 174,650 new cases will be diagnosed, and 31,620 men will die of prostate cancer. Despite all the research and preventive efforts, the numbers have been going up. On average, about one man out of every nine will be diagnosed with prostate cancer in his lifetime, and one in forty will die from it. Although, in general, it is a slow-growing cancer, the end stages can lead to a prolonged and painful death.

Researchers have found several factors that might affect a man's risk of getting prostate cancer. The likelihood of having it rises rapidly after the age of fifty, and six out of ten cases are found in men older than sixty-five. Although the reasons for racial and ethnic differences are not clear, it affects more men of African than of European ancestry. It definitely runs in some families — my family, for example — indicating an inherited or genetic basis.

High alcohol consumption and smoking are associated with aggressive prostate cancer. Other factors are diet, obesity, chemical exposure, and chronic inflammation of the prostate.

Although digital rectal examination (DRE), which keeps many men from seeing the doctor, has been helpful, the discovery of the blood test evaluating the blood level of prostate specific antigen (PSA) has revolutionized the early detection of prostate cancer. PSA was first measured in the lab in 1980, and I clearly remember Dr. Stamey's presentation at the AUA annual meeting on his initial work on the clinical use of PSA as a marker for prostate cancer. It was not until early 1986 that the first commercial PSA test was available to us. I started using it widely on all my male patients over the age of fifty. Although there can be false positive results because of BPH and prostatitis, the year-to-year change is very helpful in the early detection of prostate cancer. As urologists, we can detect the change and proactively do prostate biopsies to identify patients in the early, treatable stages of prostate cancer.

In 1986, I saw a new patient in the office. Ron was an African-American male who had just turned fifty and had his first PSA evaluation. The numbers were extremely high. I performed the prostate biopsy, and, to my utter surprise, it came back as extensive high-grade prostate cancer. He took my advice, and the following week, I removed his prostate surgically. Luckily, the disease had not spread. We kept him on supplemental hormone therapy for a while, and his PSA went down to less than 0.1. Ron has continued faithfully coming to the office every year for his follow-up and PSA test for thirty years. He graciously thanks me for saving his life. Despite the hard work and long hours, happy stories like these have kept me going over the years.

Current studies have shown that PSA alone has led to many cases of early detection and has reduced the mortality from prostate cancer by at least 25 percent. Over the years, further refinement of the PSA has led to evaluation of free PSA and IsoPSA, which was recently reported by a team of researchers from the Cleveland Clinic. It detects prostate cancer more precisely and also identifies patients with high-grade cancer. Many genomic tests such as Polaris, Oncocyte Dx, Confirm MDx, and 4K score are also available to us. Early in 2018, a new urine-based molecular diagnostic test, the SelectMDx liquid biopsy test, was introduced and adopted by the European Urology Association guidelines. It involves simply collecting a urine sample in the office and sending it to a special lab. It not only predicts patients with increased risk of prostate cancer, but also those who will have aggressive disease that may turn lethal. It is available for a very reasonable cost and will save many patients from having to undergo an invasive prostate biopsy. Overall, it is estimated to cut down the health dollars spent on prostate cancer by 50 percent.

Because of my strong family history, I had the test done on my own urine. It came back as "very low risk for prostate cancer, and extremely low risk for high-grade cancer." The results gave me a sigh of relief and a great sense of contentment that I would be spared from the trauma that many of my family members and patients have had to go through. Both my brothers, four uncles on my mother's side, and even some of my cousins have been diagnosed and treated for prostate cancer. From my early life, as I became aware of these facts, I have continued to make changes in my diet and lifestyle. I never smoked or consumed alcohol. I have always tried to exercise regularly and to maintain my weight. My red meat and fat consumption has been minimal, and I avoid carbs as much as possible in favor of alternatives like couscous, quinoa, freekeh, and cauliflower rice. Annette has figured out great replacements, and we have never starved for a good meal. We rarely eat processed food and stick to organic fruits and vegetables. Eating fast food is probably down to once or twice a year. Not only is the quality of food important, but so is the quantity. I believe we all eat too much and too frequently. We need to learn to eat healthy snacks like nuts, fruits, and vegetables. It is not essential to follow a planned commercial dieting regime. We need to eat intelligently, with knowledge of what we are eating. Most drastic weight-loss measures end up in a regaining of the lost weight. The most important thing to understand is the ratio of calories in and calories out. If it is positive, you are going to gain weight, and if it is negative, you are going to lose weight. Just like the mirror, the bathroom scale never lies. So find a well-thought-out diet that you can live with, and stick to it, remembering that a steak or a donut once in a while will not kill you.

There is a mistaken perception that exercise has to be strenuous, with sweat pouring from all pores. Exercise should be moderate but sustained, and done on a regular basis. Jogging on hard pavement can have a jarring effect on your joints, and brisk walking can provide the same results with less trauma. Always wear comfortable and supportive shoes. Toning and stretching exercises are good, again within limits. The practice of yoga can be adjusted to your age and health condition and also brings meditation and spirituality into our lives. It all boils down to balance and moderation, which should be the standard principle of our lives.

In the early 1980s, a famous urologist at the Cleveland Clinic, Dr. Bruce Stewart, was diagnosed with prostate cancer. He had done a lot of research on this dreadful disease himself, and I had had the privilege of attending a course given by him at the Cleveland Clinic. His cancer also came in a very aggressive form, and Dr. Stewart died of metastatic prostate cancer on February 15, 1983, at the age of fifty-three. Bruce was a brilliant urologist and a mentor to many urologists in that era. He was born in Flint, Michigan, received his education at the University of Michigan, and earned his medical degree in 1954. He then received training under the distinguished professor of urology Dr. Reed Nesbitt. He was a prolific writer and, at his young age, had written 213 published papers and 27 chapters in several books. His greatest contribution was a two-volume book called *Operative Urology*, which became a bible to the urology community. Besides being a superbly organized team player and natural leader, Bruce always kept his priorities straight. Family came first, and this remained true throughout his life. He was a blessing to all who knew him. The American Urological Association honored him by establishing the yearly Bruce H. Stewart Lecture.

*

Dr. H was another surgeon in his early fifties, originally from India, who had a busy practice in our hospital. One day in the mid-1990s, I was sitting in the surgeons' lounge, waiting to be called for my next surgery, when Dr. H came and sat next to me. "I have never had my prostate checked," he began. "I am fifty-two years old now. What do you suggest?" I advised him to come by my office to have a PSA blood test drawn, and I would also check his prostate with a rectal examination.

He came two days later. To my utter surprise, I felt a hard lump on his prostate, the size of a marble. I advised him to have a needle biopsy of his prostate under ultrasound guidance, which we routinely did in our office. The blood test came back normal, but I insisted on the prostate biopsy, which was performed the following week. Two days later, the results came back from the pathologist. Dr. H had extensive high-grade prostate cancer. I called him immediately to ask that he come to the office with his wife.

The next day, we sat down and went over the results. I strongly advised him to go to the University of Michigan, knowing that his cancer would require every weapon we had. At the university, he received a full course of radiation, followed by a surgical removal of his prostate. During the surgery it was found that the disease had spread beyond the prostate, into the lymph nodes and even further. The Tumor Board advised him to go through a course of strong chemotherapy, but it was all in vain. The cancer had spread far and was too stubborn to respond to anything. His health started to deteriorate rapidly, and within six months, he passed away. I still remember the faces of his wife and young children at the funeral. Nobody would ever have imagined that Dr. H would be gone so soon. Since then, I have never taken prostate cancer lightly, and over the years have saved many lives.

I have had the privilege of giving talks on prevention of prostate cancer over the years to physicians as well as non-physicians. It has been conclusively shown that the incidence of prostate cancer worldwide has been strongly associated with differences in diet and lifestyle. The lifetime risk of dying from this cancer is 1 percent among Asians, 3.5 percent in Caucasians, and 4.5 percent among African Americans. Diet is clearly implicated in the origin of many cancers. There is a higher incidence with increased consumption of red meat, animal fat, and rich carbs, while the incidence is reduced by consumption of vegetables, fiber, and natural starch. These factors make prostate cancer an ideal target for prevention. Some foods, like broccoli, have even been shown to slow or reverse the progression of premalignant lesions. Specific foods like saw palmetto, lycopenes, green tea, turmeric, and flaxseed have been recommended, though without much scientific evidence. Broccoli, Brussels sprouts, cauliflower, cabbage, spinach, wild caught salmon, pomegranate, blueberries, and soy and oat products have been shown to have beneficial effects in preventing prostate cancer.

In 2018, the sale of vitamins and supplements was estimated to be a $30 billion industry. A recent large 'umbrella review' of many randomized studies has come to the following conclusion: "there is no high quality evidence that any vitamin or supplement has a beneficial effect on overall mortality." It has been shown that regular exercise is associated with a lower risk of dying with prostate cancer. The good news is that what is good for your prostate is also good for your heart, your brain, your liver, and your kidneys.

Lifestyle changes truly make a difference in prostate cancer prevention. A high-calorie diet, sedentary habits, and obesity, which all go hand in hand, are proven to promote prostate cancer. To prevent cancer, maintain a healthy weight by lowering your body mass index (BMI) and waist-to-hip (WHR) ratio, and by maintaining blood pressure and cholesterol levels and exercising regularly and adequately. I am extremely fortunate to have a dear friend, Dr. Mark Moyad, who is the Jenkins/Pokempner Director of Complementary and Alternative Medicine at the University of Michigan Medical Center in Ann Arbor. I take his advice as gospel. He has authored hundreds of articles and several books that are simple and enlightening. I especially recommend the latest edition of his book *Promoting Wellness for Prostate Cancer Patients.*

Now, back to my own story. As I mentioned, prostate cancer runs very high in my family and has been genetically acquired from my maternal side. My own PSA levels have been like a yo-yo, up and down, but never persistently going up. I have done the latest SelectMDx urine test, and that has been negative too. For the time being everything is good, but it is like sitting under the sword of Androcles.

Annette and I lead a very healthy life. We try to follow the old saying "Eat breakfast like a king, lunch like a prince, and dinner like a pauper." Our breakfast consists of one boiled egg (white only), half a ripe avocado, a small banana, a small high-fiber muffin, a small cup of probiotic *kefir* (yogurt drink), and a cup of regular coffee with supplement pills suggested by Dr. Moyad. Lunch is usually a small salad or a handful of nuts, and for early dinner we have a couple spoonfuls of a super grain like quinoa, freekeh, or cauliflower rice, half a cup of a vegetable like broccoli, beans, or Brussels sprouts, and a small piece of fish or chicken. Before bed, a cup of chamomile tea with a bite of something sweet brings the day to an end. We sleep six to eight hours on average. I exercise daily for thirty to forty minutes, either doing laps in our pool or on the treadmill. Annette and I walk briskly everyday at least a couple miles around the sub-division. I also try to maintain my weight. When I came to the United States, I weighed 120 pounds, and forty-six years later, I was between 132 and 136 pounds. I can still fit into boys XL size clothing.

In December 2018, my PSA went up to twice of what it used to be. It definitely got me worried. I felt it was a result of inflammation of the prostate, and to clear that, I took a course of antibiotics for a month. Then I repeated the SelectMDx specialized test, and the result came back suggesting that there was no evidence of cancer. I repeated the PSA test four months later, and thank God the numbers have gone down. Vigilant monitoring is the key to early detection and treatment.

CHAPTER 20

Role of Family

It is a simple, universal truth that if each family took care of their own, there would be no community problem, either national or international. The word "family" can encompass spouses, children, relations, in-laws and go on to include households, clan, race, and any person who you become acquainted with. I like to classify it as immediate family and extended family. I have mentioned before that any patient who came to see me became a part of my extended family. What makes us family are the bonds of love and care for each other.

As humans living on this earth, we have certain responsibilities to the immediate family. The most important person is the mother. She is the only one who carries us in her womb for over nine months, protecting us and sharing everything including her blood and nutrition. After we are born, she takes the best care until we can literally stand on our feet and does everything needed until a time comes when we can take care of ourselves. Besides the physical care, she fulfills our emotional needs lovingly. Our faith tells us, "Heaven lies under the feet of the mother," and there is no amount of service you can do to repay her back.

The father has his own major contributions in grooming us to what we become, by providing for our needs and also being the role model and disciplinarian. He shows his love and affection in different ways, no less than the mother. Again, in an ideal parenting relationship, all the roles are shared and balanced. My belief is that your children will treat you the same way as they saw you treat your parents. I have seen it with my own children and those of my friends.

I have often heard a person say, "My mother is so self-centered" or "She has never done her part as a mother, so how should I treat her?" My reply to them has been very simple: "It is not about her. Your responsibilities are yours irrespective of what she does. You are answerable for your actions and she will be for hers." It is sometimes difficult to understand this concept, but we have to realize that we cannot change the behavior of others. Remember to be forgiving of ourselves and others. Our internal peace will come when we do the right things. The other scenario that sometimes happens is there is anger and arrogance from both sides, which leads to a complete breakdown of many relationships. Of course, if the mother or anyone tells you to do something wrong or against your conscience, you definitely need to refuse to do it.

Unfortunately, our society in general is becoming more and more self-centered and thereby breaking with long-held values. Many families are separated because of work, divorce, and so many other factors.

I remember a heart-breaking story from five years back. It was Christmas Eve of 2012, and I was on call for the emergency room at the hospital. Around 5:00 p.m., I received a call from the ER doctor about an eighty-seven-year-old gentleman who was brought down by his son for some cough and burning in his urine. I asked the physician the usual question: "So what are your findings?" "Well," he replied, "all the blood tests and X-rays were normal. He has a mild urinary tract infection, but other than that there is nothing wrong with him." "Let's send him home with an antibiotic prescription. We will wait for the urine culture results and I will follow up with him in the office," I suggested. After some hesitation, the ER physician said, "I totally agree, but the big problem is that the son dropped him off and left. He told the nurse to admit his dad for a few days in the hospital as he and his family were going to be very busy with Christmas celebrations." I got the son's phone number and called him, explaining that there was no major issue and his dad did not need to be admitted to the hospital. The reply I got totally stunned me. "Hey Doc! He has Medicare and we would rather have him in the hospital. He will bother all of us at home during Christmas." "But isn't Christmas all about having the family together?" I asked in a loud tone. "Well, I'm not coming to pick him up. You do what you want," and he hung up on me.

Needless to say, we had to admit him. I told the nurses on the floor to make sure they arranged a special Christmas dinner for him.

By the same token, I have seen thousands of patients and relatives who cared for each other immensely. Many sons and daughters would take time off from work to bring their loved ones to see me. I always made it a point to thank them for it. Husbands did it for their wives, and wives for their husbands. I learnt a lot from following these relationships over the years of my practice. Connecting deeply through our shared humanity, no matter our differences, is one of the most precious gifts we offer and receive as physicians.

It was January of 2002, and I had been taking care of Sam for over thirty years. He was now eighty-two and had come for his routine prostate cancer checkup. After examining him I said, "You are doing great! The PSA is stable and your urine is nice and clear. We will see you in one year." Sam looked at me in a wanting way. "Dr. Hai, do you have a few minutes to talk about something personal?"

Although I was running behind with time, I said "Sure, go ahead."

"Well, it is a very long story, but I will tell you in brief," Sam went on. "When I was nineteen years old, I fell in love with a seventeen-year-old girl who lived across the street from me. We were so passionate about it that we just wanted to get married. My family was Polish and she was of Italian heritage. Her father vehemently opposed it. I was heart-broken, but then I got drafted to the army as World War II was going on. I was gone from home for three years but not a day went by that I did not think of her. On my return, I found out that her father had got her married to an Italian boy.

A few years later, she moved to Chicago with her husband and two kids. It took me five years to get over her and I finally got married.

"One of my neighbors had remained in contact with her family and, once in a great while, I would get news of her that she was doing well. Thirty years later, her husband passed away and by this time I had three kids of my own who were grown up and had left home. I often thought of her and how life would have been if we had got married. Two years back, my wife had a major heart attack and we lost her. In my loneliness, I thought of my first love even more. Yesterday my neighbor told me that he got news that my first love had passed away."

Tears were flowing from his eyes. "I had no one to tell this story to and cry with," he said. I hugged him firmly and my own tears were running down. In a broken voice, he murmured, "I could never stop loving her."

Once he settled down, I thanked him for sharing his beautiful story. True love is forever.

Getting back to the other family members, most of us have siblings who can be a friend, a guide, or a mentor. My eldest brother, who is just five years older than me, has been an outstanding example and mentor to me. After my dad passed away, I always look up to him for guidance, and he has always been there for me. After I graduated from medical school, we always had mutual consultations and did not take any major decisions in life without getting each other's advice. There is great solace and comfort in this kind of relationship. When I was leaving home in 1973, I signed a document giving him full power of attorney for all my inheritance and, to this day, have never regretted it. His honesty and integrity have always been unquestionable. By the same token, I have seen many families completely torn apart because of inheritance and other emotional issues. When dealing with siblings, we need to show utmost compassion. I have always thought, *What would I expect if the roles were reversed?*

In the summer of 2002, Annette and I were teaching laser surgery in London. It was unusual that Annette's younger brother, Danny, called from

Atlanta, Georgia. "Hey Annette, I went for my routine physical and the family doctor felt a lump in my abdomen. He referred me to an oncologist who did some X-rays and has done a biopsy of the lump." "Have you made an appointment to get the results of the tests?" Annette asked. "Yes, I'm seeing him next Monday in his office." "Danny, this is something serious. We are flying back home tomorrow and I will fly over this weekend and we'll go to the appointment together."

Danny was a Porsche master technician and for many years had passionately worked at the Jim Ellis dealership in Atlanta. After his wife became an alcoholic, he went through divorce and had custody of his two sons, ten-year-old John and eight-year-old Michael. Life was tough with his work and being a single parent. He loved them immensely, and they had adjusted well to the new lifestyle. Danny did everything in his control to bring happiness to the kids.

The following Sunday, after our return, Annette flew down to Atlanta. On Monday morning after dropping the kids to school, they went to the oncologist's office for Danny's appointment. From what Annette told me later, the doctor was an easy-going guy. He told Danny, "You have a big tumor in the abdomen, the size of a football, and the biopsy shows it to be a sarcoma. But don't worry; we will give you some Gleevac pills and it will dissolve it. You will be fine. We will make a follow-up appointment for you." Being a surgical nurse and knowing the severity of the condition, Annette was shocked at the laissez-faire attitude of the oncologist. On their drive home, Annette had already planned everything in her mind. "Danny, you need to give notice to Jim Ellis that you'll be on medical leave for a few months. Once we get home, you and the boys need to pack. You're coming to Michigan. They have a special program there for the treatment of sarcomas. You have a big battle ahead of you." It took Danny a few minutes to grasp everything, but he knew his sister was right and would always give him the best advice. Annette flew back home to get everything ready for their arrival. Danny and the kids spent the next few days packing up their big black Chevy Tahoe to drive up to Michigan.

It was a nice warm summer day in June 2002 when Danny, John, and Michael drove up to our new home in Canton, Michigan. Fortunately, we had two bedrooms with attached bathrooms on the second floor.

Annette had already made an appointment for Danny at the University of Michigan (U of M), and within a few days the whole care plan had been worked out. Danny would be started on chemotherapy first, followed by a course of radiation, and then a very major surgery for removal of the tumor and adjacent organs. It would be a long road to recovery, provided everything went as planned.

John and Michael liked their new environment, and they would be under the loving care of their favorite aunt. We had been empty nesters at this time; our children were grown up. We had to make some adjustments in our lives, too. We registered the kids at the local elementary school as we had no idea how long Danny's treatment would take.

While all this was going on, our first grandson Belaal was born on August 22, 2002, to our daughter-in-law Amera and our son Yusuf. We were extremely happy to welcome him into our family. The irony of life goes on: a newborn joins the family and a brother is in the clutches of death. One interesting fact was that, when baby Belaal would cry and none of us could console him, Danny would take Belaal in his arms and quickly get him into a deep slumber.

Danny's rigorous treatment plan started the very next week. This meant driving to U of M in Ann Arbor every weekday. The kids had to be dropped and picked up from school. Annette was now cooking for a family of five, including occasional special meals for Danny when he could not eat regular food. The kids needed help with their homework. Laundry had tripled. We did it together, but needless to say, the majority of these duties fell on Annette's shoulders. We were both still working, and sometimes I wonder how everything got done in time.

There were times when Danny would be nauseated, vomiting, and weak from chemotherapy and needed extra assistance even to get out of bed. He was on several medications, which needed to be given in a timely fashion. We had him on supplements like Ensure and Boost to give him extra energy. The chemotherapy helped shrink the tumor and, as planned, Danny went through a long thirteen-hour surgery. The big mass was completely removed together with his spleen, left kidney, lymph nodes, and all the surrounding tissues. The recovery was long and brutal.

What was a two-month plan had now been thirteen months. All the doctors and nurses at the U of M loved Danny. Despite all what he went through, he was always cheerful, cracking jokes and keeping the other cancer patients uplifted. He had lost all his hair, and one day when I commented on it, he started laughing and, putting his palm on his bald head, said, "Mahmood, this is the solar panel for my sex machine." The doctors gave him a green light. He was cancer-free, but he would need close monitoring of the disease as it is known to come back. Annette and I still wonder how this miracle took place. We felt sure God was by our side through the journey.

After his return to Atlanta, Danny had his three-month checkup. It came back free and clear. He returned to work, the kids started school, and life was getting back to normal. At the six-month checkup, the chest X-ray showed some new spots. The doctors in Atlanta just wanted to keep an eye on it. We had a family meeting, and it was decided that he should come back. This time he would come to the Cleveland area where Annette's dad, mom, and sister's family lived. Danny and the kids would move in with his younger sister as they had two boys fairly close in age to John and Michael.

Evaluation and treatment started at the Case Western University Hospital, but the disease had come back with a vengeance. It had spread to the lungs and other organs. The doctors had nothing much to offer other than supportive treatment and pain relief. Danny went back to Atlanta for a weekend to take care of some important issues. On his flight back, he became so short of breath that he had to be taken to the hospital by ambulance.

Once things stabilized, Danny and the family decided to have him in a room in Annette's mom's house under the care of hospice. His wish was to spend the last few days of his life with John and Michael and the rest of the family around him.

Annette and I had an important GreenLight laser presentation at an international meeting in Argentina. Everything had been booked months in advance, but considering Danny's condition, we were very reluctant to go. We even talked to Danny, who said to us, "Please go; I will wait for you."

We were at the meeting for two days when Annette's dad called us urgently. "You guys should come back as soon as possible, Danny is not doing well."

We immediately called American Express Business Travel, which always did our bookings, and they were able to get us back within fourteen hours. We rushed from the airport to see Danny. He was still alert, said good-byes to everyone, and, within a few hours, went into deep coma. It seemed he was living up to his promise, just waiting for us to return. Three days later, Danny passed away peacefully. It was the end of his journey at a young age of forty-five. It seems like God recalls His Loved one sooner than others.

I am reminded of a beautiful sonnet in Elizabethan English by John Donne (1572–1631), which I memorized in high school. It is interesting to note that the poem was written in 1609, but was first published two years after Donne's death.

DEATH BE NOT PROUD

Death, be not proud, though some have called thee
Mighty and dreadful, for thou art not so;
For those whom thou think'st thou dost overthrow,
Die not, poor Death, nor yet canst thou kill me.
From rest and sleep, which but thy pictures be,
Much pleasure; then from thee much more must flow,

And soonest our best men with thee do go,

Rest of their bones, and soul's delivery.

Thou art slave to fate, chance, kings, and desperate men,

And dost with poison, war, and sickness dwell;

And poppy or charms can make us sleep as well

And better than thy stroke; why swell'st thou then?

One short sleep past, we wake eternally,

And death shall be no more; Death, thou shalt die.

John Donne

CHAPTER 21

Life's Lessons Learned

"They may see the good that you do as self-serving. Continue to do good. They may see your generosity as grandstanding. Continue to be generous. They may see your warm and caring nature as a weakness. Continue to be warm and caring. For you see in the end, it was never between you and them. It is always between you and God."

—Anonymous

In the pursuit of learning, I read a lot and apply the advices that resonate with my thinking. Now that you have read my life's story, let me summarize what I have learnt over the span of seventy-two years.

Whatever station of life you are at, it is never too late to stop for a few moments, look back, assess the present, and plan your future going forward. What is past is history and you cannot change it, but the present and future is yours to decide.

Human beings have an amazing capacity to learn, adapt, and adjust the course of their lives. The old dictum "You can't teach an old dog new tricks" is not true. We are not destined to a life of habits and selfishness, because we have the ability, with disciplined repetitive action, to construct new habits of thought, feeling, and behavior. You have only one life to live; let it be your best.

I would suggest a weekend retreat in a quiet nature location where you can think clearly without the stress of external factors. This is where you can analyze the major events of your life and evaluate the lessons you have learnt. Accept reality, be truthful to yourself, and do not dwell on false hope. Think of what excites you and make notes.

Once you have a clear picture, you can discuss it with someone unbiased that you trust, preferably one who has no conflict of interest, or even a professional. It is not a matter of public discussion. Once you have a complete picture with personal, social, and financial considerations, develop a short-term and a long-term plan that you think is doable. Then put a timeline to it. You are now ready to start the journey.

In her beautifully written book *Twelve Steps to a Compassionate Life*, Karen Armstrong describes the survival instincts of the reptilian brain that "neuroscientists have called the Four Fs: feeding, fighting, fleeing, and — for want of a more basic word — reproduction. Our reptilian ancestors were, therefore, interested only in status, power, control, territory, sex, personal gain, and survival." We have to grow beyond, into honest, loving, and caring human beings.

For our betterment, she further proposes two versions of the Golden Rule: the positive version, "Treat others as you would wish to be treated yourself," or the negative version, "Do not do to others what you would not like them to do to you."

The acquisition of knowledge and wisdom starts from infancy and many psychologists believe that the human personality gets well defined even before we reach our teens. In a recent Time magazine article, I read the story of Esther Wojcieki. She was the mother of three highly successful women who turned out to be accomplished, caring, and capable people: a doctor and two CEOs of high-profile companies. On being asked to share her parenting strategies, Esther affirmed that she focused more on character traits instead of academic accolades. Her values were reflected in the acronym TRICK, representing Trust, Respect, Independence, Collaboration, and Kindness. She did not define her children's success by the amount of money they had made or the grades and degrees they received, but by the individuals they had grown to become: "Adults who give back, evolving human consciousness with an awareness that the greatest reward comes from making someone else's life better."

Deep within each of us is a spiritual longing. It is a thirst unquenched, a hunger unfulfilled and a vision only partly seen. Life's journey is made individually. Each person dances to the beat of a different drummer and hears a unique tune. In the quest for spiritual understanding we pass through many phases of experience. To some it comes through scripture, ritual and litany, fostered by rule; while others find the message in admiring nature and being free. The spiritual quest, whatever its course, has elevated the human spirit. It has produced genius, created music, inspired poetry, nurtured ethical systems and become our philosophy of life.

Let us first talk about being healthy. This encompasses physical, mental, and spiritual health. We have total control, other than hereditary factors, which can also be modulated. Even if both your parents were diabetic or had cancer, most times you can overcome it by diet and lifestyle changes. The other good news is that what is good for your heart is also good for your brain and other parts of your body. Diet and exercise are the foundations on which you build. The American Medical Association suggests six simple lifestyle changes:

1. Identify small, measurable goals: this relates to diet and exercise.
2. Adopt tactics for eating well.
3. Eat a variety of foods.
4. Drink plenty of water.
5. Manage emotions.
6. Maintain physical fitness.

All these have been discussed at length in this book.

Meditation, prayer, and relaxation practices have a major role in obtaining long-term happiness. Remember, being happy does not mean you have it all; it simply means you're thankful for all you have.

In a recent interview with the Robb Report magazine, when asked one thing he did daily to stay sane, Stefano Domenicali, chairman and CEO of Automobili Lamborghini, replied, "I need to start the day with an hour to an hour and a half doing some exercise, just for me to refresh and think about myself." I have followed a similar routine in my life. The morning exercise and meditation set the pace for the whole day. When asked about characteristics he looks for in new employees, he mentioned trust, professionalism, being a team-player, and one who never gives up. So it all boils down to basic honesty as the prime mover in life.

Life is a journey with problems to solve and lessons to learn but most of all experiences to enjoy. Don't rely on luck; believe in hard work. Don't let anyone's ignorance, hate, drama, or negativity stop you from being the best person you can be.

- Stand up for your principles; don't let your ego guide your decision.
- The more you give, the more you will receive.
- Love, kindness, and compassion can never be compromised.
- Learn to be compassionate with everyone and at all occasions.
- Be creative and think out of the box.
- Love your neighbors and give them their rights.

In the small subdivision where we live in, Michigan, we have sixty homes. In our Home Owners Association (HOA), we have appointed a Care and Concern Committee that assists neighbors who need help. Earlier this year, the wife of an older couple was diagnosed with terminal cancer. The husband was unable to cook. Thirty of us signed up to help by providing two complete meals by rotation. All we had to do was cook for two extra people once a month, but for the needy family, it was two tasty, healthy meals everyday until she recovered and is now back and active in the community.

I will end my book with advice from two great people: a very successful businessman, and a Harvard professor of psychology.

The last words of Steve Jobs, the billionaire CEO of Apple, as he was dying of pancreatic cancer at the age of fifty-six, were, "I reached the pinnacle of success in the business world. In others' eyes my life is an epitome of success. However, aside from work, I have little joy. In the end, wealth is only a fact of life that I am accustomed to.

At this moment, lying on the sick bed and recalling my whole life, I realize that all the recognition and wealth that I took so much pride in, have paled and become meaningless in the face of impending death.

You can employ somebody to drive the car for you, make money for you, but you cannot have someone to bear the sickness for you.

Material things lost can be found. But there is one thing that can never be found when it is lost — *life*.

When a person goes into the operating room, he will realize that there is one book that he has yet to finish reading — *book of healthy life*.

Whichever stage in life we are right now, with time, we will face the day when the curtain comes down.

Treasure love for your family, love for your spouse, love for your friends . . . Treat yourself well. Cherish others.

As we grow older, and hence wiser, we slowly realize that wearing a $300 or $30 watch, they both tell the same time. Whether we carry a $300 Or $30 wallet/handbag, the amount of money inside is the same. Whether we drive a $150,000 car or a $30,000 car, the road and distance are the same, and we get to the same destination. Whether we drink a bottle of $300 or $10 wine, the hangover is the same. Whether the house we live in is 300 or 3000 square feet, loneliness is the same.

You will realize your true inner happiness does not come from the material things of this world. Whether you fly first or economy class, if the plane goes down, you go down with it.

Steve Jobs continues:

Therefore, I hope you realize, when you have mates, buddies and old friends, brothers and sisters, who you chat with, sing songs with, talk about north-south-east-west or heaven and earth, *that is true happiness!*

Five undeniable facts of life:

1. Don't educate your children to be rich. Educate them to be happy. So when they grow up, they know the value of things, not the price.
2. Best awarded words in London: "Eat your food as your medicines. Otherwise you have to eat medicines as your food."
3. The one who loves you will never leave you for another, because even if there are a hundred reasons to give up, he or she will find one reason to hold on.
4. There is a big difference between a human being and being human. Only a few really understand it.
5. You are loved when you are born. You will be loved when you die. In between, you have to manage!

Note: If you just want to walk fast, walk alone! But if you want to walk far, walk together!

Eight best doctors in the world:

1. Sunlight
2. Rest
3. Exercise
4. Diet
5. Temperance
6. Water
7. Air
8. Trust in God

Maintain them in all stages of life and enjoy a healthy life.

Sent with smiles, affection and love!"

The last line says it all: "He passed away happily."

Tal Ben-Shahar PhD, a young professor at Harvard, teaches one of the most popular and successful courses: "The Positive Psychology". He has written several books that have been on the bestsellers list of *New York Times*. In his class, he highlights fourteen key tips for improving the quality of our personal status and contributing to a positive life.

Tip 1. Thank God for everything you have.

Tip 2. Practice physical activity: exercising helps improve your mood.

Tip 3. Eat breakfast: it gives you energy, helps you think and perform your activities successfully.

Tip 4. Be assertive: ask what you want and say what you think. It helps improve your self-esteem.

Tip 5. Spend money on experiences rather than buying things.

Tip 6. Face your challenges. Write short weekly lists of tasks and complete them.

Tip 7. Put nice memories, phrases, and photos of your loved ones everywhere.

Tip 8. Always greet and be nice to other people — smile.

Tip 9. Wear comfortable shoes.

Tip 10. Always maintain good posture.

Tip 11. Listen to music and praise God.

Tip 12. Eat healthy, do not skip meals, avoid excess white flour and sugar, eat everything, and vary your food.

Tip 13. Take care of yourself and feel attractive.

Tip 14. Fervently believe in God.

My book has come to an end. Good luck as you start on your new journey. You know what you need to do, and May God help you and guide you.

About the Author

Dr. Mahmood Hai was born in Patna, India and completed his early education at the Jesuit run St. Xavier's High School. He earned his medical degree with distinction in Anatomy and Surgery from the Prince of Wales Medical College in 1969. In 1973 he completed his Master in Surgery (M.S.) degree from Patna University and proceeded to USA to complete his surgical residency in Boston and urology residency in Detroit.

Dr. Hai has been practicing urology for over forty years. He is a leading expert in the field of prostate diseases. He is internationally known for his pioneer work with the Green Light laser. He has been a visiting professor at many universities in North and South America, Europe, Middle East, Asia and Australia. He has trained urologists around the globe. Dr. Hai has been called upon to perform laser surgery on various diplomats, celebrities and world leaders.

Dr. Hai has a long list of publications and awards including: A fellowship from the International College of Surgeons and the Association of Surgeons of India, the Dr. Edwin L. Thirby award for the best presentation at the American Urological Association annual meeting, and the 'Distinguished Award for Philanthropy' by the Institute for Social Policy and Understanding, a Washington-based think-tank.

He is a founder and trustee of Michigan Educational Council, the Surgical Institute of Michigan, the Interfaith Community Outreach and the Hai Medical Research Institute.

He has variously served on the advisory board of Boston Scientific Corporation, American Medical Systems, Bayer Pharmaceutical, Storz corporation and Endo Pharma. He serves on the board of Unity Productions Foundation and on an advisory board affiliated with the Lilley School of Philanthropy, Indiana University.

Currently Dr. Hai is the President and Executive Director of the Surgical Institute of Michigan. In addition, he is actively involved in service to the community at large.